Union and Unionisms

Although the dominant political ideology in Scotland between 1707 and the present, unionism has suffered serious neglect. One of the most distinguished Scottish historians of our time looks afresh at this central theme in Britain's history, politics and law, and traces the history of Scottish unionist ideas from the early sixteenth century to the present day. Colin Kidd demonstrates that unionism had impeccably indigenous origins long predating the Union of 1707, and that it emerged in reaction to the English vision of Britain as an empire. Far from being the antithesis of nationalism, modern Scottish unionism has largely occupied a middle ground between the extremes of assimilation to England or separation from it. Nor is unionism a simple ideology to interpret: at its most articulate, Scottish unionism championed the British-Irish Union of 1800, not the uncontroversial Anglo-Scottish Union of 1707. At a time when the future of the Anglo-Scottish union is under scrutiny as never before, its history demands Colin Kidd's lucid and cogent examination, which will doubtless generate intense and profound debate, both within Scotland and beyond.

COLIN KIDD is Professor of Modern History at the University of Glasgow, and Fellow of All Souls College, Oxford. His previous publications include *Subverting Scotland's past* (1993), *British identities before nationalism* (1999) and *The forging of races* (2006).

UNION AND UNIONISMS

Political Thought in Scotland, 1500–2000

COLIN KIDD

CAMBRIDGE
UNIVERSITY PRESS

CAMBRIDGE UNIVERSITY PRESS
Cambridge, New York, Melbourne, Madrid, Cape Town, Singapore, São Paulo, Delhi

Cambridge University Press
The Edinburgh Building, Cambridge CB2 8RU, UK

Published in the United States of America by Cambridge University Press, New York

www.cambridge.org
Information on this title: www.cambridge.org/9780521706803

First published 2008

Printed in the United Kingdom at the University Press, Cambridge

A catalogue record for this publication is available from the British Library

Library of Congress Cataloging in Publication data

Kidd, Colin.
   Union and unionisms : political thought in Scotland, 1500–2000 / Colin Kidd.
      p.   cm.
   Includes bibliographical references and index.
   ISBN 978-0-521-88057-2 (hardback)
1. Scotland – Politics and government.   2. Scotland – History – Union, 1707.
3. Nationalism – Scotland – History.   I. Title.
   JN1228.K53   2008
   320.54094109411 – dc22   2008025532

ISBN 978-0-521-88057-2 hardback
ISBN 978-0-521-70680-3 paperback

CONTENTS

v

The purpose of this book is not to produce a comprehensive history of Scottish unionism as a political phenomenon, but to offer a taxonomy of Scottish unionist discourses from the vantage point of the historian of political thought. Indeed, the book is an expanded version of the Carlyle Lectures in the History of Political Thought given in the University of Oxford during Hilary Term 2006 under the title, 'The varieties of unionism in Scottish political thought, 1707–1974'. I am grateful to the Carlyle Electors for their invitation, and particularly to George Garnett, who organised the social side of things, including the Carlyle Dinner, and to Peter Ghosh, who steered me towards the neglected topic of Scottish unionism. I also feel an enormous debt to the Warden and Fellows of All Souls who took the opportunity presented by the Carlyle Lectures to rescue me from a prolonged period of quondamnation. Several Fellows of the College were staunch supporters of the lecture series, and I owe special thanks to the political scientists, Peter Pulzer and Chris Hood, for congenial discussions of problems beyond the immediate ken of the historian, to Fergus Millar for generous support on several fronts and to Charles and Carol Webster and the wider Webster family for their kindness and hospitality. Elsewhere in Oxford John Robertson and Brian Young welcomed my participation in the wider life of the University, and I have very fond memories of the seminars at the Voltaire Foundation. Back in Glasgow, I should like to thank my

Heads of Department, Thomas Munck and Don Spaeth, and my teaching colleagues, Martin MacGregor and Irene Maver, for their indulgence of my lecturing jaunts to Oxford. I should also like to thank Dauvit Broun for discussions over many years on the origins of Scottish political thought, Karin Bowie for conversations on the Union itself and Gerry Carruthers for insights into the Scottish literary tradition. I also owe a special debt to my colleagues in Law at Glasgow, especially Lindsay Farmer who first showed me several years ago how one might put together a lecture series on this topic and who read a couple of chapters in draft, Adam Tomkins, Tom Mullen, Scott Veitch, John Finlay, Ernie Metzger and Mark Godfrey. Furth of Glasgow John Cairns, Paul Brand, Clare Jackson and Kenneth Campbell have been helpful in matters juridical. I owe a special debt of thanks to Ewen Cameron of the University of Edinburgh for his kind offer to read the entire text in draft. Roger Mason read chapter 2, which is profoundly indebted to his own pioneering work in this field. Any mistakes that remain are entirely my responsibility. It has been an unalloyed pleasure to work with Richard Fisher at Cambridge University Press. I should also like to thank Teresa Lewis, Rosanna Christian, Jo Breeze and Linda Randall at Cambridge University Press for their various endeavours. Valerie Wallace did another splendid job on the index. Lucy, Susan and Adam tolerated – or perhaps relished – my absences, though they also made a trip to Oxford over half-term, and I am grateful to all those people who made them most welcome in Oxford. My daughter's first question on arrival at All Souls was: 'Does this College have cheerleaders?' Special thanks, therefore, to Gerry Cohen who improvised an All Souls cheerleaders' routine to amuse my children.

The text of this book had been completed and I was tinkering with footnotes and the like when in the summer of 2007 I experienced a brain haemorrhage. I was overwhelmed by the messages of support I received from so many quarters, and I should like to thank family, friends and colleagues for their kindness during that difficult period. To two of my hospital visitors I already had enormous obligations stretching back over thirty years: to my cousin, David McIver, who hosted my first visits to the archives in Edinburgh, and to my former Latin teacher at Glasgow Academy, Vic Hadcroft.

My father, George W. Kidd, died suddenly a few months after the lectures were delivered. He did good by stealth; possessed a fund of fine jokes, which he knew how to tell; and had a boundless enjoyment of the antics of animals, babies and small children. This book is dedicated to his memory.

Introduction: the problems of Unionism and banal unionism

Does Scottish unionist political thought merit serious historical analysis? Is there, in fact, a body of unionist political thought worthy of the name? Certainly, the topic has not generated much enthusiasm in the field of Scottish studies. While not all Scottish historians or literary scholars are partisan nationalists, Scottish history and Scottish literature as subjects nurture a non-doctrinaire nationalist outlook by way of their understandable emphases on the distinctiveness of Scotland and Scottish historical and cultural trends from wider developments in the rest of Britain. Unsurprisingly, Scottish academics have paid vastly greater attention to nationalism than to unionism, out of all proportion to the former's representativeness of public opinion. It would be hard to gauge the overwhelming dominance of unionism in Scottish political culture between the 1750s and the 1970s if one read widely in Scottish historiography, even harder if one immersed oneself in Scottish literary studies. The perceived stolidity of unionist values would appear to hold less attraction for academics than the romantic stirrings of nationalism, however faint the electoral ripples. While a few books have examined the political phenomenon of Scottish unionism, there has been no study of the ideas which underpinned it. An assumption appears to prevail among Scottish academics that unionism is dull and monochrome, and its political thought unlikely to exhibit much in the way of originality or sophistication – an intellectual dead end. After all, the Scottish intelligentsia as a whole tends to view unionism as un-Scottish and inauthentic, a form of false consciousness which is passively derivative of English values, aims and interests. As such, Scottish unionism is held not to be a branch of indigenous political thinking so much as it is a parrot cry, which mimics the voice of its English masters.[1]

It is not difficult to trace the source of these received assumptions. They arose during the Scottish Renaissance, a movement for literary renewal which began during the inter-war era, and were most clearly articulated by its presiding genius, the poet and polemicist Christopher Murray Grieve (1892–1978), who is better known by his pen name Hugh MacDiarmid. His bequest to Scottish intellectual life was an uncompromising and Manichean nationalism which viewed Anglo-Scottish relations in rigid black-and-white terms. MacDiarmid's *Who's who* entry gave his hobby as 'anglophobia', and for him, unsurprisingly, Scottish unionism constituted nothing more than a form of capitulation to an alien oppressor. Indeed, he considered unionism to be an object rather than a subject, symptomatic of colonial passivity and 'the whole base business of people who do not act but are merely acted upon'. Unionism involved merely a kind of collaboration on the part of the cravenly provincial establishment of what MacDiarmid mocked as the colony of 'Anglo-Scotland': the politicians, divines, professors and teachers he denounced as the 'toadies and lickspittles of the English Ascendancy'.

---

[1] See e.g. Hugh MacDiarmid, *To circumjack Cencrastus* (Edinburgh, 1930), 'The parrot cry', p. 22.

Unionists were inevitably drab, conventional and uninspired, for 'English Imperialism' had induced a cultural cringe among Scots, compelling 'conformity' with English attitudes and inhibiting the free creativity of the Scottish psyche. Unionist culture – except as a kitsch deformation of Scottish tradition – was a misnomer.[2]

Unionism retains these pejorative associations for the Scottish intelligentsia. MacDiarmid's legacy endures, largely unchallenged, in Scottish studies, a field which operates on binary principles, namely that there is an antithetical relationship – and always has been – between Scotland and England. This notion leads to the further conclusion that nationalism is somehow natural and that unionism, assumed to be a pale imitation of an alien Englishness, is, by contrast, an unnatural perversion. Tom Nairn, for example, has described 'British Unionism' as a 'short-lived pseudo-transcendence' of the basic national unit.[3] Furthermore, MacDiarmid's view that Scotland's experience within the Union was colonial, has been recycled by a new generation of intellectuals influenced by post-colonialism. As far as the post-colonialists are concerned, the ideology of Scottish unionism existed only as a rhetoric of negativity, a strain of inferiorism which denounced pre-Union Scotland as backward and praised the colonial power for improving and enlightening the natives. It is worth pointing

---

[2] A. Bold, *MacDiarmid* (1988: London, 1990 pbk), p. 469; Hugh MacDiarmid, *Lucky poet: a self-study in literature and political ideas* (1943: London, 1972), pp. 148–9; Hugh MacDiarmid, *The rauchle tongue: hitherto uncollected prose*, III (ed. A. Calder, G. Murray and A. Riach, Manchester, 1988), pp. 213, 289.

[3] T. Nairn, *After Britain* (2000: London, 2001 pbk), p. 154.

out here that the very terms 'improvement' and 'enlightenment' – conventionally used to describe economic and cultural developments in eighteenth-century Scotland – have also become taboo. These terms have acquired pejorative connotations – indeed are reputed unionist shibboleths – because they seem to convey the implication that Scotland before the Union of 1707 was unimproved and unenlightened.[4]

Unfortunately, articulations of unionism in recent decades – at least since the coming of Thatcherism – have done little but confirm nationalist caricatures of the phenomenon. Today's Scotland knows the phenomenon largely by way of the lopsided unionism of the Thatcher era when it came to mean simply resistance to a Scottish parliament, or even to the idea of any reconstruction of the Union or the British constitution. Moreover, Thatcherite unionism also upheld a stridently unitarist conception of the British state, which left little scope for the defence of Scottish particularity within the Union. Unitarism was a reflection of political realities: a Conservative government, which drew its electoral support predominantly from England, was determined to remake Scotland in its own image, but was faced with a Scottish people reluctant to honour it with a mandate. As the sociologist David McCrone noted: 'By the late 1980s Unionism as a political creed had grown thrawn and defensive, and reduced to its most simple meaning of doing Westminster's bidding.'[5] Unionism – in its reduced

---

[4] C. Beveridge and R. Turnbull, *The eclipse of Scottish culture* (Edinburgh, 1989).

[5] D. McCrone, *Understanding Scotland: the sociology of a stateless nation* (London and New York, 1992), p. 144.

Thatcherite formulation – prescribed the narrow conformity of recalcitrant corporatist or socialist Scots to the free market values of the south of England. Stridently integrationist and relentlessly negative in its implacable opposition to devolution, Thatcherite unionism had turned into the cartoonish unionism depicted by its opponents, an un-Scottish fifth column within Scottish public life bent on the assimilation of Scottish society to English norms and values.

But was Scottish unionism always like this? Under the twin influences of Hugh MacDiarmid and Margaret Thatcher Scottish intellectuals had forgotten the fluidity of older strains of Scottish unionism, some of which were highly sensitive to the claims of Scottish nationhood. A caricature unitarism had obliterated the contours of traditional unionism from popular memory. Unionism was not necessarily about capitulation, assimilation, integration or emulation – though, to be fair, it could be sometimes – but was more often about the maintenance of semi-autonomy or nationhood within Union, by means of compromise, adjustment and even nationalist assertion when required.[6] Pre-Thatcherite unionism had contained many mansions.

This book will present the case that there were a variety of unionisms in modern Scottish history. Not only did formulations of unionism vary significantly over time and in different political contexts, but unionism also took divergent forms in the major arenas of Scottish discourse – juridical,

---

[6] Cf. N. Phillipson, 'Nationalism and ideology', in J. N. Wolfe (ed.), *Government and nationalism in Scotland* (Edinburgh, 1969); L. Paterson, *The autonomy of modern Scotland* (Edinburgh, 1994).

constitutional and ecclesiastical – as well as in ethnological and historical writings. The volume eschews an overly narrow definition of the history of political thought to embrace political argument in its broadest sense as debate over the institutions of a society, including its legal system and its established churches. Scholars have hitherto been oblivious of these important variations in unionist discourse; nor have they attempted to offer a taxonomy of unionisms, which is one of the central aims of this book.

Another important objective is to show how some of the varieties of Scottish unionism overlapped significantly with certain expressions of Scottish nationalism. The unionist spectrum ranges from assimilation and anglicisation to the outspoken defence of Scottish rights within a strict construction of the Union – a position which verges on nationalism and is sometimes interpreted as such. It is a category error, therefore, to think of unionism and nationalism as opposites. Rather the relationship of unionism and nationalism is very complicated and defies easy parsing. Nationhood as well as provincialism have both been conspicuous – and integral – aspects of the Scottish unionist tradition. For much of modern Scottish political history there was an ill-defined – and neglected – middle ground where moderate unionism and moderate nationalism were in surprisingly close proximity.

As we shall see, unionism's grammar of assent did not preclude criticism of England. Unionists loudly criticised English misinterpretations of Union, in particular the casual assumption that the Union was indeed a kind of English empire. On occasions, the excesses of anglicisation also provoked outbursts from otherwise loyal unionists. Nor did unionism preclude a healthy amount of outright anglophobia, when required. David Hume (1711–76), a supporter not only of Union but also of the anglicisation of eighteenth-century Scotland, complained that the unenlightened 'barbarians who inhabit the banks of the Thames'[7] remained in thrall to the dangerous errors and delusions of English political mythology, having failed to absorb the lessons of Hume's own corrective philosophy. Yet in general it was the ecclesiastical sphere which resounded to the most vigorous protests from Scottish unionists against English iniquities. As the volume will make clear, the fundamental faultline within the Union was for most of its history religious rather than political. Against the legend of unionist lethargy and complacency needs to be set the out-spokenness of Scottish unionists in their critique of English Erastianism and the ways in which it had been insinuated into the British constitution in defiance – as they saw it – of the Union of 1707. Indeed, the more seriously Scots read the hallowed texts of 1706–7, the more likely they were to challenge conventional assumptions of British statehood. Strict unionism was a potential solvent of the Union, at least as the English understood it.

Unionism was, moreover, quite compatible with strains of cultural nationalism, including legal nationalism and, most defiantly, religious nationalism. The contentious ecclesiastical expression of unionism serves as a reminder that Scots unionists often defined Britain and the Union with a Scots inflection which was incomprehensible or even

---

[7] David Hume to Rev. Hugh Blair, 26 Apr. 1764, in J. Y. T. Greig (ed.), *The letters of David Hume* (2 vols., Oxford, 1932), I, p. 436.

offensive to English ears. The chapters which follow will attempt to show the deep native roots of Scottish unionism. Unionism has been a venerable and indigenous element in the Scottish political tradition, though rarely honoured as such. Although the late Thatcherite variant of unionism was a clear exception to the general rule, unionism was not a programme imposed from without or an ideological import. Rather unionism was very much a Scottish coinage. Indeed, it is one of the central arguments of this book that Scottish unionism originated long before the English connection: it predates not only the parliamentary Union of the Kingdoms of 1707, but also the Union of the Crowns of 1603. Deep-rooted and native, Scottish unionism was no English transplant, which partly accounts for the ways in which unionists for long happily deployed what have come to be appropriated as exclusively nationalist positions.

The book will also highlight Scottish assertiveness *within* the Union: sometimes, of course, Scottish unionists were calling for more anglicisation than was on offer, at others for decentralisation and greater autonomy. Above all, Scots insisted on equality within the Union. In the eighteenth century this took the form of reformist claims that the civil and political rights of Britons should be the same on both sides of the border, in particular that the Scots should be liberated from the burdens of their distinctive feudal laws and institutions. The focus during the age of Enlightenment was on the equal rights of the individual, whether Scots or English. Thus an open emulation of English ways and practices, rather than the prickly defence of Scottish distinctiveness, characterised the

8

eighteenth-century Scottish aspiration to equality.[8] However, during the nineteenth century the emphasis shifted towards the collective rights and privileges of the Scots as a nation, and Scots now invoked the equality of Scotland as a nation with England in a partnership of equals. National dignity within the Union – now including the very preservation of Scottish institutional distinctiveness which an enlightened North Britain had disdained – had come to supplant an earlier conception of political equality.[9] Nevertheless, it is important to notice that the demand for equality – of one sort or another – has been a consistent theme of Scottish unionist argument within the Union. What follows is not, therefore, as conventional wisdom might have it, the story of timid and defensive Scottish unionists and the narrow parameters within which they were circumscribed, but a history of unionist agency and creativity within a loosely defined multi-national state and empire. The history of unionist political thought turns out to be richly – and unexpectedly – cross-grained. However, before we embark properly upon the story of Scottish unionisms, there are further obstacles to its telling which we need to confront.

---

[8] C. Kidd, 'North Britishness and the nature of eighteenth-century British patriotisms', *Historical Journal* 39 (1996), 361–82.

[9] H. J. Hanham, 'Mid-century Scottish nationalism: romantic and radical', in R. Robson (ed.), *Ideas and institutions of Victorian Britain* (London, 1967); C. Kidd, 'Sentiment, race and revival: Scottish identities in the aftermath of Enlightenment', in L. Brockliss and D. Eastwood (eds.), *A union of multiple identities: The British Isles c. 1750–c. 1850* (Manchester, 1997); G. Morton, *Unionist-nationalism: governing urban Scotland 1830–1860* (East Linton, 1999).

The problem of Unionism

For a start, the historian needs to be aware of the problem that Unionism had a very specific meaning in modern Scottish history. Unionism was the creed of the Unionist Party – a fusion of Scottish Conservatives and Liberal Unionists – which was a serious force in Scottish electoral politics between 1912, when the party formed as the Scottish Unionist Association, and 1965, when the party changed its name to the Scottish Conservative and Unionist Party. From our perspective, the problem of Unionism is not only that Unionism stands both for a general acceptance of the Union and for a particular party known as the Unionists, but that in this secondary and more precise meaning, the Union being referred to is not the Anglo-Scottish Union of 1707. The Union alluded to in the name of the Unionist Party is the British-Irish Union of 1800, the Liberal Unionists having broken with the Liberal Party in 1886 over Gladstone's plans for Irish home rule.

This slippage of terms bedevils the study of Scottish unionism. Most studies of Scottish unionism inevitably focus upon an institutionalised Unionism (at the expense of the less clearly defined culture of unionism), and as a consequence have relatively little to say about the Anglo-Scottish Union of 1707 compared to the British-Irish Union of 1800 and the problems of Irish home rule. In addition, they tend to concentrate upon the constitutional views of Scottish Conservatives to the comparative neglect of their political rivals, which leads to the casual assumption – perhaps reinforced by the politics of recent decades – that the Conservatives monopolised unionism.[10] Of course, the history of Unionism is only a small, though revealing, portion of the history of Scottish unionism. Nevertheless, with the blurring of Unions and unionisms, it becomes very difficult for historians and political scientists to disentangle Unionism as a partisan platform from unionism as a non-partisan or cross-partisan discourse about the British state. Yet the Liberals and Labour were unionist parties for whom home rule was a way of reordering the Union for its ultimate preservation. Indeed, during the period from 1958 to 1974 the Labour Party explicitly repudiated Scottish home rule and was at this stage a more decidedly centralist party than the Unionists.[11] However, as Michael Keating and David Bleiman note, there was a significant difference between Labour's instrumental commitment to the British state and the Unionism of the Unionists. Labour, with its emphasis on the unity of the working class, never developed 'a coherent ideology of the British state' beyond a 'contingent' support for the state in which it found itself operating, unlike the Conservatives, or Unionists, for whom the United Kingdom was a cherished value in itself.[12]

The historiographical eclipse of unionism by Unionism is closely related to the further problem of banal unionism, which will be discussed more fully later in this chapter. Prior

[10] Catriona Macdonald's fine edited collection *Unionist Scotland 1800–1997* (Edinburgh, 1998) deals largely with the impact of the Ulster question on Scotland and on the history of the Unionist Party.

[11] M. Keating and D. Bleiman, *Labour and Scottish nationalism* (London, 1979), pp. 146–68.

[12] *Ibid.*, pp. 16–17.

to the emergence of the Scottish Question in the 1970s, there had been no pressing need to articulate the case for the Union or to analyse the nature of the Union. A few platitudes about the importance of the Union in laying the foundations of Scottish commercial and industrial prosperity within the Empire sufficed. On the other hand, the British-Irish Union of 1800 and the Irish Question had been a dominant feature of late nineteenth- and early twentieth-century British constitutional debate, in Scotland as much as at Westminster. Irish migration into Scotland during the nineteenth century had sharpened indigenous Lowland Protestant hostility to Ireland's Catholic nationalism and encouraged sympathies with the predicament of Ulster Scots. Articulate Scottish Unionism took the curious form of an ideology supportive of the British-Irish Union of 1800 – not the uncontroversial Anglo-Scottish Union of 1707.

This curious set of affairs provides a useful warning that the historian of Unionism in Scotland should not fixate on the Anglo-Scottish relationship to the exclusion of British-Irish and Scottish-Irish relationships. Bill Miller in his classic study *The end of British politics?* notes that, however important 1707 is to an understanding of Scottish government, the 'visitor to Scotland is most unlikely to find "1707" chalked or painted on the walls of derelict buildings. Indeed he would be much more likely to come across "1690".'[13] This is a reference, of course, to the Battle of the Boyne, an event in Irish history. Graffiti reveal a stark truth about Irish influences on Scottish popular political

---

[13] W. L. Miller, *The end of British politics? Scots and English political behaviour in the seventies* (Oxford, 1981), p. 1.

culture. Indeed, historians are aware that Unionism emerged in late nineteenth- and early twentieth-century Scotland not as a response to Scottish nationalism – which was then a very marginal phenomenon – but to the more potent threat of Irish nationalism to the territorial integrity of a United Kingdom which comprehended Ireland as well as England and Scotland. Ironically, the strong Scots presbyterian associations of this form of Unionism meant that – much more than a nascent and still politically irrelevant Scottish nationalism – it was Unionism which for some decades thereafter became, arguably, the primary party political vehicle for the expression of the values of Scottish nationality – albeit within the Union. Michael Dyer has argued that during the early parts of the twentieth century 'Irish nationalism was more important in Scotland than Scottish nationalism', and that at this period the Unionists emphasised 'their defence of traditional presbyterian institutions and cultural values' against 'the secularism and Roman associations of Labour'.[14] According to Graham Walker, one of its leading historians, Unionism 'fused the appeals of Empire, religion, Ulster, and a definition of Scottishness which derived to a large extent from Presbyterian mythology'.[15]

This strain of Unionism was far removed from the co-option of an anglicised elite imagined by MacDiarmid. Although Unionism was indeed an anti-nationalist ideology,

---

[14] M. Dyer, *Capable citizens and improvident democrats: the Scottish electoral system 1884–1929* (Aberdeen, 1996), p. 177.

[15] G. Walker, 'Varieties of Scottish Protestant identity', in T. M. Devine and R. Finlay (eds.), *Scotland in the twentieth century* (Edinburgh, 1996), pp. 250–68, at p. 260.

its inflections were neither English nor metropolitan,[16] but rather those of an embattled presbyterian provincialism somewhat distrustful of the motives of the English core of the United Kingdom. Unionists celebrated connections with kith and kin in Ulster and, further afield, in the white dominions of the Empire. On the other hand, Unionism was inescapably linked to Protestant sectarianism and was fuelled by a powerful anti-Catholic nativism which was one of the most pronounced features of nineteenth-century Scottish culture. Already by 1851 there were 207,367 Irish-born immigrants out of a total population of 2,888,742.[17] Although the Irish-born constituted only 7.2 per cent of the Scottish population, this population was unevenly distributed within Scotland – being concentrated in the major industrial centres, such as Glasgow, Greenock, Paisley and Dundee, and the figure does not include people of Irish descent born in Scotland. While the majority of immigrants from Ireland were Roman Catholic, there was also a significant minority of Ulster Protestants who imported the Orange movement into Scotland, further reinforcing an indigenous Scots hostility towards Roman Catholicism.[18] The Liberal Unionist split in 1886 was not simply a matter of constitutional principle for Scots, but also capitalised upon Scots Protestant antipathy to the pretensions of Irish nationalism and aligned itself with a contemporary movement for the defence

[16] C. Harvie, 'Introduction', in Harvie, *Travelling Scot: essays on the history, politics and future of the Scots* (Glendaruel, 1999), p. 13.

[17] J. E. Handley, *The Irish in modern Scotland* (Oxford, 1947), p. 43.

[18] E. McFarland, *Protestants first: Orangeism in nineteenth-century Scotland* (Edinburgh, 1990).

of the established Church of Scotland against Liberal calls for disestablishment.

Settlement of the Irish Question – for the time being at least – compelled a subtle degree of Unionist reorientation. The Anglo-Irish Treaty of 1921 provoked some dissent among Unionists, but was generally accepted by the party. Acquiescence in the new Anglo-Irish relationship opened up room for the party to disengage from its primary commitment to Irish issues and to broaden its electoral appeal, if not immediately to Scotland's large Catholic electorate at least to elements of progressive or polite opinion alienated by overt expressions of sectarianism. Although the party did not lose its sectarian overtones, it maintained a polite distance from the militant anti-Catholic movements which emerged in Edinburgh and Glasgow during the inter-war era. Nevertheless, Unionism as an ideology continued to be inflected by religious bigotry and a preoccupation with Scotland's relationship to Ireland. In 1923 the Church of Scotland – arguably the Unionist Party at prayer – approved a special report by a committee of kirkmen entitled *The menace of the Irish race to our Scottish nationality*.[19] The leadership of Unionism shared some of the petty bigotries of the rank-and-file. Sir John Gilmour, who became the first Secretary of State for Scotland, also served as Deputy Grand Master of the Orange Order.[20]

[19] See S. J. Brown, 'Outside the covenant: the Scottish presbyterian churches and Irish immigration, 1922–1938', *Innes Review* 42 (1991), 19–45.
[20] D. Seawright, *An important matter of principle: the decline of the Scottish Conservative and Unionist Party* (Aldershot, 1999), p. 80.

Notwithstanding its associations with sectarianism and a reactionary commitment to the unity of the British Isles, Unionism was in several respects a progressive ideology with a broad social catchment. The Unionists somehow contrived to appeal not only to anti-Catholic sentiment (though without alienating respectable opinion) but also to the radicalism of the Liberal Unionists. After all, the Unionist Party was a hybrid which owed its existence to the fusion of the Conservatives with a wing of the Liberals. The electoral appeal of the Unionists was not confined to the middle class and the party won a number of working-class constituencies – including the Glasgow constituencies of Govan, Glasgow Central, Maryhill and Partick – at different times between 1918 and 1959. Another case in point is Motherwell, which the Unionists won in 1918, 1923 and 1931, though losing it to the Communists in 1922.[21] Nor was the Unionist appeal simply an anti-intellectual one based on brute sectarianism. Iain Hutchison notes that during the inter-war era there was a 'well-supported' Glasgow Unionist Teachers' Association, which by 1933 had 800 members.[22]

The inter-war Unionists were not simply the Scottish wing of English Conservatism. The party's intellectual leaders – Walter Elliot (1888–1958) and Noel Skelton

---

[21] J. Kellas, 'The party in Scotland', in A. Seldon and S. Ball (eds.), *Conservative century: the Conservative Party since 1900* (Oxford, 1994), pp. 671–93, at p. 678.
[22] I. G. C. Hutchison, *Scottish politics in the twentieth century* (Houndmills, 2001), p. 34.

(1880–1935) – were progressive and statist. They favoured public sector housing, land reform and state intervention in the economy – including the establishment of industrial estates, the application of science and planning to social problems and the fostering of a welfare state. Elliot, indeed, was a self-described 'White Marxist', capable of appreciating Marxist arguments and of responding to them with a progressive conservatism informed by modern science and sociology. This outlook was apparent both in his influential book *Toryism and the twentieth century* (1927) and in his ministerial career which encompassed the Ministries of Agriculture and Health, as well as the Scottish Office.[23] The Unionists made a distinctive and enduring contribution to political thought. In *Constructive Conservatism* (1924) Noel Skelton coined the expression 'property-owning democracy' which would become an important term of art in conservative political argument. Skelton's original prescription was envisaged as a plan to restore equilibrium to a political system dangerously unbalanced by the accession of newly enfranchised groups through a broader extension of property-holding. Conservatives, so Skelton warned, had responded in a sensitive and progressive fashion to the rise of democracy.[24] Katharine, Duchess of Atholl (1874–1960), who sat as Unionist MP for Kinross and West Perthshire adopted

[23] Harvie, 'Walter Elliot: the White Marxist', in Harvie, *Travelling Scot*, esp. p. 127; P. Ward, *Unionism in the United Kingdom, 1918–1974* (Houndmills, 2005), ch. 2.

[24] Noel Skelton, *Constructive Conservatism* (Edinburgh and London, 1924), p. 17.

a pro-Republican stance during Spanish Civil War and introduced the Unionists to women's rights by way of her book *Women and politics* (1931).[25]

The Unionists are not easily pigeon-holed. Nor were they any less slippery on the question of Scotland's place in the United Kingdom. Indeed, it would be a mistake to presume Unionist consistency on the subject of a Union – that of 1707 – which was little thought of by Scottish Unionists, at least until the emergence of the Scottish nationalist movement in the late 1920s and early 1930s; and even then Unionists did not regard that Union as under any serious threat. In general, Unionists were opposed to Scottish home rule as a threat to the integrity of the United Kingdom. Nevertheless, during the first two decades of the twentieth century some Unionists did explore the possibilities of home rule all round – that is devolved government for all the nations of the United Kingdom, not just for the Irish – or a federalist reordering of the United Kingdom as potential solutions to the Irish Question. A subordinate parliament for Scotland was not out of the question. Indeed, the willingness to explore any avenue which might bring about a resolution of the Irish problem created some ideological space within Unionism for a measure of Scottish home rule, albeit as a means to a larger constitutional end. There was an awareness among Unionists that the maintenance of the Union required some breathing space for the nationalities of the United Kingdom.

[25] S. Ball, 'The politics of appeasement: the fall of the Duchess of Atholl and the Kinross and West Perth by election, December 1938', *Scottish Historical Review* 69 (1990), 49–83; Hutchison, *Scottish politics*, p. 50.

The standard Unionist interpretation of Scotland's constitutional position within the Union combined a straightforward commitment to the status quo, a concern for administrative as opposed to legislative devolution and an awareness that the overall needs of the British Empire might necessitate some reordering of the constitutional relationships of the home countries. Nor did Unionism preclude all expressions of Scottish nationalism. Skelton took the view that Scottish MPs of all parties should form a Scottish lobby for Scottish interests. When the House of Commons discussed Scottish home rule in November 1932 the occasion brought out variations in the tone and mood music of the Unionist response to the Scottish nationalist movement. Sir Robert Horne (1871–1940), the Unionist MP for Hillhead, took the view that, on balance, much as he disagreed with socialist policy, he would 'rather have the United Kingdom governed by a body which was Socialist than I would have different political legislatures in the two ends of the island'. On the other hand, John Buchan (1875–1940), who sat for the Scottish Universities, proclaimed that 'every Scotsman should be a Scottish nationalist' and that, if it could be demonstrated that the merits of a Scottish parliament outweighed the disadvantages, then 'Scotsmen should support it.' Nevertheless, there was agreement on practicalities. Both Horne and Buchan favoured further measures of administrative devolution as the preferred method of soothing nationalist grievances.[26]

---

[26] Hansard HC Debs. Vol. 272, 24 Nov. 1932, cols. 235–53, 259–67, esp. 248, 261.

Unionists were no less prone to exploiting Scottish national consciousness than other political parties. Certainly, Unionist commitments did not entail surrendering the Scottish card when it was there to be played. During the late 1940s, for example, the Unionists ostentatiously defended Scottish nationhood against Labour's misleading policy of 'nationalisation', which was as far as Scots were concerned really a form of remote centralisation. In 1949 the Unionists issued a policy paper entitled 'Scottish control of Scottish affairs', which promoted administrative devolution in preference to straightforward nationalisation at the United Kingdom level.[27] Administrative devolution to Edinburgh was a shibboleth of Unionism throughout its history.[28] By the 1940s it had become a way of differentiating Unionism from Labour's policy of centralism. Moreover, the Unionists had also encouraged initiatives such as the Grand Committee which carved out a semi-autonomous role for Scottish legislation under the umbrella of a united Westminster parliament. Nationhood just short of legislative devolution was a constant element of Scottish Unionism.

Clearly, it is important to point out that Unionism was very far from being the antithesis of Scottish nationalism, despite what is sometimes assumed. Indeed, some former Unionists played an influential role in the partial reinvigoration of Scottish nationalist politics during the 1930s. In the winter of 1932–3 the Cathcart Unionist Association on

---

[27] Cf. *Scotland and the United Kingdom: the Unionist Party's practical policy for Scottish administration of Scottish affairs* (1948).

[28] For administrative devolution, see J. Mitchell, *Governing Scotland: the invention of administrative devolution* (Houndmills and New York, 2003).

Glasgow's south side established an Imperial Committee led by Kevan McDowell, a Glasgow solicitor, committed to reform of the Empire. The Cathcart Unionists subscribed to the unity and cohesion of the Empire but believed that this greater cause also required Scottish legislative autonomy in domestic affairs. In 1932 the dissident Cathcart Unionists joined with other right-leaning Scottish nationalists to form the Scottish Self-Government Party, which in turn united with the existing National Party of Scotland to form the Scottish National Party in 1934. After 1932 Unionist rhetoric – including hibernophobia – surfaced in Scottish nationalist polemic, not least in the writings of Andrew Dewar Gibb, who had been a Unionist candidate in the elections of 1924 and 1929.[29]

Unionism – with its allusions to the Irish Question – retained its ideological purchase in Scotland much longer than it did south of the border. During the 1940s the Conservative Party chairman Lord Woolton favoured changing the name of the Conservative Party in England to the Union Party, because some felt that Conservative was a vote loser. This plan came to nothing, fortunately in the view of the Conservative historian, Lord Blake, because of the 'similarity to the old but now irrelevant name of "Unionist"'.[30] However, the Unionist label was far from outdated, it seems, north of the border, notwithstanding the passage of time and events since the Liberal Unionist

---

[29] L. Farmer, 'Under the shadow over Parliament House: the strange case of legal nationalism', in L. Farmer and S. Veitch (eds.), *The state of Scots law* (London, 2001), p. 155.

[30] R. Blake, *The Conservative Party from Peel to Churchill* (1970: London, 1979 pbk), p. 261.

schism and the Irish settlement of the early 1920s. Only in 1965 did the Unionists change their name to the Scottish Conservative and Unionist Association. The name change appears to have been a deliberate decision by Sir John George, the party chairman in Scotland, to modernise the party. In particular, it seems the change of name was intended to widen the party's electoral base by distancing it from the sectarian overtones of Protestant Unionism.[31]

The huge electoral decline of the Scottish Conservatives between the mid-1950s and the mid-1990s throws up a curious puzzle very relevant to this enquiry. In the general election of 1955 the Unionists took thirty-six seats out of seventy-one – evidence indeed that there was nothing particularly un-Scottish about Unionism, at least in the eyes of the electorate. However, in the general election of 1997 not a single Conservative was returned across the whole of Scotland. By the 1990s the Conservatives – the leading party by now of an unreformed Anglo-Scottish Union, had lost significant electoral appeal. Historians agree that the Conservatives became unpopular in Scotland not only for opposing devolution, but also because they changed their name from the Unionists, in addition to several other factors including secularisation and the decline of Protestant working-class politics, the retreat from Empire and the corporatist disenchantment of otherwise conservative-minded Scots from Thatcherite political economy.[32] It might

[31] Seawright, *Important matter of principle*, p. 81.
[32] J. Mitchell, *Conservatives and the Union* (Edinburgh, 1990); D. Seawright, 'The Scottish Unionist Party: what's in a name?', *Scottish Affairs* no. 14 (winter 1996), 90–102.

seem paradoxical that the Conservative defence of the Union of 1707 and the relegation of the Unionist name in 1965 are both held to have lowered the Scottish profile of the party, were it not for the fact that the Unionist label did not refer to the Union of 1707. This historic disconnectedness between articulate organised Unionism and the Union of 1707 is itself indicative of a further problem.

The problem of banal unionism

In addition to the problem of the Unionist Party, the historian of unionism also needs to confront the problem of banal unionism. The term banal unionism is intended to be analogous to a key term of art in the sociology of nationalism, the category of 'banal nationalism' coined by Michael Billig. By banal nationalism Billig meant a nationalism which is so dominant that it does not need to be demonstrative. Banal nationalism diverges radically from the vociferous nationalism of threatened particularisms or embattled minorities, outspoken flag-waving irredentisms or programmes of national unification and state-building. Rather Billig uses banal nationalism to classify the low-key, unthreatened nationalisms of established and stable nation states, where nationhood is so deeply and subconsciously taken for granted that it does not require coherent articulation. In the absence of ethnic frictions or national hostilities, banal nationalism flourishes as the undramatic, unreflective acceptance of nationhood as an 'endemic condition'.[33]

[33] M. Billig, *Banal nationalism* (London, 1995).

23

This brand of understatement was also a common feature of Scottish political culture within the Union.[34] The Union, indeed, was part of the wallpaper of Scottish political life. Banal unionism alludes to the very marginal presence played by the Anglo-Scottish Union of 1707 in modern Scottish political discourse, at least until the rise of Scottish nationalism in the 1970s. Whereas the Irish Question has loomed prominently in the foreground of British politics since the British-Irish Union of 1800, the Anglo-Scottish Union of 1707 did not lead to the formulation of a Scottish Question. Rather the Union of 1707 followed by the defeat of Jacobitism at Culloden in 1746 largely settled the question of Scotland's relations with England. Between the mid-eighteenth century and the emergence of the Scottish Question in the 1970s there was no credible, sustained or widely supported Scottish critique of the Anglo-Scottish Union, and as such no call for an articulate ideology of Anglo-Scottish unionism.

Even with the eventual emergence of a national movement, beginning with the Scottish Home Rule Association in 1886, which reformed after the Great War, and then the National Party of Scotland in 1928, which merged with the short-lived Scottish Party (1932–4) to form the Scottish National Party in 1934, nationalism remained firmly at the fringes of Scottish politics, posing little in the way of a serious threat to the Union. The early history of nationalism is a saga of lost deposits. Nationalism occupied the margins of the

[34] Another exploration of the affinity between Scottish unionism and Billig's category of banal nationalism comes in J. Mitchell, 'Contemporary unionism', in Macdonald (ed.) *Unionist Scotland*, p. 118.

margins of Scottish politics. It was certainly more marginal during the inter-war era than the Communist Party of Great Britain, a unionist party which eschewed the socialist nationalism of John Maclean. The nationalists took only 1.3 per cent of the vote in the 1935 general election, and lost deposits in five of the eight seats they contested. A very similar result occurred in the general election of 1945. Before the 1970 general election, the Scottish National Party had won only two seats, and both of these in by-elections, Motherwell in 1945 and Hamilton in 1967. In the elections of 1951 and 1955 two seats were contested yielding below 0.5 per cent of the total poll.[35] Only in 1970 with the capture of the Western Isles seat did the SNP win a constituency in a general election campaign. The early nationalist challenge – such as it was – did little to dent the complacencies of banal unionism.

The Union occupied a position of such unchallenged dominance in Scottish life between about 1750 and 1970 that there was no need to make a vigorous case on its behalf. Banal unionism existed as a background noise in Scottish politics for most of this period, except for some occasional interruptions when the Anglo-Scottish relationship assumed an ephemeral salience in political argument. For instance, there was a brief flurry of interest in the Anglo-Scottish Union in 1799–1800 in the run-up to the Union with Ireland.[36] The Union also assumed considerable prominence in the ecclesiastical debates

---

[35] Hutchison, *Scottish politics*, pp. 83–5.

[36] J. Smyth, 'Arguments for and against union: Scotland and Ireland, 1700–2000', in L. McIlvanney and R. Ryan (eds.), *Ireland and Scotland: culture and society, 1700–2000* (Dublin, 2005), pp. 23–37, at pp. 29–31.

of the Ten Years' Conflict of 1834–43 which preceded the Disruption of 1843, when the Free Church broke away from the Church of Scotland.[37] Similarly, discussion of Irish home rule, home rule all round and imperial federation during the last two decades of the nineteenth century inevitably brought the Union of 1707 into clearer focus.[38] However, this clarity was atypical, as one contemporary, the historian James Mackinnon, recorded:

> Taken in connection with the Irish Home Rule controversy, in the course of which the Union settlement of 1707 has been so industriously referred to by the controversialists on both sides, it is not too much to say that the great measure which has blended the imperial history of England and Scotland for nearly two centuries, has, during the last ten years, enjoyed a singular prominence, as remarkable as the obscurity to which it had long been consigned.[39]

For most of the first three-quarters of the twentieth century the Union was once again uncontentious and invisible to the generality of Scots, except to those in particular areas of professional life. The settlement of the constitutional status of the Scottish Kirk establishment in 1921 meant that the Union assumed a high profile in ecclesiastical discourse, while the celebrated case of *MacCormick* v. *Lord Advocate* in 1953 caused jurists to look afresh at the constitutional ambiguities

---

[37] M. Fry, 'The Disruption and the union', in S. J. Brown and M. Fry (eds.), *Scotland in the age of the Disruption* (Edinburgh, 1993), pp. 31–43.

[38] J. Kendle, *Federal Britain* (London, 1997).

[39] James Mackinnon, *The Union of England and Scotland* (London, 1896), p. 514.

of the Union of 1707. On the other hand, the centenaries of the Union in 1807 and 1907 passed without much fanfare, despite or perhaps because of the ingrained unionism of Scottish culture at these points. Otherwise the history of Anglo-Scottish unionism as an articulate ideology is largely to be found in two distinct periods – in the two centuries prior to the Union of 1707, and in the period since the modern rise of the Scottish National Party. Between these two periods banal unionism prevailed – an inarticulate acceptance of Union as part of the barely noticed but enduring backdrop of British politics.

Banal unionism did not entail the total invisibility of the Union – or, more precisely, of the advantages of the Union – in Scottish political thought. From the mid-eighteenth century onwards it was an uncontested commonplace of Scottish unionist culture – particularly in histories of Scotland or in economic tracts – to celebrate the transformative effects of the Union on Scottish agriculture, trade and industry. The Union, it was believed, had given Scots access to a transatlantic empire and by injecting incentives into Scotland's hitherto precarious economy had put the nation on a new path to agrarian improvement, commercial prosperity and industrialisation. There was also some commentary throughout the eighteenth and nineteenth centuries on the liberalising consequences of the Union on Scottish feudal society, and the ways in which the benign anglicisation of Scotland's archaic feudal institutions had conferred new liberties and freedoms on the Scottish people. However, such discussions focussed on the economic and social benefits of Union; they were not accompanied by any attempts to discuss the nature of the Union or the contours of the state created in 1707. Notwithstanding the place of political theory in Scottish intellectual life, from the era of the Scottish Enlightenment through its long nineteenth-century afterlife, theoretical approaches to the Union were conspicuous by their absence. Political commentators generally ignored the Anglo-Scottish relationship, except to discuss the internal consequences of the Union for Scots. Nor did pluralism or the status of minorities strike much of a chord with Scottish writers on political themes. More curiously still, during the era of banal unionism, from the writings of Adam Ferguson (1723–1816) and Adam Smith (1723–90),[40] by way of Thomas Chalmers (1780–1847),[41] through to the work of the Scottish Idealists – most prominently, David G. Ritchie (1853–1903) and the brothers John (1820–98) and Edward Caird (1835–1908) – in the late nineteenth and early twentieth century,[42] there has been a pronounced communitarian aspect to Scottish social and political thought. Yet, despite an ongoing fascination with citizenship and the bonds of community, Scottish moral and political philosophers generally said very little about the Union or indeed about Scottish nationhood – surely the most obvious form of community within it. Even the Scottish Idealists

[40] Adam Ferguson, *An essay on the history of civil society* (Edinburgh, 1767); Adam Smith, *The theory of moral sentiments* (1759: ed. D. D. Raphael and A. L. Macfie, Indianapolis, 1982); J. Dwyer, 'The construction of community in eighteenth-century Scotland', *History of European Ideas* 16 (1993), 943–8; J. Dwyer, *Virtuous discourse: sensibility and community in late eighteenth-century Scotland* (Edinburgh, 1987).

[41] Thomas Chalmers, *The Christian and civic economy of large towns* (3 vols., Glasgow, 1821–6); S. J. Brown, *Thomas Chalmers and the godly commonwealth* (Oxford, 1982).

[42] D. Boucher (ed.), *The Scottish Idealists* (Exeter, 2004).

who were centrally concerned with the organic relationship of state and society seemed altogether oblivious of the potential challenge to their outlook posed by Britain's multi-national polity. Silences of this sort are characteristic of banal unionism. It is as if the status quo were so taken for granted, that Scots developed an amnesia about the component parts out of which the British state was composed.

Indeed, banal unionism comprehended different levels of inarticulacy and neglectfulness. The most conventional type was an instinctive unionism where the nature or reasons for one's loyalty to the British state were never quite spelled out. But there was also a much deeper level of amnesia associated with banal unionism. Some Scots became forgetful of their own Scottishness or even that the Union state was a multinational entity. David Hume, for instance, referred to himself as an Englishman and turned his *History of Great Britain* into a *History of England*. Similarly, John Millar (1735–1801) included Scottish and Irish elements within his *Historical account of English government* (1787). In response to the radical threat of the 1790s Thomas Hardy (1748–98), the Professor of Ecclesiastical History at Edinburgh, published a pamphlet provocatively titled *The Patriot* in which he called for the preservation of the status quo in decidedly anglocentric terms: '*nolumus leges Angliae mutari*'.[43] On the other hand, Hardy's opponents among the Scottish radicals of the 1790s exhibited a similar obliviousness of their Scottish heritage, calling as they did for the restoration of the ancient Anglo-Saxon constitution of their Saxon forefathers which had been suppressed under the

---

[43] Thomas Hardy, *The Patriot* (2nd edn, Edinburgh, 1793), pp. 9–10, 16.

Norman Yoke of 1066.[44] Almost a century later this vein of amnesia was still characteristic of this deeper kind of unionist inarticulacy. In a lecture entitled *The British parliament* delivered in 1887 to Liberal Unionists in Glasgow the jurist Alexander McGrigor advanced a totally anglocentric account of British constitutional history. McGrigor traced the continuity of the parliament from 'the Witenagemot of *our* ancestors', namely '*our* Anglo-Saxon fathers', through to the modern British parliament. The Union was mentioned only in passing, and there was no suggestion that the history of the British parliament embraced the constitutional history of the pre-Union Scottish parliament.[45]

The historian of Scottish unionist political thought needs to be sensitive to such evasions and silences, to approach unionism obliquely and indirectly. Moreover, the complacent contentment of banal unionism served to circumscribe the ideological ambitions of Scottish unionists. While controversial aspects of the Union gave rise to discrete debates in the various arenas of ecclesiology, jurisprudence and constitutional theory, there was no serious attempt to synthesise these within a grand totalising ideology of unionism. Rather, unionist political thought existed in the form of a series of discourses about the nature of the Union and the British state, which is

[44] J. Brims, 'The Scottish Jacobins, Scottish nationalism and the British Union', in R. A. Mason (ed.), *Scotland and England 1286–1815* (Edinburgh, 1987), pp. 247–65, at p. 252.

[45] Alexander McGrigor, *The British parliament, its history and functions: an address delivered to the Liberal Unionist Association of the College Division of Glasgow, on 28th January, 1887* (Glasgow, 1887), pp. 34, 36.

why the chapters which follow, apart from the second chapter which deals with the period preceding the onset of banal unionism, eschews chronology for a thematic treatment of its subject. Unionism did not equate simply to the sum of its parts.

The defence of the Union

Banal unionism was the default position of Scottish unionism almost from the Union's inception until the final quarter of the twentieth century. However, at this point circumstances changed dramatically, and unionism was forced to become more articulate. The 1970s mark a watershed in the history of unionism. For with the rise of the SNP and the emergence of a new raft of constitutional issues in politics ranging from the Ulster problem to EEC accession, the defence of the Union now required something more robust than banal unionism.

The rise of the SNP was assisted by the appearance of the Report of the Royal Commission on the Constitution in 1973, which conferred a degree of political credibility on devolution as a policy option. Scottish nationalism was no longer viewed as the unrealistic vision of cranks and romantics. In the two British general elections of 1974 the SNP made a significant electoral breakthrough. Indeed, in October 1974 it captured eleven seats, taking 30 per cent of the overall vote in Scotland. In 1974 Labour had also reconverted – admittedly after considerable prompting from Downing Street rather than any compelling nationalist desires on the part of Labour's Scottish rank-and-file – to a devolutionist stance. However, Labour was moving too slowly for the former Labour unionist turned convinced home ruler, Jim Sillars (b. 1937), MP for South Ayrshire, who left the party to set up his own Scottish Labour Party in 1975. On the other hand, Tam Dalyell (b. 1932), then Labour MP for West Lothian, posed the West Lothian Question: how could Scots MPs at Westminster continue to vote on matters of domestic English concern when these very same matters, insofar as they concerned their own constituents in Scotland, had been devolved to a Scottish Assembly? Dalyell, a staunch Labour unionist, also made the case for an unreconstructed Union in his book *Devolution: the end of Britain* (1977). Meanwhile, the political scientist and MP for East Lothian, John P. Mackintosh (1929–78), author of *The devolution of power* (1968) and various other books and articles on the constitution, explored the growing importance of regionalism in the UK economy and contemplated the ways in which the Union might be made more responsive to its needs. In Labour circles, the Union had become a matter for serious discussion and debate.

Similarly, the Unionism of the Conservative and Unionist Party was discreetly redefined to encompass both the traditional stance on the Irish – now Northern Irish – question and the hitherto neglected issue of how the Union of 1707 might be maintained. In the aftermath of the SNP's first post-war victory in a by-election, at Hamilton in 1967, Edward Heath, the Tory leader at Westminster, attempted to outflank Labour by supporting a measure of legislative devolution for Scotland in his Declaration of Perth at the Scottish

Conservative conference in 1968.[46] In 1970 the Home Committee which Heath set up to explore some form of devolved legislative machinery for Scotland recommended the establishment of a Scottish Convention which was to have the unusual status of a specialised third chamber of the United Kingdom parliament.[47] Although falling short of the promise of devolution, this solution indicates nonetheless the creativity Heathite Conservatism brought to the acknowledged problem of how the Union might be updated in the vastly changed circumstances which prevailed 260 years or so after its passage. However, Heath's successor Margaret Thatcher imposed, as we have seen, a more rigid conception of Unionism.

Unionism now became a contested issue within the Conservative Party, with Thatcherite unitarists standing at one extreme of the party and Heathite devolutionists at the other. By the late 1980s another intermediate strain had developed – associated with Malcolm Rifkind and later John Major – which attempted, in the spirit of the Home Committee, to explore ways of revitalising the institutional structures of the Union. Despite Thatcher's description of herself as an 'instinctive unionist', she was not a unionist in the traditional mould. Indeed where others saw a potential constitutional problem in the series of election results which left the Tories in power but a small minority party in Scotland, Thatcher and some of

---

[46] There is an edited version of the speech in L. Paterson (ed.), *A diverse assembly: the debate on a Scottish parliament* (Edinburgh, 1998), pp. 26–30.

[47] P. Seaward and P. Silk, 'The House of Commons', in V. Bogdanor (ed.), *The British constitution in the twentieth century* (2003: Oxford, 2004 pbk), pp. 139–88, at p. 178.

her ministers saw only ungrateful Scots who had forgotten the wisdom of Adam Smith. In a speech in Glasgow in November 1987 the Chancellor of the Exchequer Nigel Lawson complained that too many sectors of Scottish society were 'sheltered from market forces and exhibit a culture of dependence rather than that of enterprise'.[48] Thatcherites – in Scotland as much as England – rejected devolution as a means of rolling back the unwanted intrusions of the state, preferring instead authoritarian individualism, the economic freedom of the individual beneath the protective canopy of a strong indissoluble British state. Nor was there much sympathy for asymmetries in government, whether regional policies or legislative devolution; though the Scottish Office survived. Thatcherite unitarism obliterated the contours of traditional unionism, for the New Right believed that the entrepreneurial values of the prosperous south-east of England ought to be exported to Scotland, whether the Scots wanted them or not. However, such views provoked opposition at the heart of government. Malcolm Rifkind – an open devolutionist during the 1970s but by the late 1980s an otherwise discreetly non-Thatcherite Secretary of State for Scotland in Thatcher's government – spoke out against a rigidly unitarist conception of the Union in a speech delivered in Aberdeen on 15 April 1988. Rifkind argued that Unionism was and should be 'supportive of Scottish institutions'. Rifkind did not repudiate the 'common destiny' of the British peoples. However, he qualified this position by insisting that the Union was not a straitjacket which restricted the national

[48] Quoted in Mitchell, *Conservatives and the Union*, p. 113.

aspirations of the various peoples of the United Kingdom. 'The unity of the kingdom', Rifkind declared, 'is strengthened by diversity and does not require uniformity.' The Union was a 'partnership'. In a sharp rebuke to the integrationist view of the Union propounded by Lawson, Rifkind argued that the Union 'neither requires, nor would benefit from, the Anglicisation of Scotland'.[49] By the late 1980s banal unionism was dead.

Thatcher's successor as Prime Minister, John Major, was a close political ally of Malcolm Rifkind, and though himself from the south-east of England, was sensitive to the Union as a partnership. After the 1992 general election which again saw a Conservative government in power, though largely rejected by the electorate in Scotland, Major promised a Taking Stock exercise. In 1993 his government – in which Ian Lang now served as Secretary of State for Scotland – published a White Paper entitled *Scotland in the Union: a partnership for good*, which contained chapters on 'An evolving Union' and 'Bringing the Union alive'.[50] The highly articulate 'new unionism' of Major – who devoted a whole chapter of his memoirs to the Union of 1707 and its salience in British politics[51] – and his allies Rifkind and Ian Lang[52] marked a significant shift from the banal unionism of the past.

---

[49] *The Scotsman* (16 Apr. 1988), p. 5.

[50] *Scotland in the Union: a partnership for good*, Cm 2225.

[51] John Major, *The autobiography* (1999: London, 2000 pbk), ch. 18, 'The Union at risk', pp. 415–30.

[52] Ian Lang, *Blue remembered years* (London, 2002), esp. pp. 202–6 for the Taking Stock exercise.

Unionism in political science

This growing self-consciousness about the workings of the Union was paralleled by a transformation of the conceptual universe of British political science. As late as 1967 Peter Pulzer, who went on to become Gladstone Professor of Government at Oxford, was correct in his analysis that class was the determining theme of British politics, and that all else was 'mere embellishment and detail'. After all, in the 1966 general election the SNP had won only 5 per cent of the vote in Scotland. Class, moreover, as Pulzer recognised, was 'a factor making for national unity'.[53] However, in the decade which followed political scientists re-educated themselves in the wake of the seismic shocks which the rise of the nationalists posed to political understanding: there was no longer, it seemed, a 'British nation' divided by classes but a multi-national British state created out of a series of Unions.[54]

Foremost among the pioneers of the new political science was Richard Rose who emphasised that in a multi-national polity the territorial dimension of government was no less important than its functional operations. Rose not only explored the multi-form character of the British state – a 'union without uniformity' – but also began to uncover the banality of unionism: the 'inarticulateness' of the 'unthinking

---

[53] P. Pulzer, *Political representation and elections in Britain* (1967: 3rd edn, London, 1975), p. 102.

[54] See e.g. J. Kellas, *The Scottish political system* (1973: 4th edn, Cambridge, 1989); T. Nairn, *The break-up of Britain* (London, 1977); J. Mitchell, 'Scotland in the Union, 1945–95: the changing nature of the Union state', in Devine and Finlay (eds.), *Scotland in the twentieth century*, pp. 85–101.

unionism' which reigned in what Rose nicely called the 'steady-state united kingdom' of the period between the Irish settlement of the 1920s and the emergence of nationalism in the late 1960s. Previously, only Northern Irish Unionists and nationalists had taken the Union seriously; but now the old tacit unionism which had previously flourished under an unwritten constitution during a long period of constitutional stability had become a self-indulgence. Rose was also alert to the diversity of constitutional positions compatible with the maintenance of the Union. In his taxonomy of modern unionism he distinguished traditional unionists from devolutionary unionists and federal unionists.[55]

Unionism also acquired a more precise technical vocabulary. In a major advance in political analysis, the Norwegian political scientist Stein Rokkan and the Scot Derek Urwin made the crucial distinction between unitary states and union states. A unitary state, they argued, is 'built around one unambiguous political centre which enjoys economic dominance and pursues a more or less undeviating policy of administrative standardization. All areas of the state are treated alike.' A union state, on the other hand, was one where 'integration is less than perfect', yet administrative standardisation generally prevails. Nevertheless, within such states one can perceive survival of 'pre-union rights and institutional infrastructures which preserve some degree of regional autonomy'. The United Kingdom, quite clearly, was not a unitary state, but a union state. The unionism of a union state was clearly not a

---

[55] R. Rose, *Understanding the United Kingdom: the territorial dimension in government* (London, 1982), pp. 1–8, 35–6, 50–1, 68, 209–10, 222.

straightforward drive for national standardisation, but was compatible with the tolerant indifference of its centre to institutional variation in its peripheries.[56]

By a curious irony at the very point when Thatcherite unitarism had become the most visible version of unionism, political scientists had begun to recover the nuances of an older unionism. More recently, Ian MacLean and Alistair McMillan have further refined the vocabulary of unionism, with their distinction between 'instrumental' and 'primordial' unionisms,[57] and Graeme Morton has coined the term 'unionist-nationalism'[58] to describe the Scottish assertiveness within the Union in the 1850s. Yet the full richness of Scottish unionism has yet to be explored, not least because political scientists and historians have not engaged with the arcane and difficult terrains of jurisprudence and ecclesiology, where the most sustained arguments took place over the status of the Union within the British constitution; nor have they noticed the fertility of Scottish unionist argument in the troubled centuries which preceded Union and the complacent eighteenth-century lapse into banal unionism.

[56] S. Rokkan and D. W. Urwin, 'Introduction: centres and peripheries in western Europe', in Rokkan and Urwin (eds.), *The politics of territorial identity* (London, 1982), p. 11. See also Urwin, 'Territorial structures and political developments in the united Kingdom' in the same volume.

[57] I. Maclean and A. McMillan, *State of the Union: Unionism and the alternatives in the United Kingdom since 1707* (Oxford, 2005).

[58] Morton, *Unionist-nationalism.*

2

Unionisms before Union, 1500–1707

It is sometimes assumed that Scottish unionism is un-Scottish; that the ultimate provenance of this lap-dog ideology lies in an English desire to control the whole island of Britain, an alien cause which some self-interested or hireling Scots have nevertheless been willing to propagate. By extension, so this train of assumptions runs, Scottish unionism lacks native inspiration, being, at best, a de-factoist design to win over Scots to the brute fact that they find themselves in an English-dominated Union. However, Scottish unionism should not be crudely identified with English imperialism. As will become clear, historically these were antithetical positions. Indeed, Scottish unionism developed as a counterweight to English imperialism, proposing various schemes of Anglo-Scottish association as an alternative to claims of English dominance over Britain. Moreover, unionism also has an impeccably Scottish pedigree. Scottish unionism did not simply emerge in the aftermath of the Union of 1707 as a set of arguments to reconcile Scots to the British state. Neither, indeed, did it take its rise in the years immediately preceding the Union of the Parliaments in 1707, nor around the Union of the Crowns of 1603. Rather unionism predated Union. Articulate unionist political thought has a long history in Scotland which dates back to the early sixteenth century when Scotland was still an independent kingdom and union had no more substance than a utopian vision.

Unionism was not, of course, the dominant voice in early modern Scottish political thought. The main tradition in Scottish political discourse focussed on the defence of Scotland's autonomy as a sovereign, independent kingdom. Indeed, the origins of Scottish political thought are to be found in the arguments mustered by the kingdom's clerics in response to English claims of overlordship over Scotland. These surfaced in pleadings at the papal curia of Boniface VIII in 1299–1300 when Baldred Bisset replied to Edward I's assertion of rightful dominion over the whole island of Britain. Edward I had used Geoffrey of Monmouth's history of ancient Britain to justify an English *imperium* over Scotland. This, in turn, had necessitated the deployment of an alternative history of Scotland which explained the ethnic origins of the nation and the establishment of an independent kingdom of Scotland without any reference to the Galfridian account of British antiquity. In response to the accepted legend found in Geoffrey that Brut the first emperor of Britain had been of Trojan descent, a Scottish counter-mythology developed which traced the ultimate origins of the Scottish nation in the elopement of the Greek prince Gathelos and his Egyptian bride Scota, daughter of the Pharaoh, with their followers across the Mediterranean to Spain. The descendants of this Iberian nation, who were of course distinguished by their glorious Graeco-Egyptian pedigree, had eventually come to Scotland via Ireland, so the late medieval Scottish legend ran, and had established an independent monarchy there around 330 BC under the first king of Scotland Fergus MacFerquhard. This mythical history was set out in full for the first time between the early 1370s and the mid-1380s in the *Chronica gentis Scotorum* by John of

Fordun. Fordun's account of the origins of the Scottish monarchy in 330 BC became the standard version of Scottish history. It was perpetuated by Walter Bower, whose *Scotichronicon* of the 1440s built upon Fordun's interpretation of early Scottish history; presented in elegant Renaissance Latin by Hector Boece in his *Scotorum historiae* (1527); and – shorn of the fantastical Gathelos–Scota legend – repackaged in an enduring form in the *Rerum Scoticarum Historia* (1582) of the historian and political theorist George Buchanan (1506–82). Buchanan's reworking of Fordun's interpretation of Scottish history survived as a canonical element of Scottish political discourse until the early eighteenth century. Throughout the early modern period the principal arguments of Scottish political debate were framed by the facts of Scotland's purported origins as an independent monarchy in 330 BC. Scots of all political and religious persuasions agreed that the nation had enjoyed sovereign independence from these ancient origins. However, they disagreed about the nature of the monarchy founded in 330 BC. A line of royalist writers, including James VI and Sir George Mackenzie of Rosehaugh (1636/8–91), contended that Fergus I had established the kingdom as an indefeasible, hereditary monarchy. Others, including Buchanan, held the view that Fergus I had been elected Scotland's first monarch by the phylarchs, or clan chiefs, of the Scottish nation, and that by the terms of this ancient constitution of 330 BC the kings of Scotland were accountable to the nation (or, at the very least, its leading men) for their actions, and that it was legitimate to overthrow those kings of Scotland who degenerated into tyrants. The history of Scotland since 330 BC became a vast storehouse of precedents for royalist and anti-royalist interpretations of Scottish history.

An independent Scottish antiquity provided the primary matter of political debate in early modern Scotland. Despite wide divergences in the use that they made of the legend of 330 BC, most Scottish controversialists subscribed to the basic idea of an independent Scottish nationhood.[1]

Nevertheless, a lively minority tradition emerged during the sixteenth and seventeenth centuries which questioned the value of Scottish independence and sought some form of union with England. Its proponents, as Professors Roger Mason and Arthur Williamson have shown,[2] championed union for a variety of different reasons. Some were quietly pragmatic, arguing that on a small island such as Britain, union was a sensible option for the two warring kingdoms of Scotland and England. There was an idealistic element in this case: union would, after all, bring peace to the island.

---

[1] John of Fordun, *Chronica gentis Scotorum* (ed. W. F. Skene, 2 vols., Edinburgh, 1871–2); Hector Boece, *Scotorum historiae a prima gentis origine* (1527: Paris, 1574); George Buchanan, *Rerum Scoticarum historia* (1582), in Buchanan, *Opera omnia* (2 vols., Edinburgh, 1715); James VI, *The trew law of free monarchies* (1598), in James VI and I, *Political writings* (ed. J. P. Sommerville, Cambridge, 1994), p. 73; George Mackenzie, *Ius regium* (1684); C. Kidd, *Subverting Scotland's past* (Cambridge, 1993), ch. 2.

[2] R. Mason (ed.), *Scots and Britons* (Cambridge, 1994); R. Mason, 'Lineages of Unionism: early modern Scots and the idea of Britain' (an inaugural lecture delivered at the University of St Andrews, published in a shortened version as 'Posing the East Lothian question', *History Scotland* 8 (Jan.–Feb. 2008), 40–8); A. Williamson, 'Scotland, Antichrist and the invention of Great Britain', in J. Dwyer, R. Mason and A. Murdoch (eds.), *New perspectives on the politics and culture of early modern Scotland* (Edinburgh, 1982), pp. 34–58; A. Williamson, *Scottish national consciousness in the age of James VI* (Edinburgh, 1979), pp. 97–107.

Indeed, some Scots, on the defensive against English claims to suzerainty over the kingdom of Scotland, saw a genuine union of equals as a realistic alternative to English imperial domination of the whole island. Unionism, for some far-sighted and anxious Scots, was the opposite of English empire, not only of Scottish independence. Some Scots wondered whether providence provided clues as to God's design for the peoples of Britain. Was not the island of Britain destined to enjoy a united government? The cause of the Reformation reinforced this argument. After the success of the Reformation in England, several Scots Reformers anticipated its extension into the unreformed church in Scotland, and wondered at the prospect that Britain as a whole might become a beacon of the reformed religion. This became likelier after the success of the Scottish Reformation in the 1560s, and the happier co-existence of two Protestant realms in Britain. To some Scottish Protestants, the wider needs of the Reformed movement appeared to demand some kind of association between the English and the Scots. This acknowledgement of cross-border religious interests was formalised during the Civil Wars of the 1640s. The Solemn League and Covenant of 1643, an agreement between the Scots Covenanting presbyterians and the English Long Parliament to unite the British Isles – in religion, though not in government – was the culmination of a long tradition of religious unionism in early modern Scotland. Moreover, the fortuitous Union of the Crowns in 1603, when James VI of Scotland succeeded to the throne of England's childless spinster-queen, Elizabeth I, seemed to confirm expectations that providence had foreordained a union of the two Protestant kingdoms. Over the course of the sixteenth and seventeenth centuries this minority tradition, which embraced various kinds of unionism, became less peripheral, and by the very end of the seventeenth century had come to challenge the ideology of Scottish independence, though not yet to eclipse the legend of Scotland's ancient origins.

The origins of Scottish unionism

The founding father of Scottish unionism was the scholastic philosopher and historian John Mair (1469–1550), whose surname is sometimes found Latinized as Major). In 1521 Mair published his *Historia maioris Britanniae*, a title which played cleverly on his name. In this history of Greater Britain Mair rejected the preposterous origin myths of the English and Scottish nations, though not the – then – more plausible claim that the Scottish kingdom had originated under Fergus I. The story of Gathelos and Scota, reckoned Mair, was as risible as the English legend of Britain's founding under Brut. The Scots had concocted a pedigree back to the Greek prince Gathelos as a piece of oneupmanship, to rival the vaunted pedigree of the English, who had confabulated their own myth of Trojan origins. Not only were the respective Gathelos–Scota and Brut legends fanciful, these national myths had contributed to the disorders and internal convulsions which had wrecked the peace and prosperity of Britain. Indeed, it was Mair's contention that a common British interest – the common good of those who inhabited the island of Great Britain – transcended the particular, conflicting and tragically misunderstood interests of the Scottish and English kingdoms.

Only a union, Mair believed, would bring about a true alignment of Scottish and English interests. Not only did right
reason and common sense trump the inordinate love of Scotsmen and Englishmen for their particular patch of Britain, but
all the peoples of Britain – not just the descendants of the
original Britons, the people of Wales – were properly Britons
and interested – whether they knew it or not – in the fate of
the island as a whole. Indeed, the linguistic divisions of the
island, Mair noted, did not match political boundaries. The
conquered Welsh subjects of the English crown spoke Welsh;
Irish was spoken in the Highlands and Islands of Scotland;
and English was the lingua franca of Lowland Britain, of the
civilised Scots of the Lowlands and the people of England. Mair,
it was clear, did not subscribe to the view that Scotland had
been since its origins in 330 BC a Highland kingdom which had
since absorbed the rest of northern Britain. Unlike sixteenth-
century champions of Scottish independence, such as Boece
and, later, Buchanan, Mair took no delight in the pristine
and uncorrupted virtues of Highland Scotland. Instead, Mair
identified two distinct ways of life in Scotland: the wild Scots
of the Highlands seemed a people apart from the domestic,
householding Scots of the Lowlands. Nevertheless, although a
unionist and a debunker of national legends, Mair was steadfast
in his defence of a genuine history of Scottish independence
from English claims to an imperial authority over the whole
island. Union did not entail capitulation so much as a common acknowledgement of partnership and shared interests.
This would not be absorption as in the case of Wales, which
was entirely distinct from the Scottish case. The best hope for
the realisation of the common good lay in a marriage alliance

between the ruling dynasties of both kingdoms, which would bring about the rule of a single British monarch. This united British monarchy would be in the best interest of the peoples of both kingdoms, though the nobility – Mair's bugbear – would oppose such a scheme out of their own selfish interests, for, a law unto themselves, the nobles disliked the prospect that union might create a stronger pan-British monarchy which would manage to tame the overmighty subjects of the weaker and warring monarchies of England and Scotland. Welcome liberation from the evils of centuries-long Anglo-Scottish warfare provided more than adequate compensation for the loss of bogus origin legends and delusive national attachments which drew English and Scots alike away from their common interests as Britons.[3]

The advent of Protestantism persuaded some Scots unionists that the project of godly reformation overrode any concerns Scots might have about English imperial ambitions in Scotland. Indeed, a couple of Scottish unionist propagandists – the Highlander John Elder (fl. 1533–65) and the Edinburgh merchant James Henrysoun – became turncoats in the cause of English imperialism. Yet in neither case did such apparent treachery entail an abandonment of principle, for now English imperial claims over Scotland served to reinforce arguments for the extension of the English Reformation to England's northern neighbour, where Protestantism had made less headway and the Scots laity remained in the thrall of

---

[3] John Mair, *A history of Greater Britain* (transl. A. Constable, Scottish History Society, Edinburgh, 1892), esp. pp. 1–4, 17–18, 48–56, 127–8, 143–4, 167–8, 189–90, 216–19, 287–9, 333–5, 358–62.

a benighted priesthood. In short, imperialism was a vehicle of Reformation. In the early 1540s, after the Scots' defeat at Solway Moss and the death of James V, Elder wrote a letter to Henry VIII of England, calling for the amalgamation of England and Scotland under the rule of the Tudor monarch. Elder accepted the proposition – whose very rejection had been and otherwise remained the cornerstone of Scottish political thought – that Scotland was part of 'the empire of England'. However, Elder believed that a godly union under Henrician auspices promised to cleanse Scotland of old-style Catholicism, to purge Scotland of obnoxious French influences and to inaugurate an era of peace between the Scots and the English. A similar ensemble of arguments surfaced in Henrysoun's *Exhortacion to the Scottes to conforme themselves to the honourable, expedient and godly union betweene the realmes of England and Scotland* (1547). Henrysoun, like Elder, enjoyed a pension from the English government, having chosen to remove to England after the English invasion of Scotland in 1544. On the eve of a further English campaign in Scotland in 1547, planned by Protector Somerset on behalf of the godly boy-king Edward VI, Henrysoun earned his keep by publishing his case for a godly union of Britons under an English Protestant *imperium*. Indeed, Henrysoun argued for the re-establishment of a godly British imperial monarchy whose original foundation he traced back to the first Christian emperor of Rome, Constantine, who, according to Galfridian legend, had also been a king of the Britons. This line of argument conflated the mythical history of the Britons with the authority of the Roman emperorship to make a powerful case that the kings of Briton enjoyed an imperial status. The prospect that a marriage might be arranged between the infant Mary, Queen of Scots, and Edward VI of England – or compelled, in what Scots referred to contemptuously as the Rough Wooing – would restore Britain's ancient godly empire. It would also bring about the reunion of the divided and warring peoples of Britain – most of whom, Henrysoun claimed, were in fact descended of aboriginal British stock, notwithstanding the 'hateful' names of Scots and English by which they were now known. At bottom, however, Henrysoun's rhapsodies on empire were based upon deeply held Protestant commitments. God, he argued, had made Britain an island, and that island reunited under a single Protestant monarchy, would become – as it was destined to be – a bastion of Protestantism.[4]

However, the Rough Wooing of the 1540s was to be a lost opportunity for Anglo-Scottish reconciliation, a sad fact lamented by John Knox (c. 1514–72), the inspirational figure behind the Scottish Reformation and a champion of union. Yet, as Roger Mason has argued, there was a significant gulf

[4] John Elder, 'A proposal for uniting Scotland and England, addressed to King Henry VIII', *Bannatyne Miscellany* (Edinburgh, 1827), pp. 1–18; James Henrysoun, *An exhortacioun to the Scottes to conforme themselves to the honourable, expedient and godly union between the two realmes of Englande and Scotland*, in J. A. H. Murray (ed.), *The complaynt of Scotlande* (London, 1872), pp. 207–36; R. Mason, 'The Scottish Reformation and the origins of Anglo-British imperialism', in Mason (ed.), *Scots and Britons*, pp. 161–86, at 170–8; R. Mason, 'Scotching the Brut: politics, history and national myth in sixteenth-century Britain', in R. A. Mason (ed.), *Scotland and England 1286–1815* (Edinburgh, 1987), pp. 60–84; M. Merriman, 'James Henrisoun and Great Britain: British Union and the Scottish commonweal', in Mason (ed.), *Scotland and England*, pp. 85–112.

between the Scottish unionism of the Rough Wooing in the 1540s and the unionism of the Scottish Reformation of 1560.[5] The imperialism of Elder and Henrysoun was missing from the Knoxian vision of union. Nevertheless, there remained the same pragmatic rationale for enlisting English support for the Scottish Protestant movement, and the same desire to effect a harmonious relationship – whether confederacy, amity, league or perpetual friendship – between the Protestant peoples of Scotland and England. Although Knox has become an icon of the Scottish Reformation and a symbol of a harsh, authoritarian and unattractive version of Scottishness, it is important to remember that the fate of English Protestantism also loomed very large in his thoughts. Indeed, Knox was an important figure within the history of English Protestantism. In 1549 after his release from penal servitude in the French galleys, he sought refuge in England and became part of the community of 'assured Scots'[6] in north-east England. His first wife Marjory – to whom he was betrothed in 1553 and whom he eventually married in 1556 – was from Norham, and his two sons from this marriage grew up in England and were educated at Cambridge, where they both became fellows. Knox became committed to the cause of uncompromising reformation within Edward VI's England, and in 1551 moved to London to become a royal chaplain. It was only the unfortunate death of the young Edward VI in 1553 and the accession of his

---

[5] Mason, 'Scottish Reformation and the origins of Anglo-British imperialism', p. 181.

[6] M. Merriman, 'The assured Scots: Scottish collaborators with England during the Rough Wooing', *Scottish Historical Review* 47 (1968), 10–34.

Roman Catholic sister Mary to the English throne which drove him into exile from his English home. Knox's most notorious work of political thought, *The first blast of the trumpet against the monstrous regiment of women* was directed primarily not against Mary, Queen of Scots, but against Mary I of England and her attempts to re-Catholicize England. For most of the 1550s – at least until 1558 – the work of reformation in Scotland was peripheral to his central aim of reversing England's apostasy. Only with his return to Scotland in 1559 did Knox plunge back into the Reformation of his native land, a cause which relied heavily upon the support of the newly Protestant England of Elizabeth I, who had succeeded her sister Mary in 1558. Given the depth of Knox's immersion in English religious life, it should occasion little surprise that the Scots Reformation of 1560 should draw so heavily upon English inspiration, albeit of a more advanced and less compromising kind of Protestantism than prevailed within the English establishment itself.[7]

English, moreover, became the language of the Reformation in Scotland. Everywhere the Reformation encouraged the rise of a Bible-reading laity – a universal priesthood of believers – to replace the narrow Roman priesthood which had previously monopolised control of the Latin Vulgate scriptures and their interpretation. However, in Scotland the translation of the Scriptures into the vernacular and the spread of Bible literacy did not lead to the consolidation of the existing

[7] Mason, 'Scottish Reformation and origins of Anglo-British imperialism', pp. 179–80; John Knox, *The first blast of the trumpet against the monstrous regiment of women* (1558), in Knox, *On rebellion* (ed. R. A. Mason, Cambridge, 1994).

national tongue, Scots. Instead, it gave a tremendous boost to the spread of English. In this sense at least, if not in others, Scotland's distinctive Reformation was an epiphenomenon of England's. Even the hybrid Scots–English translation of the New Testament, which the Scots Lollard Murdoch Nisbet (fl. 1520) drew from Wycliff's English translation, circulated only in manuscript. The English Geneva Bible of 1560, first published in Scotland in 1579, was the official version of the Scots Reformation. From the early seventeenth century, the English King James Bible (1611) which carried the authority of King James VI of Scotland and I of England would become the standard translation of the Bible north and south of the border. In this way, English ceased to be foreign. The new world of print also contributed in other ways to the erosion of Scots, particularly in the area of orthography. Native printers – and authors ambitious of a wider circulation for their works – began to iron out Scots diction and phraseology into a language more closely approximating to English. Market pressures conspired to promote the silent erosion – from within Scotland – of the peculiar characteristics of Scots as a written language.[8]

Yet by no means did Scottish Protestantism speak with a single voice; nor was the dominant voice unionist. Alongside the political myth of the ancient Gaelic past there emerged a parallel ecclesiastical legend, a Protestant version of Scottish history. In his influential history of Scotland, George

---

[8] D. Murison, 'The historical background', in A. J. Aitken and T. McArthur (eds.), *Languages of Scotland* (Association of Scottish Literary Studies Occasional papers no. 4, Edinburgh, 1979), pp. 2–13, at p. 9.

Buchanan began to marry contemporary Protestant themes to the established narrative of Scotland's independent history from its ancient Gaelic foundations in 330 BC. Buchanan and his successors within the presbyterian historical tradition constructed a myth of Scotland's aboriginal Celtic Christianity which emphasised the indigenous roots within ancient Scotland not only of Protestant values, but even of presbyterian institutions. Scots presbyterian historians contended that Scotland had first received Christianity around AD 200 in the reign of (the mythical) King Donald I, significantly not from Petrine missionaries acting under the auspices of Rome, but at the hands of Johannine missionaries who represented the churches of Asia Minor. Thus, so the legend ran, the original constitution of the Church of Scotland had been independent of Rome and the Papacy. Moreover, presbyterian historians also argued that the Church of Scotland had been governed without bishops, under a kind of proto-presbyterian government. Governance of the Kirk had been a matter for colleges of monks, called Culdees, who had elected their own abbots. From the early seventeenth century in particular Scottish ecclesiastical historians turned to the early history of Gaelic Scotland as a means of justifying the Scottish Reformation. Although John Knox's *History of the Reformation of the Church of Scotland* had taken the origins of Scottish Protestantism back only as far as the Kyle Lollards of the fifteenth century, other historians, most notably David Buchanan (c. 1595–c. 1652) – ironically in his extended introduction to an edition of Knox – saw the potential to construct an illustrious indigenous pedigree for Scottish Protestantism out of existing historical materials. Similarly, David Calderwood (1575–1651) contended that a primitive Celtic Christianity without bishops had once flourished in Scotland. David Buchanan set out the system of Culdaic church government in more detail. The Culdees, who had been established in the third century by King Cratilinth, had elected overseers of the church from within their own ranks, but these superintendents had not formed a distinct order within the church. According to David Buchanan full-blown diocesan episcopacy had only made its appearance in Scotland during the eleventh century. Such arguments set out a distinctive case for presbyterianism in Scotland as part of the historic fabric of the national Church of Scotland before it succumbed to Romish corruptions.[9]

So, what then was the dominant orientation of Scottish political culture in the era of the Union of the Crowns, when James VI of Scotland inherited the separate throne of England as James I of that country? It is difficult to give a clear answer. Obviously, the influence of Protestantism had worked both to create a sense of a common cross-border Reformed interest in Britain and to construct a patriotic myth of an ancient proto-presbyterian constitution of the Scottish church. There was a Scots episcopalian variant of this myth,[10] and Scots

[9] Buchanan, *Rerum Scoticarum historia*, lib. iv, R. 27; lib. v, R. 42; lib vi, R. 69; John Knox, *The history of the Reformation in Scotland*, in Knox, *Works* (ed. D. Laing, 6 vols., Wodrow Society, Edinburgh, 1846–64), I, pp. 5–6; David Calderwood, *The history of the Kirk of Scotland* (ed. T. Thomson, 8 vols., Edinburgh, 1842–9), I, pp. 34–43; David Buchanan, 'Preface', John Knox, *The history of the Reformation of the Church of Scotland* (1644: Edinburgh, 1731), pp. lvii–lxxxiv.

[10] John Spottiswoode, *History of the Church of Scotland* (1655: 3 vols., Spottiswoode Society, Edinburgh, 1851), esp. I, pp. 2–7.

episcopalians were to be just as affronted as Scots presbyterians after 1603 by Anglican encroachments on the independent jurisdiction of the Church of Scotland.[11] Similarly, in the sphere of temporal politics Scots were exposed both to an enduring myth of independent Scottish nationhood from 330 BC and to the visionary idea that Britain might be united under an imperial figure – a modern Constantine – and that the consequence would be a regime of peace and plenty, in lieu of the Anglo-Scottish wars which had despoiled southern Scotland. In 1603 James VI and I appeared to be the prophesied modern Constantine, who would unite Scotland and England under terms favourable to Scotland.

Soon after his accession to the English throne, James VI and I – himself one of the most articulate and powerful champions of early Scottish unionism – embarked upon a project to establish a firmer union between the two kingdoms, a project which had run into the sand by 1607, largely owing to English defensiveness.[12] James's proclamations on his accession to the English throne had commanded his subjects to forget their former quarrels and expressed the wish that the union 'be perfected'.[13] James also proclaimed a symbolic change in the royal style from 'King of England, Scotland, France

---

[11] C. Russell, *The causes of the English Civil War* (Oxford, 1990), ch. 2.

[12] B. Galloway, *The union of England and Scotland 1603–1608* (Edinburgh, 1986).

[13] 'Proclamatioun anent the keeping of gude ordour in his Majesties journay touardis Londoun', in D. Masson (ed.), *Register of the Privy Council of Scotland*, VI (Edinburgh, 1884), pp. 558–61; 'A proclamation for the uniting of England and Scotland' (1603), in J. F. Larkin and P. L. Hughes (eds.), *Stuart royal proclamations*, I (Oxford, 1973), pp. 18–19.

[notionally] and Ireland' to 'King of Great Britain',[14] notwithstanding the fact that the Union of the Crowns had not – ironically – effected any such union of crowns or kingdoms. In 1604
a large Scottish delegation was appointed to negotiate with the
English regarding the possibility of a further and closer Anglo-
Scottish union, which gave rise to several Scottish unionist
tracts (several of which existed in manuscript form and went
unpublished at the time). The jurist John Russell (c. 1550–
1612) composed 'Ane treatise of the happie and blissed unioun'
in 1604. Here Russell supported further union to strengthen
Britain, and to bring about unity in religion. Had not Britain
been united once under the simple and uncorrupted religion of
the early Christian monarchs of the ancient Britons, such as –
the mythical – King Lucius?[15] The aristocratic adventurer and
Anglo-Scottish cleric John Gordon (1544–1619) also stressed
the importance of religious unity within Britain in *The Union
of Great Brittaine, or England's and Scotland's happinesse in
being reduced to unitie of religion* (1604). A united Britain,
Gordon argued, had a divine destiny within a divided Christendom.[16] In his dialogue *De unione Britanniae* (1604) Robert
Pont (1524–1606), a minister and jurist, welcomed a union
based not on conquest but upon friendship and religion, which
appeared to be a sign that God's providence favoured closer

[14] S. T. Bindoff, 'The Stuarts and their style', *English Historical Review* 60
(1945), 196, 213–14, 216.

[15] John Russell, 'Ane treatise of that happie and blessed Unioun', in B.
Galloway and B. Levack (eds.), *The Jacobean union: six tracts of 1604*
(Edinburgh, SHS, 1985), pp. 75–137.

[16] John Gordon, *The Union of Great Brittaine, or England's and Scotland's
happinesse in being reduced to unitie of religion* (London, 1604).

Anglo-Scottish ties.[17] Gordon, Russell and Pont all, in varying degrees of intensity and in slightly different idioms, envisaged union as a providential mission. The idolatries and superstitions of the past, it appeared, had been the prime causes of Anglo-Scottish estrangement. Nevertheless, religious enthusiasm for the idea of Britain remained tempered by concerns to avoid any suggestion that union might involve the imperial subjection of Scotland. Russell was especially insistent on the equality of Scotland with England; unification implied a partnership not the absorption of a Scots province into an English empire of Britain.[18]

Religion was not the only significant motivation behind the idea of closer Anglo-Scottish union. Historical, legal and institutional factors also played a part in contemporary Scottish unionist discourse, not least in the work of the Scots jurist Thomas Craig of Riccarton (1538?–1608). A commissioner for Union in 1604, Craig composed a series of important treatises on the Anglo-Scottish relationship. The sequence began before the Union of the Crowns with *De jure successionis regni Angliae*, which maintained James VI's hereditary right to succeed Elizabeth on the throne of England. There followed *De hominio*, which dealt with the question of the supposed homage owed by Scottish kings to the kings of England, and *De unione regnorum Britanniae*, which put the case for closer union. Despite some superficial divergences in their treatment of Anglo-Scottish issues, Craig's treatises preserved

---

[17] Robert Pont, 'Of the Union of Britayne', in Galloway and Levack (eds.), *Jacobean Union*, pp. 1–32.

[18] Russell, 'Treatise', esp. pp. 75, 89, 98–9, 126–8, 136.

a measure of balance between an aspiration to union and the traditional claims of Scottish independence. Craig proposed a union which would merge the existing kingdoms of Scotland and England into a single state, yet, notwithstanding this vision of British integration, insistently denied that Scotland had ever been a mere vassal kingdom of an English empire. By implication, of course, he suggested that English imperialist fantasy of this sort provided no solid basis for union. In *De unione* Craig advanced an interpretation of British history which ascribed all its calamities and reverses to the island's internal divisions. Lack of unity among the ancient Britons had allowed the Romans to conquer Britain; thereafter political disunity had been a factor in a devastating sequence of invasions – of the Scots, Saxons, Danes and Normans. Later, Anglo-Scottish warfare had been a prime reason for England's loss of her possessions in France. Indeed, most of the problems of the previous 600 years had arisen from the quarrels and rivalry of England and Scotland. Yet Great Britain was naturally fitted to be a single state. As an island, Craig contended, it was a well-defined expanse of territory, and its peoples adhered to the same basic forms of law and spoke the same language. Britain called out to be unified under a single regime, which might overcome the anarchic history of two (or more) competing powers, an unhealthy situation which had led to catastrophe after catastrophe in Britain's disordered past. The greatest of England's kings, Craig conceded, had realised that the absorption of Scotland was necessary to protect English interests, but the only means at hand had been conquest (with all its attendant miseries) or matrimonial alliance. Fortunately, it was the latter which, a century after the marriage in 1503 of James IV to the daughter of Henry VII, had, by way of the deaths without heirs of Henry VIII's offspring, Edward VI, Mary I and Elizabeth I, brought Britain under the rule of a single monarch. The succession of James VI to the throne of England allowed the inhabitants of Britain to perceive more clearly their common interests. Indeed, Craig likened Britain to a corporation in which every member had a duty towards the welfare and security of the corporation as a whole. No longer was Britain fated to be a two-headed monster confined uncomfortably to a single body. The union Craig envisaged would not be a treaty between England and Scotland which preserved aspects of their former autonomy and distinctiveness but the complete fusion of the two states into a single realm. There were several essential building blocks for a perfect union of this sort. The new kingdom required a single name (which would help to erase former national distinctions) and a single government (which would pursue impartial policies on behalf of the whole united realm), and in addition there needed to be some basic similarities in religion, language, laws and customs which might bring the old nations together as one. Fortunately, the Reformation had drawn England and Scotland together and their differences in worship were inconsiderable by comparison with the core doctrines on which they agreed. Similarly, the Scots dialect was a variant of Old English, and there were no insuperable obstacles to integration on this score. Despite obvious differences between Scots law and the English common law, Craig subscribed to the view that there were nonetheless key areas where the two legal systems corresponded. While procedures differed between England and Scotland, common feudal principles underpinned the laws of heritable property on both sides of the border. Nor did Craig accept the commonplace view that, while Scots law was indebted to civilian principles, the common law was untouched by the Roman law. Surely, Craig wondered aloud, there were more civilian influences in the English law than its champions were prepared to admit. However, Craig recognised that any union of Scots and English law would have to be based on the original principles of feudal jurisprudence, dating from an era which preceded the more recent divergences of Scots and English laws. Nevertheless the abandonment of the names of England and Scotland was vital to inhibit the revival of old enmities. Only under the name of Britons, Craig believed, could Scots and English live together happily as common subjects of the same monarch.[19]

No Scot of the time expressed a more undiluted enthusiasm for the Union than the poet and historian David Hume of Godscroft (1558–1630?), a self-described 'Scoto-Britannus'. Hume composed a two-part Latin treatise on the theme of union under the title *De unione insulae Britannicae*. The first section, which set out the general case for a united Britain, was published in 1605, while the second portion – completed in 1605 and existing in several manuscript versions – presented the institutional arrangements which Hume believed might nurture and sustain a common British nationhood. Within the united kingdom there would be a single, supreme council, dominated by the nobility, whose membership would be drawn in equal number from both countries and to which

---

[19] Thomas Craig, *De Unione regnorum Britanniae tractatus* (transl. C. S. Terry, Scottish History Society, Edinburgh, 1909), esp. pp. 207–25, 231–4, 240–2, 252, 254, 264, 281–9, 297–9, 304, 311–22, 326–7, 390–407, 460–7.

various regional councils would be subordinate, as well as a common British parliament, whose forms and procedure would run along English lines, but which would meet in the heart of the island – in York, most probably, rather than in London. There would also be a common British order of knighthood, whose membership would be drawn equally from both sides of the old, redundant border. The law of England and Scotland – which differed much less, Hume contended, than popular caricature suggested – would continue as before, while cross-border legal disputes would be settled by a special court, composed of two judges each from both England and Scotland, the *censores Britannici*. A convinced presbyterian, Hume argued that there should be one united state religion for the British people, a church whose rites and organisation would be decided by the supreme council of Britain, with an expected preference, Hume imagined, for the tried and tested methods of Scots presbyterian discipline.[20]

However, attempts by the crown to achieve a degree of religious harmony in Britain sorely tested the stability of the regal union. While James VI and I was cannily cautious in his attempts to bring Scottish religious worship into a closer alignment with those of the Church of England, his son Charles I pushed harder. Charles I's attempts to provide for the maintenance of the Scottish church at the risk of reopening the Reformation land settlement in Scotland, and his introduction

---

[20] *The British Union: a critical edition and translation of David Hume of Godscroft's De unione insulae Britannicae* (ed. P. J. McGinnis and A. H. Williamson, Aldershot and Burlington, VT, 2002), esp. pp. 176–91, 200–5, 208–9, 224–49, 252–5.

of new canons and an English-style prayer book into Scotland generated a backlash among the most anti-Anglican of Scots clerics and within the landed elite. The revolt against Charles I found expression in the National Covenant of 1638, which upheld the distinctive national traditions of the Scots Reformation against Anglican encroachments. Yet by 1640 Charles I's policies – and the haughty abruptness of their introduction – had provoked rebellion in England too. As a result, the concerns for kirk and nationhood which were uppermost in the Covenanting movement in 1638 metamorphosed into a more ambiguous approach to the Anglo-Scottish relationship, with patriotic defensiveness increasingly counterbalanced by an ambitious – if hitherto suppressed – imperialism. In 1643 the Scots Covenanters concluded a treaty with the English Long Parliament, the Solemn League and Covenant, which embodied a sacred commitment to unite the churches of England, Scotland and Ireland on the common grounds of presbyterian church government. The first article of the Solemn League and Covenant listed the treaty's pan-Britannic goals and appeared to endorse Scots presbyterian practice as a blueprint for the reformation of its neighbours in England and Ireland:

> the preservation of the reformed religion in the Church of Scotland, in doctrine, worship, discipline and government, against our common enemies; the reformation of religion in the kingdoms of England and Ireland, in doctrine, worship, discipline and government, according to the word of God, and the example of the best reformed churches; and shall endeavour to bring the churches of God in the three kingdoms to the nearest conjunction and uniformity, in religion, confession of

faith, form of church government, directory for worship and catechizing; that we and our posterity after us, may, as brethren live in faith and love, and the Lord may delight to dwell in the midst of us.

The second article authorized the 'extirpation' not only of popery, but also of 'prelacy' (apparently in all three kingdoms) in order that 'the Lord may be one, and his name one in the three kingdoms'. The Solemn League and Covenant combined respect for the historic rights of the three kingdoms with aspirations to a deeper association of the British nations. Although the third article upheld the rights and privileges of the parliaments and liberties of the kingdoms, the fifth article promoted a measure of political union:

> And whereas the happiness of a blessed peace between these kingdoms, denied in former times to our progenitors, is by the good providence of God granted unto us, and hath been lately concluded, and settled by both parliaments, we shall each one of us, according to our place and interest, endeavour that they may remain conjoined in a firm peace and union to all posterity.[21]

However, it seems clear that the projected union of 1643 was in some ways the opposite of the Union eventually achieved in 1707. The 1707 Union was a political union which encompassed religious diversity, with two separate religious

---

[21] The Solemn League Covenant is found most conveniently in an edited version in G. Donaldson (ed.), *Scottish historical documents* (1970: Glasgow, 1997), pp. 208–10. For the full text, see *Acts of the Parliaments of Scotland*, vol. VI, pt 1, pp. 41–2.

establishments; the union advocated in the Solemn League and Covenant was envisaged as a religious union of the three nations along Scots presbyterian lines, which nevertheless comprehended political variations among the three kingdoms. Bringing the nations of the British Isles into the 'nearest conjunction and uniformity in religion' did not entail any overt political amalgamation.[22]

The Solemn League and Covenant did not, in practice, live up to the Scots' initial hopes for it. English Puritanism lapsed into independency, and the goal of a presbyterian Britain evaporated. Nevertheless, there were practical achievements. The Westminster Assembly of Divines – an Anglo-Scottish body meeting in London under the auspices of the Solemn League to hammer out the framework of a common British Protestantism – managed to produce a Confession of Faith, a Larger and Shorter Catechism, a Directory of Public Worship and a Form of Church Government. These documents held little appeal for English Independents, but were eagerly adopted in Scotland as the standards of Scots presbyterianism. Moreover, many Scots Covenanters, notwithstanding the failures of the Solemn League and Covenant, continued to regard the sacred engagement of 1643 as binding in perpetuity. In other words, Scots were bound by a holy obligation to effect a religious union with England. Unionism was, henceforth, for many a core commitment of Scots presbyterianism; though union, of course, on the terms apparently agreed by both England and Scotland in 1643.

[22] E. J. Cowan, 'The Solemn League and Covenant', in Mason (ed.), *Scotland and England*, pp. 182–202.

The Cromwellian conquest of Scotland and Ireland further complicated the idea of Britain. Technically, government was carried out under the auspices of the Commonwealth of England, Scotland and Ireland; but in the eyes of episcopalians and royalists, British integration, de facto or otherwise, was no less discredited than the concept of republican government. Covenanting presbyterians, on the other hand, remained wedded to the ideal of covenanted union and a godly covenanted monarchy. The Restoration of 1660 witnessed not only the restoration of the traditional order in the Scottish state, but also a return to the loose and decentralised Union of the Crowns, and the re-establishment of separate institutions of government in the Stuarts' dominions of England, Scotland and Ireland. Scottish political thought of the Restoration era – at least the political thought of the establishment – bore the imprint of royalist, episcopalian and patriotic values. Union remained a possibility to be entertained – and indeed it was championed by the leading royalist writer of the Restoration era, Sir George Mackenzie of Rosehaugh; nevertheless the need to defend the standard mythology of ancient Scottish history from the scepticism and counter-boasts of antiquaries from other parts of the British Isles, such as Edward Stillingfleet (1635–99), William Lloyd (1627–1717) and Roderic O'Flaherty (1627/30–1716/18), pressured Mackenzie into a posture of patriotic defensiveness.[23] While union had surfaced as

---

[23] George Mackenzie, *A defence of the antiquity of the royal line of Scotland* (1685); George Mackenzie, *The antiquity of the royal line of Scotland further cleared and defended* (1686); Edward Stillingfleet, *Origines Britannicae* (London, 1685); Roderic O'Flaherty, *Ogygia* (1685: transl.

a royalist project around 1668–70,[24] by the mid-1680s British political discourse was characterised by intense debate among the champions of the various nations of Britain on the very authenticity of the claim that Scotland's origins as an independent kingdom could be traced back to 300 BC. In this milieu, unionist arguments fell from view, except as the pledge of dissident Covenanting rebels.[25] Nevertheless, circumstances were to change after the Revolutions of 1688–9 which toppled James VII and II.

The idea of Anglo-Scottish union resurfaced as a possibility during the Scottish Revolution of 1689,[26] but had become a clearer objective of policy by the end of the decade. The failure of the Scottish colonial project at Darien in central America[27] had infuriated Scots, who, correctly identified English interference against a potential imperial rival in the Caribbean. Scots mismanagement had also blighted the project and there were wider fears about the ability of a small nation such as Scotland to engage seriously in the scramble for overseas possessions in the New World. Some form of commercial treaty with England – an economic union – might win Scotland

J. Hely, Dublin, 1793); William Lloyd, *An historical account of church government as it was in Great Britain and Ireland* (London, 1684).

[24] For the 1668 scheme of economic union and the plans of 1670 for a political union, see B. Levack, *The formation of the British state* (Oxford, 1987), pp. 10–11, 14, 45–6, 151, 164, 204.

[25] C. Kidd, 'Conditional Britons: the Scots Covenanting Tradition and the eighteenth-century British state', *English Historical Review* 117 (2002), 1147–76.

[26] Levack, *Formation*, p. 11.

[27] D. Watt, *The Price of Scotland: Darien, Union and the Wealth of Nations* (Edinburgh, 2007).

admission to the trading zone regulated by the English Navigation Acts. Yet anglophobic sentiment ran high. However, the death of Princess Anne's last surviving child in 1700 created a succession crisis, which, in turn, gave the Scots some leverage with the English government. In the event of William II and III's death, Anne would succeed him; but now the line of succession expired with her. While the English entailed their crown (and the dependent crown of Ireland) on the Protestant Hanoverian line, this measure did not apply to the independent Scottish crown. The failure to persuade the Scots parliament to accept the Hanoverian succession created a further crisis. Might the Scots restore the Jacobite line deposed at the Revolution of 1689? To avoid such a perceived catastrophe, Queen Anne's politicians turned to an Anglo-Scottish Union as a means of winning Scots over to the Hanoverian succession. The momentous prospect of a Union with England generated a wide-ranging and sophisticated debate in Scotland, which featured a variety of unionist voices.[28]

The Union debates as intra-unionist conversation

Notwithstanding loud and widespread domestic opposition to the Union which was to occur in 1707, unionist voices predominated in the intense debates which gripped the Scottish political nation in the years immediately

---

[28] W. R. and V. B. McLeod, *Anglo-Scottish tracts, 1701–14* (University of Kansas Library Series 44, 1979); J. Robertson (ed.), *A union for empire* (Cambridge, 1994); K. Bowie, *Scottish public opinion and the Anglo-Scottish Union, 1699–1707* (Woodbridge, 2007).

preceding the Union of 1707. The axes of debate in the first decade of the eighteenth century were far from straightforward and defy easy reduction to the concepts of modern nationalists and unionists. Whereas today's historians – nationalist historians in particular – tend to misread the Union debates as a contest between nationalists and unionists, it will become clear that the struggle was largely one between incorporating unionists who wished to see Scotland and England united under a single parliament, and confederal unionists who wished to see a looser arrangement, with separate Scottish and English legislatures. Obviously, government controls on publication restricted the positive expression of Jacobite and anglophobic sentiments, but censorship was far from tight, and, in the massive expansion of print culture which Scotland witnessed in the decade before 1707,[29] debate ranged widely and pamphlets abounded with manifest evidence of popular irritation with English policy. Not that opposition to English policy or the dominant role of the English nation within the regal union since 1603 precluded the wish to establish a new and better form of association with England. However, on reviewing the evidence of pamphlets and printed speeches, it is hard to avoid the conclusion that unionist principles – sometimes, of course, loudly and uncompromisingly anti-incorporationist – were to be found on both sides of the debate over incorporating Union. Scottish historians have largely overlooked the discreet irony that the Union debates of 1698–1707, for one

---

[29] A. J. Mann, *The Scottish book trade, 1500–1720: print commerce and print control in early modern Scotland* (East Linton, 2000), pp. 24, 144, 147, 158–9, 165, 168, 175–6, 178–9, 186–91.

reason or another, largely took the form of an intra-unionist conversation.

On one issue, however, almost everybody agreed. There was an almost universal consensus that the Union of the Crowns had been a disaster for Scotland. But what was to be done? Independence and total incorporation stood at the extremes of the range of options facing Scots in the first decade of the eighteenth century. Between these positions Scots proposed various solutions which might rectify the problems besetting the Union of the Crowns. Suggestions included reforms of the regal union, most obviously the imposition of a scheme of Scots parliamentary limitations on the power of the dual monarch, the establishment of a proper confederal constitution to define the Anglo-Scottish connection, and – the outline of the Union eventually achieved in 1707 – a modified incorporating Union, where distinctive Scottish institutions such as the Kirk and Scots law enjoyed special protections under the – otherwise – sovereign sway of a united British crown-in-parliament.

The most articulate opponents of the Union on offer did not champion outright Scottish independence. Figures such as Andrew Fletcher of Saltoun (1653?–1716), James Hodges and George Ridpath (d. 1726) did not find themselves confronted with the stark alternatives of union or independent nationhood. In lieu of a unitary British state with a single sovereign parliament, Hodges and Ridpath preferred some kind of confederal association of England and Scotland in which a Scottish parliament would guard the privileges of the Scots presbyterian kirk, while Fletcher's proposed solutions ranged from a practical scheme of limitations on the British multiple monarchy to a utopian reordering of Europe into several leagues of modestly sized city states, one of which would comprise the British Isles reorganised into a loose federation of provinces.[30] The idea of Britain, or of some British association of states, was not anathema to the principal critics of Union. Far from obsessing about Scottish independence, they had, as we shall see, other fish to fry.

James Hodges produced a series of pamphlets arguing against incorporating Union. His primary concerns were to safeguard the autonomy of the Scots presbyterian Kirk from Anglican interference and 'to clear what kind of union is most agreeable to the true interests of both nations'. Hodges insisted that an incorporation was not a genuine union. Instead he favoured 'a confederate or federal union' whereby

> distinct, free, and independent kingdoms, dominions or states, do unite their separate interests into one common interest, for the mutual benefit of both, so far as relates to certain conditions and articles agreed upon betwixt them, retaining in the mean time their several independencies, national distinctions, and the different laws, customs and government of each.

Hodges distinguished 'interfering interests', areas in which, he believed, it would be sensible for Scotland and England to retain autonomy, with 'unitable interests' – including shared interests in peace within the island of Great Britain, common

---

[30] Andrew Fletcher, *Account of a conversation* (1704), in Fletcher, *Political works* (ed. J. Robertson, Cambridge, 1997); J. Robertson, 'Andrew Fletcher's vision of union', in Mason (ed.), *Scotland and England*, pp. 203–25.

defence, trade and the succession to the throne (or thrones) – which would be the platform for an enduring and workable union. However, there would be no security for Scotland in a supposed incorporating union, for where 'interfering interests' jarred, English interests would prevail. 'Britain', Hodges concluded, was a piece of camouflage disguising the true nature of incorporation; for, 'notwithstanding this new name, Old England is to remain as much Old England as ever', with the Scottish nation, on the other hand, dispossessed of the least 'shadow of a kingdom'. Incorporation, when its underlying mechanics were understood, stood revealed as 'no union at all'.[31] George Ridpath was an anti-incorporationist of a similar stamp. In his *Considerations upon the union of the two kingdoms* (1706) Ridpath favoured a union of parliaments, but also the retention of a separate Scots legislature. While a common British parliament would deliberate on shared issues of peace and war, trade and prosperity, Ridpath contended, the Scots parliament would deal with matters particular to Scotland, such as Scots law, and the status of a separate Scots presbyterian church.[32]

Although now appropriated by the Scottish National Party as a nationalist icon, Fletcher of Saltoun was an unconventional anti-unionist. Indeed, he had promoted a closer union between Scotland and England at the time of the

---

[31] James Hodges, *The rights and interests of the two British monarchies . . . treatise I* (London, 1703), p. 3; Hodges, *The rights and interests . . . treatise III* (London, 1706), pp. 15–17, 118–19.

[32] George Ridpath, *Considerations upon the union of the two kingdoms* (n.p., 1706), esp. pp. v–vi, 36, 40–4, 65–6.

Glorious Revolution in 1689. Nevertheless, by the early eighteenth century that moment had passed, and Fletcher had become increasingly pessimistic not only about Scotland's predicament, but about the fates of other small states like it within a Europe of leviathan powers. One solution advocated by Fletcher in a series of speeches delivered to the Scottish parliament in 1703 was to reform the Union of the Crowns through the imposition of limitations upon the crown, given that Scotland's monarchy was, in effect, an English institution which, generally speaking, advanced policies in the interests of the core English kingdom of the British multiple monarchy. However, in the broader context of European geopolitics it was clear that a reform of the Anglo-Scottish regal union would be insufficient to solve Scotland's plight. Indeed, Fletcher concluded that, given the harsh realities of the European states system, small state independence was illusory. In his utopian *Account of a conversation* (1704) Fletcher's message was neither unionist nor straightforwardly anti-unionist. He warned of the dangers of massive urban cores which sucked the life out of rural peripheries and distant provinces. But this trend was seemingly inexorable; the only hope for small entities was a complete – and unrealistic – reordering of Europe into leagues of city states. These leagues would restore the lost balance of the European states system and inhibit the growth of powerful imperial monarchies, each centred on a single metropolis. Curiously, Fletcher envisaged the British Isles as one such league, with Scotland itself broken up into two city states, one centred on Stirling, the other on Inverness. Within this utopian fantasy the loss of Scottish nationhood itself seemed a small price to pay for the end of superpower ambitions which produced endless wars and hypertrophied cities which, engrossing as these were to an urbane and well-travelled sophisticate such as Fletcher, thrived at the expense of their hinterlands. A convinced opponent of incorporation, Fletcher is nevertheless difficult to parse convincingly as an outright opponent of Anglo-Scottish association or a champion of viable independent Scottish nationhood.

Fletcher's pan-European range was far from atypical. The case against Union was strikingly cosmopolitan and far from insular. Anti-incorporationists identified models for Anglo-Scottish association in the loose confederal unions of early modern Europe. Indeed, both sides – incorporationist and anti-incorporationist – were informed by the unions, leagues and associations of the recent European past. Unions seemed to be a ubiquitous feature of European politics. Contemporary Scottish pamphlets discussed the Union of Kalmar (1397–1523) which combined Denmark, Sweden and Norway under the primacy of Denmark; the Union of Lublin (1569) which created the Polish–Lithuanian commonwealth; the United Provinces of the Netherlands; the Helvetic League of the Swiss Cantons; and the composition of the imperial monarchies of France and Spain.[33] Ridpath pointed to the equal authority enjoyed by the various cantonal assemblies in the Swiss confederal association as a model for the Anglo-Scottish relationship. He also argued that the

---

[33] Hodges, *Rights and interests I*, esp. pp. 2–4, 8; *A short account of the Union betwixt Sweden, Denmark and Norway which commenced about the year 1396 and was broke about the year 1523 . . . fit to be perus'd by Scotsmen at this juncture . . .* (Edinburgh, 1706).

Polish–Lithuanian commonwealth, the Spanish union and the United Provinces of the Netherlands all preserved important constitutional privileges within their component parts. Rigid centralisation, Ridpath argued, was not necessary for effective association. Europe provided a set of models of successful federal relationships.[34] Hodges pointed to the success of looser unions – 'well-ordered federal conjunctions' – such as found among the United Provinces of the Netherlands, Swiss cantons and Polish–Lithuanian commonwealth. In such unions 'a plurality of independencies or distinct provinces, cantons or governments' were 'knit fast together by an amicable consideration bottomed on lasting mutual interest'.[35] But a so-called incorporating union of England and Scotland would not be a proper union of interests. However, where anti-unionists saw nations, the leading incorporationists, William Seton of Pitmedden (1673–1744) and the Earl of Cromarty (1630–1714), saw the results of successful incorporating unions. Seton cited several examples of solid and enduring incorporating unions, such as the ten kingdoms of Spain, the twelve states of France and – closer to home – the English heptarchy. On the other hand, noted Seton, within looser non-incorporating unions, the weaker partner tended to lose out and eventually to separate from the larger nation, as Portugal had from the Spain of Philip IV, or Sweden from Denmark.[36] Cromarty exploded the distinction between support for nationhood and support for

[34] Ridpath, *Considerations*, pp. 37–9.
[35] Hodges, *Rights and interests I*, p. 65.
[36] William Seton, *A speech in parliament the second day of November 1706* (1706), pp. 9–10.

union. What was viable nationhood in the Europe of 1700, suggested Cromarty, but the result of a series of successful unions and amalgamations? French, Spanish and English nationhood rested on such unions. Would Aragon, say, or Britanny, Cromarty wondered, be better off as independent units? England too, he argued, was not so much a nation as a union, the historic merger of the Anglo-Saxon heptarchy into a single, indivisible national unit. According to both Seton and Cromarty, the history of Scotland itself involved a history of successful incorporation, though they differed in their accounts of this history. Whereas Seton claimed that 'Scotland itself was formerly divided into two kingdoms, which at present are incorporated into the one kingdom of Scotland', Cromarty maintained that Scottish nationhood was the outcome of a series of amalgamations of ancient tribes and ethnic groups such as the Catti, Horesti, Brigantes and Picts. Indeed, Cromarty insisted that Scottish nationality was a construct, like those of other European kingdoms. The direction of history, Cromarty seemed to be suggesting, was towards the amalgamation of smaller nations, by way of incorporating unions, into larger and more viable nation states.[37]

It is sometimes forgotten that there was also a unionist critique of the projected Union. In another of the neglected ironies of British integration, many anti-Unionist Scots presbyterians were more deeply committed to the ideal of

---

[37] Cromarty, *Paraneisis pacifica* (London, 1702), pp. 4–5; Cromarty, *Trialogus* (1706), pp. 6, 9–15; Cromarty, *A letter from E. C. to E. W. concerning the Union* (Edinburgh, 1706), pp. 3, 5–7; Cromarty, *Second letter on the British Union* (1706), pp. 2–3, 18.

74

Anglo-Scottish union than the incorporationists themselves. For some Scots presbyterian opponents of the Union the ecclesiastical integration of the British peoples was a long-term ideological goal to which they were pledged by the Solemn League and Covenant of 1643. Union – albeit not the Union actually on offer – was a Covenanting imperative.[38] Thus some Scots presbyterians viewed the Union of 1707 as a betrayal of the true Scottish unionist tradition, whose principles were set out in the Solemn League and Covenant. The very group with the most powerful and emotional connection to the idea of Britishness found itself disillusioned with the Union, despite its safeguards for securing the privileges of the Kirk. Instead Scots Covenanters supported 'a union in the Lord with England' consistent with their Covenant engagements.[39] Covenanters were to be found inside as well as outside the Kirk. Outside the Kirk were Cameronian groups who maintained an open commitment to the Covenants, while the presbyterian Kirk itself had been re-established in 1690 without reference to the Covenants. However, although the Covenants had not been renewed in 1690, neither had they been expressly repudiated. Some hardline presbyterians within the Kirk shared the view of the Cameronian minority that the Covenants – amphibiously anti-English and pro-unionist, depending upon the relative weight one attached to the sacred pledges of 1638 and 1643 – were still binding upon Scotland. The leading supporter of Covenanted union within the Kirk was the Reverend James

---

[38] Kidd, 'Conditional Britons'.

[39] *To His Grace Her Majesties High Commissioner the humble address of a considerable body of people in the south and western shires* (1706).

Webster (1658–1720) whose pamphlet *Lawful prejudices against an incorporating union with England* (1707) rejected the Union on offer as a 'manifold breach of the Solemn League'.[40] The fact that the Union was a pluralist arrangement recognising the distinct presbyterian and episcopalian establishments of Scotland and England flew in the face of Covenanting pledges to implement presbyterian government throughout the British realms. 'Should we not begin with England where we left in 1643', wondered a pamphlet attributed to the Lanarkshire minister the Reverend Archibald Foyer (d. 1710), 'and if they will not join with us upon such terms, ought we not to protest against the breach of covenant, and look to God for help in choosing a king of our own?'[41] In other words, going it alone as an independent kingdom was an alternative option in the event of England's refusing to agree the right kind of covenanted union. Ecclesiastical pluralism was not enough, not least when Scots presbyterians felt themselves committed by the Solemn League and Covenant to a kind of ecclesiastical imperialism, the remaking of Britain as a presbyterian polity. Given that Covenanters believed that they were solemnly pledged by the Covenant of 1643 to accomplish the 'extirpation' of prelacy throughout the British Isles, the ecclesiastical pluralism on offer in 1707 was an offence, they believed, against God. They were opposed to the Union of 1707 not because they were

---

[40] James Webster, *Lawful prejudices against an incorporating Union with England* (Edinburgh, 1707), pp. 4–5.

[41] [Archibald Foyer?], *Queries to the presbyterian noblemen and gentlemen, barons, burgesses, ministers and commoners in Scotland* (n.p., n.d.), p. 2.

opposed to an Anglo-Scottish union per se, but because it was an abomination. The Union of 1707 deviated in too many significant features from the template for Anglo-Scottish co-operation outlined in the Solemn League and Covenant. To be sure, presbyterian discipline was guaranteed in Scotland, but the Union also provided similar safeguards to the Anglican establishment. Worse, the framers of Union had done nothing to prevent Anglican bishops – contrary to the strict presby-terian prohibition on the interpenetration of the temporal and spiritual spheres – from sitting in the British House of Lords. Nevertheless, although they opposed the Union of 1707, Covenanters were most emphatically not separatists. Despite the fact that the Solemn League and Covenant did not envis-age an explicitly political union, the Scots Covenanters of the Union era continued to employ the rhetoric of 'the three king-doms' and tended to eschew a separatist critique of the Union. For separatism would mean, in effect, to renege on the sacred Covenant obligations which bound England, Scotland and Ire-land together.

Covenanted presbyterians were not the only true believers in Anglo-Scottish union. The incorporationist case for Union was not simply predicated on a hard-nosed accep-tance that England was determined to solve its Scottish ques-tion by way of a union, whether the Scots liked it or not. Neither did it depend on Scottish self-interest in the economic sphere, at a time when Scotland was recovering from the devastat-ing famines of the late 1690s and the collapse of the Darien scheme. There was also an idealistic case for Union, and par-ticularly for incorporation into a single British nation. As an oppositionist in 1700 William Seton of Pitmedden had already set out a blueprint for union which was more comprehensive than the modified incorporation of 1707. In *The interest of Scotland in three essays* (1700, with a second edition in 1702) Seton proposed the full integration of laws and churches in Britain as a project of enormous benefit to Scotland. Unconvinced by claims made for the divine right status of any particular form of ecclesiastical polity, the latitudinarian Seton wondered which form of church government would best conform to the post-Revolution constitution. Identifying episcopal hierarchy as a pillar of absolute monarchy, Seton concluded that, were England and Scotland to unite, as he believed they should, their liberties would be best protected by an Erastian union of their churches under either superintendency or presbytery.[42] Both in 1700 and again in his pamphlets and speeches in support of Union in 1706, the liberation of the Scottish tenantry from an oppressive and tyrannical class of feudal lords and lairds constituted a central theme in Seton's vision of a united Britain.[43] Similarly, another principled unionist, the jurist Francis Grant, concluded that the passing of Scotland's capricious unicameral parliament was no real loss; despite Scotland's paltry representation in the new British parliament, the rights of the Scottish people would actually be better protected under the guardianship of England's more robust bicameral legislature.[44]

---

[42] William Seton, *The interest of Scotland in three essays* (1700), pp. 23–35.

[43] *Ibid.*, pp. 57–8; Seton, *A speech in parliament*, pp. 7–8; William Seton, *Scotland's great advantages by an Union with England* (1706), p. 12.

[44] Francis Grant, *The patriot resolved* (1707), pp. 15, 19–20.

The most advanced incorporationist was Cromarty, who believed in full incorporation and the replacement of the old national names of England and Scotland with a wholehearted commitment to the idea of a common and undiscriminating Britishness. Cromarty ridiculed the misguided sentimentality and incoherent 'sophisms' of false patriots who 'would rather have a piece of Britain under their patrocinie, than it should be in a whole, and thereby in the state of a durable life'.[45] The Union needed to be fully incorporating or it would perpetuate Anglo-Scottish interests and divisions. It was in the interest of Scots to become full-blooded British patriots. Such reasoning applied both to the domestic sphere of politics within the new British polity and to the international scene. Working from the same analysis of European power politics as Fletcher, but reaching diametrically opposed conclusions, Cromarty argued that in a Europe of powerful territorial and maritime empires, Anglo-Scottish incorporation had become a strategic necessity for the maintenance of the European balance of power, not least when the nightmare loomed of Franco-Spanish universal monarchy. British Union was a necessary contribution to the War of the Spanish Succession. Might not the small sacrifice of Scottish nationhood – for Scottish sovereignty as such had evaporated during the century of regal union from 1603 – help to secure the liberties of Europe as a whole?[46] Cromarty's commitment to incorporation was deeper and more extensive than the compromise

---

[45] Cromarty, *Second letter*, p. 18.
[46] Cromarty, *Letter from E. C. to E. W.*, p. 3.

Union ratified in 1707.[47] Some flavours of Scottish unionism were, it seems, more unionist than the Union itself.

[47] C. Whatley, *The Scots and the Union* (Edinburgh, 2006), argues persuasively that the Union achieved in 1707 fell significantly short of a fully incorporating union.

3

Analytic unionism and the issue of sovereignty

The Union of 1707 is an enigma which defies easy constitutional analysis. This undertaking took its rise from the reluctance of the Scots parliament to fall into line with the English Act of Settlement (1701) which entailed the English crown on the Hanoverian line. The Scots rejected overtures to agree the Hanoverian succession to the crown of Scotland. An alternative strategy to bring the Scots to accept the Hanoverian succession was to offer the Scots a Union with England which involved significant trading advantages for the Scots but also incorporated their recalcitrant parliament with England's and provided for their adherence to the Hanoverian succession. In the summer of 1706 two sets of commissioners acting on behalf of Queen Anne in her two distinct regal personalities as Queen Anne of England and Queen Anne of Scotland negotiated the terms of a Union agreement. These twenty-five Articles of Union – which dealt with the Hanoverian succession, the union of the two parliaments, fiscal matters, trade and the continuation of a separate system of Scots law, but wisely avoided the contentious issue of religion – were sent to the Scottish parliament for ratification. With some modest amendments and the addition of an Act – integral to the Union settlement – which guaranteed the privileges and autonomy of the established presbyterian Church of Scotland in perpetuity, the Articles of Union were embodied in an Act of the Scottish parliament. This agreement was then ratified in an Act of the

English parliament which passed further guarantees for the security of both the Churches of Scotland and England. On 1 May 1707 a new state, the United Kingdom of Great Britain came into being, and sixteen Scots representative peers and forty-five Scots MPs joined the existing Houses of Lords and Commons respectively. There was, however, no general election in England to mark the founding moment of a new British parliament.[1]

The Union was an anomalous arrangement which is hard to align with the conventional categories of international law and political science. Problems surrounding the interpretation of the Union do not pertain only at the level of internal contradictions within the text, but also arise from a fundamental ambiguity about the character and status of the Union itself. Was the Union of 1707 a Treaty or an Act of Parliament – or even two Acts of separate and equally sovereign Scots and English parliaments? If the Union was a Treaty, did the parties to the Treaty continue to exist after 1707 and is the Treaty justiciable in international law? Indeed, when was the Treaty agreed and when did it expire, if at all? Did the Union constitute the fundamental law underpinning the British state, or did the English, now British, parliament remain untrammelled in

---

[1] For the text of the Union agreement, see G. S. Pryde, *The Treaty of Union of Scotland and England 1707* (London and Edinburgh, 1950), pp. 81–120. Alternatively, *Acts of the Parliaments of Scotland 1124–1707* (ed. T. Thomson and C. Innes, 12 vols., Edinburgh, 1814–75), XI, pp. 402–3, 406–13; *The Statutes at Large*, IV (London, 1769), 5 Anne c. 8, pp. 223–34. An edited version is available in G. Donaldson (ed.), *Scottish historical documents* (1970: Glasgow, 1997), pp. 268–77.

its sovereign capacity to amend legislation, the Act of Union included? Or, even if the latter were indeed the case, was the Church of Scotland a specially protected matter which was untouchable by an otherwise omnicompetent British parliament? What was the constitutional significance of the fact that some (but not all) Articles of Union and the Act for Securing the Kirk of Scotland appeared to be entrenched by language describing certain provisions as unalterable in all time coming? Did entrenchment really mean forever? Were there, moreover, degrees of constitutional entrenchment? Did the Union create a new set of political institutions in the United Kingdom or were Scots members of parliament and representative peers simply absorbed within pre-existing English institutions? Did the Union destroy the legal persona of either Scotland or England? Does the fact that there is no British legal system, but rather separate legal institutions for England and Scotland, mean that there is no single body of British constitutional law, but rather two, one Anglo-British, the other Scoto-British? Moreover, is the United Kingdom – contrary to popular belief and current political practice – bound to a written constitution, one to be found in the Treaty of Union?

Until recent decades, however, these problems had no purchase whatsoever in English constitutional and legal thought. The doctrine of unlimited parliamentary sovereignty reigned supreme. In particular, the constitutional wisdom of the eminent English jurist A. V. Dicey (1835–1922) went unchallenged, south of the border at least until the final quarter of the twentieth century. Dicey had famously claimed that 'neither the Act of Union with Scotland, nor the Dentists Act, 1878, has more claim than the other to be considered a supreme law'.[2] This apothegm was by no means Dicey's last word on the Union, and, as we shall see later, he did attempt, elsewhere in his writings, to honour the special significance of the Act of Union – though without yielding the irresistible point of untrammelled parliamentary sovereignty. Nevertheless, it was the cruder maxim which became the orthodox standard of the Diceyan tradition of constitutional law. There was, indeed, a compelling logic to Dicey's view that in the last resort there were no truly fundamental laws within the British constitution and that, however they appeared to differ in constitutional significance, the Act of Union and the Dentists Act (1878) stood on the same footing with regard to the authority of a sovereign parliament. Nevertheless, the accession in 1973 of the United Kingdom by treaty ratified in parliament to the new legal order of the European Community seemed to bear some affinity to the neglected Union of 1707.[3] Moreover, the courts were soon faced with the intractable problem – most notably in the Factortame fishing dispute[4] – of adjudicating in cases where the expressed will of parliament in domestic legislation openly contradicted the writ of European law, which further loosened English constitutional thinking from the constraints

---

[2] A. V. Dicey, *Introduction to the study of the law of the constitution* (10th edn, Basingstoke, 1959), p. 445.

[3] Cf. J. D. B Mitchell, 'What happened to the constitution on 1 January 1973?', *Cambrian Law Review* (1980), 69–86.

[4] There were seven Factortame cases, of which the most important was the first, 'R. v. Secretary of State for Transport ex parte Factortame Ltd. and others (no. 1)' (1989), *Common Market Law Reports* 55 (1989), 353–409.

of Diceyan orthodoxy. Was the Communities Act (1972) of no more significance than the Dentists Act (1878)? Now, by analogy with problems raised by accession to the European Community, the Union of 1707 was again in play as a matter of vexed constitutional interpretation.

Thus, the constitutional dilemmas which arise out of the Union of 1707, far from having been resolved – as Diceyans had once complacently assumed – remain a matter of intense debate. There is no agreement in the current academic literature as to whether post-1707 Britain was a brand new state constituted by the Treaty of 1707 or whether the British state embodied continuities from the pre-1707 states out of which it was formed. Furthermore, these unanswered questions raise vital issues about the entrenchment of Scottish differences within the Union and about the location of the ultimate source of authority within the United Kingdom. Thus, although for many Scottish unionists, unionism – banal unionism indeed – involved nothing more complicated than a straightforward loyalty to the British state, for a small articulate minority unionism entailed inquiry as well as allegiance. Profound questions about the very being of the Union and the institutions which – supposedly – derived from it, have, at certain points over the past three centuries, intrigued some of the more constitutionally literate elements of Scottish unionism, particularly jurists, political theorists and historians.

These attempts to define the nature of the Union and the British state are different in kind from other strains of unionist political thought, and might be described as analytic unionism. By analytic unionism I do not mean to suggest that this type of unionism is necessarily detached and objective.

Some exponents of analytic unionist arguments were deeply committed to advancing particular interpretations of Scotland's place within the Union; others treated the Union as a matter of genuine perplexity within the fields of law or political science. On some occasions one detects a mixture of motivations including both a decided ideological stance on the Union and a desire to understand the Union or the British constitution as objectively as possible. Given this difficulty of disentangling pure inquiry from polemical purposes, this chapter will explore analytic unionism in its various modes, from the academic to the partisan.

There is another crucial problem of definition to consider. At certain points analytic unionism shades into nationalism. Indeed, some of the most penetrating questions about the nature of the Union have come from nationalists.[5] While banal unionists take the Union for granted, nationalists, like analytic unionists, take it very seriously indeed. This chapter will highlight the subversiveness which lurks within analytic unionism and its close proximity in certain areas to positions adopted by Scottish nationalists. Analytic unionism is but a step away from deconstructive unionism. This is because the events and key documents of 1706–7 do not easily fit into conventional English understandings of the British state and its constitution, but seem in fact to contradict them. Thus the attempts of analytic unionists to understand the Union risk subverting the shibboleths of British statehood.

---

[5] See below, chapter 7.

Parliamentary sovereignty in the Union debates

The issue of parliamentary sovereignty – the sovereignty of the pre-Union Scottish parliament and, by extension, though secondarily, the future sovereignty of the British parliament – had already been debated by Scots at the time of Union. In the first instance, Scots asked whether it was within the remit of the Scottish parliament to incorporate Scotland's sovereignty with England's without some process of wider communal consultation. Anti-incorporationists called for representatives to consult with their constituents before proceeding to alter Scotland's fundamental constitution, a step which, they claimed, would otherwise be *ultra vires*.

The presbyterian writer Robert Wyllie resurrected and republished the earlier arguments of the eminent seventeenth-century jurists Sir George Mackenzie and Sir John Nisbet of Dirleton (1610–88) about the procedure which ought to be followed in case of a Union negotiation with England. Mackenzie had claimed that 'commissioners for shires and burghs' within the Scots parliament were 'the same with us that *procuratores universitatis* are in the civil law', namely that they 'could not alienate the rights of their constituents without a special mandate for that effect'. He had also insisted upon a *liberum veto* within each parliament – English as well as Scots – on the matter of Union. Whereas legislation was a matter for a 'plurality' within the parliament, membership within the legislature was a form of dominion or property which could not be voted away by a majority, but only with the consent of every single member. As a result Wyllie contended that the Scots parliament cannot find it within the compass of their power, to ratify any treaty, that may import the everting of our constitution, and the cutting us off from being a nation, as well as a church, without consulting the whole nation. Which may be done, by printing the treaty for general information; and after a recess and competent time to advise, returning again next session with the fresh sentiments and instructions of their constituents, upon so essential and fundamental an affair.

Wyllie maintained that 'parliaments cannot overturn fundamentals', insisting upon a distinction between fundamental and ordinary laws, with the former – essentially a type of dominion or property rather than the matter of lawmaking – 'above the reach' of parliamentary legislation. Wyllie also foresaw that acceptance of an unrestrained parliamentary sovereignty in the Scottish legislature had significant consequences for Scotland's security within a future united kingdom. If the Scots parliament 'could by a plurality of voices, overturn the fundamentals, and destroy the very being of our parliament; how shall it be possible to secure our parliament, when it is joined in with the parliament of England?' Might a majority in the British parliament not cavalierly decide to 'overturn any fundamentals that shall be condescended upon?'[6]

Thus the debate over the sovereign authority (or otherwise) of the Scottish parliament also raised the issue of how

---

[6] Robert Wyllie, *A letter concerning the Union, with Sir George Mackenzie's observations and Sir John Nisbet's opinion upon the same subject* (1706), pp. 5, 7, 9–12, 14–15, 17.

far a united British parliament might be constrained by the Articles of Union. The most compelling answers to Wyllie's charges came from David Symson and the Earl of Cromarty. Symson countered the civil law argument that members of the Scottish parliament enjoyed merely procuratorial authority by arguing that procurators were empowered to do everything that might be to the advantage of their community, and that if the Union were in their interest it was right for them to consent to it without further consultation. Nor did Symson accept Wyllie's claim that the veto of a single member was sufficient to stop the Union. Rather Symson invoked the authority of the Dutch jurist Hugo Grotius to argue that the sovereign power possessed *dominium eminens* – 'eminent domain' – the authority to dispose of his subjects' rights for the common good.[7]

Cromarty rejected Wyllie's powerful interrogation of the sovereign powers of the Scottish parliament. Cromarty reasoned that

> in every nation, there is an absolute necessity of government, of governors and governed, in distinction without reciprocation or confusion in these two; of a sovereign supreme, in whom, the last result of authority doth reside. And that such a supreme government, being absolutely necessary, must of necessity reside somewhere, but not in the governed; nor can it possibly be by delegation, or, of its nature.

---

[7] David Symson, *Sir George Mackenzie's arguments against an incorporating Union particularly considered* (Edinburgh, 1706), pp. 9–10, 13.

Cromarty insisted that the sovereign authority held by the Queen and parliament included the power to redraw the constitution. There were no fundamental laws beyond the reach of sovereign power. Delegation, Cromarty noted, was logically inconsistent with sovereignty. Sovereign power – by its very nature – could not be held to account. The alternative – including a hypothetical 'primitive independent convocation of the governed' – was in effect a form of anarchy. Cromarty located the sovereignty of Scotland in the crown-in-parliament and maintained that, far from being delegates, the representatives of the shires and the royal burghs were 'true integrant parts of the sovereign constituted body'.[8]

Indeed Cromarty and another prominent unionist writer William Seton of Pitmedden were quite content to acknowledge the sovereign competence of crown and parliament untrammelled by any notions of fundamental law. In his speech of 18 November 1706 on the Third Article of Union, Seton directly informed the parliament that there was no validity in the claim that the representatives of the burghs and shires could not approve this Article of the Treaty – which dealt with the incorporation of parliaments – without the assent of their constituents. 'Our government', Seton declared, 'is not a Polish aristocracy founded on *pacta conventa*, whereby all the gentry are impowered in their particular meetings to prescribe rules to their representatives in a general diet.' Nor, Seton reminded the parliament, was the government 'a common democracy,

---

[8] Cromarty, *A friendly return to a letter concerning Sir George Mackenzie's and Sir John Nisbet's observation and response on the matter of the Union* (1706), esp. pp. 6–7, 15, 18, 21, 25, 29.

whereby every subject of Scotland may claim a vote in the leg-islature'. Seton was a convinced believer in the untrammelled authority of sovereign bodies. He argued in this same speech to parliament that there were 'no fundamentals of government in any nation, which are not alterable by its supreme power, when the circumstances require'. Although the destruction of the natural rights to liberty and property went beyond the competence of any legislature, Seton was clear about the oth-erwise unlimited sovereign competence both of the crown and parliament of Scotland and of the proposed new united king-dom of Great Britain, welcoming the prospect of 'our liberty, property and religion, secured under the protection of one sovereign, and one parliament of Great Britain'.[9]

On the other hand, Seton's fellow incorporationist, the jurist Francis Grant (1658 × 63–1726), who would later be elevated to the Scots judicial bench as Lord Cullen, argued that the future British parliament was limited in its powers in the same way that an estate held in entail did not confer unconstrained rights of property upon its possessor:

> In point of right, the united parliament erected by the
> Articles [of Union], hath no power as to what is made
> ours, by these, not being in the case of a parliament
> originally constituted without limitation; which hath the
> command of simple alterable laws, though never so well
> hedged by preceding parliaments. Whereas *quoad* the
> interests reserved by an unchangeable contract in a

---

[9] 'An abstract of the proceedings on the Treaty of Union within the parliament of Scotland', in D. Defoe (ed.), *History of the Union of Great Britain* (Edinburgh, 1709), pp. 79–80.

primitive constitution, it is no parliament at all, *pro tanto*;
but private men. The same way as an heir in a tailzied
estate differs from him who receives an illimited fee from
his predecessor.[10]

Grant's main objective was to persuade Scots that their rights
would be better protected in a united British parliament, which
was explicitly constituted with guarantees for Scottish rights,
than in a Scots parliament unconstrained in its powers to alter
Scots law. However, the Union was far from explicit about how
issues of constitutional law might be resolved. John Spottiswoode (1667–1728) in *The trimmer* (1706) thought that the Articles of Union were defective because they made no provision
for reserved powers to summon a Scottish parliament (or, more
properly, the Estates) in the event that an English-dominated
British legislature might at some future point attempt to make
a fundamental alteration to the Articles. Nevertheless, in lieu of
such provisions (including the referral of any intended change
in the Kirk's to a General Assembly of the Kirk), Spottiswoode
was nevertheless clear that parliamentary sovereignty was
limited – implicitly – by the Articles of Union:

> If the British parliament shall, contrary to the Articles of
> Union, usurp a power to overthrow our separate and
> peculiar interests (which is scarce possible) then Scotland
> by the law of all nations may have recourse to their
> parliaments and meetings of estates for their own security
> and safety, as freely and lawfully as if no Union had ever
> been concluded betwixt the two kingdoms; for this is a

---

[10] Francis Grant, *The patriot resolved* (1707), p. 11.

condition implied in all leagues, treaties and contracts
betwixt different states and kingdoms, that the breach of
one article (especially if it be a substantial and
considerable one) makes the whole league, treaty or
contract void and null.[11]

Given the lacunae of the Treaty on the mechanics of how a dispute between England and Scotland might be resolved within
the institutions of the Union, there was no clear consensus,
even among Scots incorporationists, regarding the sovereignty,
or otherwise, of the new British parliament.

Imperial crowns

Questions of sovereignty had also surfaced in another
crucial theatre of pre-Union disputation, what has become
known to scholars as the imperial crowns debate.[12] This concerned the claim of some English historians and pamphleteers
that the English monarchy had historically enjoyed a measure
of suzerainty over the kingdom of Scotland, which was, in
fact, dependent upon an English imperial crown. Although
the form and matter of the imperial crowns debate now seem
antiquarian and apparently remote from the mainstream of
political thought, contemporaries realised that the stakes were
high. If Scotland was already subordinate in this way, then
any Union would not be a proper treaty in international law

---

[11] John Spottiswoode, *The trimmer* (Edinburgh, 1706), pp. 8–9.
[12] W. Ferguson, 'Imperial crowns: a neglected facet of the background to
the Treaty of Union of 1707', *Scottish Historical Review* 53 (1974), 22–44.

between co-equal sovereign kingdoms, and this would in turn leave a question mark over the validity of the Union agreement.

The origins of the imperial crowns debate lay far back in the history of Scotland's troubled awareness of the imperial pretensions of its neighbour. As early as the tenth century it had been the boast of the Anglo-Saxon kings that they were overlords of Britain as a whole: the coinage of Athelstan described him as *rex totius Britanniae*. The fact that from 1124 Scottish kings held lands in England as vassals of the English crown appeared to lend credence to the continuing claims of the monarchs of England that they were the overlords of Scotland. Moreover, the twelfth-century chronicle of Geoffrey of Monmouth lent historical legitimacy to the claim of the kings of England to be the suzerain high-kings of the whole of Britain, if not the British Isles as well. In 1174 the Scottish king William the Lion found himself the captive of Henry II, and won his freedom only by the open concession in the Treaty of Falaise that Scotland was in a state of feudal subjection to the English crown. However, the issue came to a head in the reign of Edward I, who attempted to make real his pretensions to a pan-Britannic sovereignty. Having conquered Wales, Edward exploited a succession crisis in the Scottish royal line to insist upon his pretended rights as suzerain over the Scottish kingdom. Edward assumed the role of umpire in the matter of the Scottish succession; then, when his chosen nominee King John Balliol refused to serve in the army of his overlord, Edward invaded Scotland and attempted to incorporate it within his English realm. Edward's invasion was soon followed by a propaganda campaign, which drew inspiration from Geoffrey of Monmouth's mythical history of Britain. In reaction, Scots constructed their own rival history of Scottish independence as a counter to English claims of suzerainty.[13]

The ideological battles of the late thirteenth and early fourteenth centuries were explicitly revived during the Union debates. In 1695, responding to the discovery and publication by Thomas Rymer, the king of England's historiographer, of archival evidence that Malcolm Canmore had performed homage to Edward the Confessor, George Ridpath published an edition of Thomas Craig's treatise on homage, *De hominio*, under the unambiguous title *Scotland's soverainty* [sic] *asserted: being a dispute concerning homage, against those who maintain that Scotland is a feu, or fee-liege of England, and that therefore the king of Scots owed homage to the king of England*. Scottish sovereignty was presented in such a way that it answered the pretensions of those who questioned the existence of an independent Scottish sovereignty. The next phase of the debate was launched by the English whig polemicist William Atwood in his book *The superiority and direct dominion of the imperial crown of England over the crown and kingdom of Scotland* (1704), which was followed by a sequel in 1705. Atwood claimed that the monarchs of England were heirs to an ancient pan-Britannic *imperium* and that the kingdom of Scotland was a feu held by the sub-kings of Scotland from an English

[13] R. R. Davies, *The first English empire: power and identities in the British Isles, 1093–1343* (Oxford, 2000), chs. 1, 2; C. Kidd, 'The matter of Britain and the contours of British political thought', in D. Armitage (ed.), *British political thought in history, literature and theory, 1500–1800* (Cambridge, 2006), pp. 47–66. For the origins of English imperialism within the British Isles, see D. Armitage, *The ideological origins of the British Empire* (Cambridge, 2000).

feudal superior. The Scots parliament ordered Atwood's work to be burnt by the public hangman and paid the lawyer and antiquary James Anderson (1662–1728) handsomely for his riposte, *An historical essay shewing that the crown and kingdom of Scotland is imperial and independent* (1705).[14]

While, on the one hand, the Union agreement itself seemed an implicit rejection of England's imperial claims over Scotland, Scots remained concerned lest the English come to assume that the Union was anything less than a treaty between sovereign equals. Thus, although the Scottish side of the imperial crowns debate had deep and historic associations with the cause of Scottish independence, it now became a central plank of Scottish unionist argument. During the Scottish Enlightenment of the eighteenth century anxieties about sovereignty centred on the impression that English historians still seemed in thrall to the idea that England had enjoyed an imperial suzerainty over the whole of Britain. Scots were aware that false memories of another Treaty – the extorted Treaty of Falaise (1174) – lurked behind English assumptions about the real meaning of the Treaty of Union. A strict and honest construction of the Union of 1707 required Scottish unionist historians

---

[14] Thomas Craig, *Scotland's sovereignty asserted* (ed. and transl. George Ridpath, London, 1695); William Atwood, *The superiority and direct dominion of the imperial crown of England over the crown and kingdom of Scotland* (London, 1704); William Atwood, *The superiority and direct dominion of the imperial crown of England . . . reasserted* (London, 1705); *Acts of the Parliaments of Scotland*, XI, p. 221; James Anderson, *An historical essay shewing that the crown and kingdom of Scotland is imperial and independent* (Edinburgh, 1705). See also James Anderson, *Selectus numismatum diplomatum Scotiae* (Edinburgh, 1739).

to expose the emptiness of English imperial pretensions and their total irrelevance to a modern Britain which was founded on treaty. Scots unionists were not prepared to concede that the Union state was, in effect, an English empire. The cleric and historian William Robertson spelled out the benefits of Union in his *History of Scotland* (1759), but insisted upon a strict construction of the events of 1706–7: 'If the one crown had been considered not as imperial and independent, but as feudatory to the other, a treaty of union could not have been concluded on equal terms, and every advantage which the dependent kingdom procured, must have been deemed the concession of a sovereign to his vassal.'[15] The same issue exercised David Hume, who used his *History of England* to explode the damaging myth of an English imperial crown. Hume has a very pointed passage which discusses Edward I's quest for evidence to support his claim of feudal superiority over Scotland. Hume was in no doubt that this was a 'pretended superiority' which lacked the authority of any 'authentic testimony' in the English crown's archival record of homages performed by the kings of Scotland. As a result, Hume noted, Edward I 'ransacked' the monasteries 'for old chronicles and histories written by Englishmen, and he collected all the passages, which seemed anywise to favour his pretensions'. Hume reckoned that Edward I's methods 'must have discovered to himself the injustice of his claim'. For the Saxon materials 'when stripped of the bombast and inaccurate style of the monkish historians' amounted only to the fact that 'the Scots had sometimes been defeated

---

[15] William Robertson, *History of Scotland*, in Robertson, *Works* (London, 1831), p. 54.

by the English, had received peace on disadvantageous terms, had made submission to the English monarch, and had even perhaps fallen into some dependance on a power, which was so much superior, and which they had not at that time sufficient force to resist'. The records of the Norman era, Hume contended, were 'if possible, still less conclusive'. Chroniclers did recount homages performed by the kings of Scotland, 'but no one of them says that it was done for his kingdom, and several of them declare, in express terms, that it was relative only to the fiefs which he enjoyed south of the Tweed'. There was one unambiguous exception to this meagre record. Hume does concede that when William the Lion found himself prisoner of Henry II in 1174 'he was obliged, for the recovery of his liberty, to swear fealty to the victor for his crown itself'. Nevertheless, Hume was at pains to stress that this homage was 'the only one of the kind, and as historians speak of this superiority as a great acquisition gained by the fortunate arms of Henry II there can remain no doubt, that the kingdom of Scotland was, in all former periods, entirely free and independent.'[16]

In the standard early nineteenth-century history of Scotland, *Caledonia* (1807), its staunchly unionist author, George Chalmers (1742–1825), felt obliged to reprise these arguments. After all, the issue of imperial crowns was still alive, the English historian George, Lord Lyttelton, having discussed in his *History of the life of King Henry the Second* (1771) how the peace of Falaise had secured 'the feudal subjection of

---

[16] David Hume, *History of England* (6 vols., Indianapolis, 1983), II, pp. 88–9; Note A, II, pp. 526–8.

Scotland to the crown of England'.[17] Chalmers recounted how
the unfortunate surrender of Scottish independence by the
Treaty of Falaise (1174) had been only temporary in its effect,
for it had been promptly followed by the Quitclaim of Canterbury (1189) in which Richard the Lionheart 'made a formal restitution of the independence of Scotland, with all her
rights . . . and as the kingdom was bounded, at the captivity of
William'. Although Chalmers highlighted this formal English
concession of Scottish autonomy, he thought it 'was to be
lamented, that William accepted what Richard agreed to convey, the earldom of Huntingdon, and other English territories',
because the performance of feudal ceremonies on behalf of
these lands seemed to create the impression that the Scottish
kingdom as a whole depended upon the English crown. Nor did
the Quitclaim of Canterbury stand alone as an official English
acknowledgement of Scotland's historic independence. The
Treaty of Northampton (1328), which brought a formal end
to the first Scottish War of Independence, had, according to
Chalmers, 'settled the peace, between Scotland, and England,
as two independent states; and which was also confirmed by
Parliament, who again acknowledged the sovereignty of Scotland, according to its limits, at the demise of Alexander III'.
This was the necessary platform, it appeared, for the oppor-
tune moment almost four centuries later when, in Chalmers's
careful description, commissioners were appointed 'to treat of
an union between the sister kingdoms'.[18]

---

[17] George, Lord Lyttelton, *The history of the life of King Henry the Second*
(4 vols., London, 1767–71), III, p. 171.

[18] George Chalmers, *Caledonia* (London, 1807), pp. 629, 632, 819, 865.

This language of 'sister kingdoms' would become a common trope of nineteenth-century Scottish unionist rhetoric; a happy coinage, perhaps, but one which served to rebut English assumptions that the Union was an English empire, a position set out with insensitive force by a number of leading English historians over the course of the nineteenth century. In *The rise and progress of the English Commonwealth* (1832) Francis Palgrave attacked the traditional Scottish interpretation of Scotland's historic relations with England. Moreover, he claimed that the Scots had acknowledged the king of the Anglo-Saxons to be the 'Basileus of Britain', the emperor of the whole island, and that after the Norman Conquest the new kings of England continued to hold the Scottish Lowlands in a state of feudal vassalage.[19] This prompted an immediate response from the London-based Scot, John Allen (1771–1843), a Holland House whig, whose *Vindication of the ancient independence of Scotland* appeared in 1833. Palgrave long remained a target of Scottish unionist hostility. As late as the 1860s, James Hannay rejected Palgrave's claim that 'Scotland was a mere part of the Saxon empire, and that Edward had a just claim to its suzerainte.'[20] Palgrave's slurs were repeated by Edward Freeman (1823–92) in his *History of the Norman Conquest of England*, the first volume of which was published in 1867. Freeman contended that from the tenth through to the fourteenth

---

[19] Francis Palgrave, *The rise and progress of the English Commonwealth: Anglo-Saxon period* (2 vols., London, 1832), I, pp. 444, 473, 476–7, 480–1, 562–4, 598–624.

[20] James Hannay, 'The Scot at home', *Cornhill Magazine* 14 (Aug. 1866), 238–56, at 240.

century 'the vassalage of Scotland was an essential part of the public law of the Isle of Britain'.[21] The Free Churchman, the Reverend James Begg (1808–83), who had his own special complaint about perversions of the Union in the ecclesiastical sphere, but was otherwise a unionist, albeit a very strict constructionist, stoutly resisted the 'false theory' that Scotland had become a 'kind of Yorkshire on this side of the Tweed'. Scotland, Begg argued, should not be 'regarded as a conquered province of England, but as a distinct independent kingdom, which was united with England on equal terms, and under a clear and solemn treaty'.[22] By the late nineteenth century some of the first stirrings of Scottish nationalism, unsurprisingly, took the form of assaults on the theories of English empire propounded by the likes of Palgrave and Freeman. What is perhaps more surprising is that the arguments of the first modern Scottish nationalists bore a very close similarity to a long-established *unionist* response to English imperial pretensions.

Parliamentary sovereignty

In the long run, however, it was to be the other problematic aspect of sovereignty – the issue of parliamentary sovereignty within the constitution of the Union state – which was to arouse controversy within the Scots unionist intelligentsia of jurists and clerics. However, there was no debate over parliamentary sovereignty during the eighteenth century,

---

[21] Edward Freeman, *The history of the Norman Conquest of England*, I (Oxford, 1867), p. 61.

[22] James Begg, *A violation of the Treaty of Union the main origin of our ecclesiastical divisions and other evils* (Edinburgh, 1871), p. 3.

when it attracted much less attention from eighteenth-century Scottish commentators than the question of imperial crowns. Not that Scottish constitutional theorists spoke with a single voice on the topic of sovereignty. The eminent jurist, Lord Bankton, who sat on the judicial bench, claimed that the Scots presbyterian Kirk was an entrenched part of the British constitution, beyond the reach of parliament: 'no infringement can be made upon that establishment without breach of the Union, whereas formerly it was alterable at pleasure of the legislature, having no other than an act of parliament for its security'.[23] More broadly, though in a similar vein, John Bruce (1745–1826), the Professor of Logic at Edinburgh, noted in an aside that the 'treaty of union [was] now held to be a fundamental law of both realms'.[24] On the other hand, John Erskine, the Professor of Scots Law at Edinburgh, subscribed to the logic of parliamentary sovereignty:

> The right of legislation is vested in the sovereign alone, or the supreme power of the state; for none other but the supreme power has a right to exact our obedience. No independent state can subsist without a supreme power, or a right of commanding in the last resort; and supreme power cannot restrain itself. No enactment, therefore, of the legislative power in one age, can fetter that power in any succeeding age; for the legislature of every age, as it has the unlimited power of making laws, must have the same

---

[23] Lord Bankton, *An institute of the laws of Scotland* (3 vols., Edinburgh, 1751–3), I, p. 22.

[24] John Bruce, *Report on the events and circumstances, which produced the Union of the Kingdoms of England and Scotland* (2 vols., 1799), I, p. 401.

right of abrogating or altering former laws; otherwise it would cease to be supreme. . . . [25]

By Erskine's lights, the very notion of fundamental law – inhering in the Union or elsewhere – was a nonsense.

During the eighteenth century there was clearly some divergence of opinion over the constitutional status of the Union, though this did not generate any serious debate. Nevertheless, the Ten Years' Conflict of 1834–43 in the Church of Scotland brought sharply into focus issues of parliamentary sovereignty and the entrenchment of Treaty rights as well, of course, as their ultimate incompatibility. Those ministers and lay members of the Church of Scotland, known as the Non-Intrusionists, who now directly challenged the parliamentary imposition of lay patronage on the Kirk, a festering sore in church politics since the Patronage Act of 1712, invoked the Treaty of Union to support the claim that the Church of Scotland enjoyed a sphere of autonomy independent of the British parliament. The Reverend William Hetherington of Torphichen (1803–65), for instance, claimed that the Act for Securing the Kirk of Scotland which accompanied the Union of 1707 was 'creative' of the British parliament and that any infringement of it was therefore a 'suicidal deed'; after all, 'no jurist will ever prove that the British parliament ever did or can pass an act greater than that to which it owes its existence'.[26] Hetherington's confidence in juridical reasoning

---

[25] John Erskine, *An institute of the law of Scotland* (2 vols., Edinburgh, 1773), I, p. 6.

[26] William Hetherington, *History of the Church of Scotland* (Edinburgh, 1842), p. 602.

was misplaced. The Non-Intrusionists' opponents within the Kirk – most notably the lawyers in the Moderate camp of the Church of Scotland led by John Hope – accepted the cold logic of parliamentary sovereignty. Notwithstanding these correctives the Kirk issued a Claim of Right in 1842 asserting that the guarantees of the privileges of the Church of Scotland which had been 'inserted in the Treaty of Union, as an unalterable and fundamental condition thereof' were 'reserved from the cognizance and power of the federal legislature created by the said Treaty'. Parliament did not acknowledge the pretensions of the Kirk, and the result was the Disruption of 1843. The withdrawal of around two-fifths of the Kirk ministers and members to form the Free Church of Scotland was a matter not only of ecclesiology, as we shall see in chapter 6, but also involved questions of parliamentary sovereignty and fundamental law. Parliamentary sovereignty was one of the compelling facts of British life, as Moderates recognised. Yet, tragically, Non-Intrusionists took the Union at face value as an unalterable entrenchment of the Kirk's spiritual autonomy – a position which, however impeccably unionist in principle, turned out to conflict irreconcilably with the prevailing norms of British political culture.

Nevertheless, in the aftermath of the Disruption the philosopher J. F. Ferrier (1808–64) produced a remarkable attempt to fuse the Kirk's claim of self-government with the doctrine of parliamentary sovereignty. In his *Observations on church and state suggested by the Duke of Argyll's Essay on the ecclesiastical history of Scotland* (1848) Ferrier founded a complex edifice of constitutional argument on the Protestant theory of the state. The Romanist and Reformed theories of government and ecclesiology, he argued, had been fundamentally dissimilar. The Reformation had abolished the notion that the sacerdotal function belonged to a distinctive group within society whose privileges and status ought to be specially protected. Rather the Protestant idea of the priesthood of all believers rendered church and state virtually synonymous. No longer did civil and ecclesiastical government belong to distinct temporal and spiritual realms. Extrapolating from this general insight to the particular case of the Scottish Reformation, Ferrier insisted upon 'the unclerical character of the General Assembly in its original idea and constitution'. The General Assembly of the Church of Scotland had not been a clerical council, but a genuinely national body, exemplified by the presence of a lay element in its composition. Far from being a synod, indeed, it constituted 'an extra House of Parliament, a second supreme national assembly, organised for the treatment of ecclesiastical topics'. Ferrier spelled out the constitutional implications for sixteenth-century Scotland: 'The one Scottish Parliament became, under the agitation of the Reformers, two Scottish Parliaments. And our General Assembly of the present day, however much it may have altered its character, is the second and junior of these Scottish Houses of Parliament.'[27]

Ferrier went on to argue that the Union of the Parliaments had been a limited one, encompassing the Scottish Estates but failing to comprehend the General Assembly, a forgotten element of the old Scots parliament which continued

---

[27] J. F. Ferrier, *Observations on church and state suggested by the Duke of Argyll's essay on the ecclesiastical history of Scotland* (Edinburgh and London, 1848), pp. 6–15.

under the aegis of the Union to enjoy a separate existence as an unacknowledged chamber of the British parliament. Ferrier reasoned that if, as he believed, the General Assembly was none other than 'our old Scottish Parliament existing under the phasis in which it transacted ecclesiastical business, it is obvious that it is responsible to no higher authority – that no authority higher than itself exists'. Of course, the old Scottish parliament appeared to have been incorporated within the British parliament; but this was only part of a complex story which had not been properly parsed. After all, conceded Ferrier, the Scottish parliamentary assemblies failed to understand 'even the alphabet of their own constitution'. The Union had seen only the abolition of the Scottish Parliament '*quoad civilia*'; but the Scottish parliament, Ferrier contended, 'never was abolished *quoad sacra*. It still exists for the transaction of ecclesiastical business.' Ferrier had discovered a hidden principle of the British constitution, 'that one and the same body sits in the General Assembly and in the House of Commons'.[28]

Ferrier boasted that his 'theory entirely justifies (although by a reasoning very different from its own) the General Assembly in its late resolute opposition to the decrees of the Court of Session'. The General Assembly was not an 'inferior tribunal', but one which enjoyed the sovereign powers of parliament with regard to ecclesiastical matters. It stood 'by birthright on a level with the highest court in the realm'. The House of Lords was not superior in a judicial capacity to the General Assembly, and had not – properly speaking – enjoyed the authority to overrule the General Assembly in the disputed

[28] *Ibid.*, pp. 19, 23, 30.

106

patronage cases of Ten Years' Conflict. Rather the relationship of these two Houses of Parliament – the Lords and the General Assembly – was analogous to that of the House of Commons and the House of Lords. One could apply a 'legislative check' to the other, no more. The House of Lords could not sit in judgement on the General Assembly, for the General Assembly, Ferrier insisted, 'is itself the state'.[29]

Ferrier argued that both state and church had behaved unconstitutionally during the Ten Years' Conflict. Instead, he steered a path between the rival claims of theocracy and Erastianism which had brought the Church of Scotland to implosion in 1843. The General Assembly, he argued, possessed 'supreme spiritual jurisdiction' – not from God, not from the state, but 'as the state'. Indeed, the Non-Intrusionist doctrine of the two kingdoms was, Ferrier claimed, fundamentally un-Protestant and a usurpation upon parliamentary sovereignty. Free Churchmanship and the traditional presbyterian doctrine of the two kingdoms were based – unconsciously, of course – on Romanist conceptions of the relationship of church and state which, although discredited at the Reformation, had crept back into the polities of Reformed states. The Non-Intrusionists had been in the right, but they had totally misunderstood their own position. These deluded clerics had imagined their rights to be clerical, when they were, in fact, parliamentary. Ferrier had shown how the doctrine of parliamentary sovereignty might be restated to vindicate the substance of the Non-Intrusionist position, but, equally clearly, he did not accept that Scots presbyterians might evade the authority of

---

[29] *Ibid.*, pp. 18, 21–2.

the sovereign. Nor did Ferrier stand as an orthodox defender of parliamentary sovereignty, not so long as he insisted that the General Assembly – like the rest of the British parliament was 'amenable to no earthly power'. The only way of rectifying this constitutional anomaly, Ferrier reckoned, was through the formal incorporation of the General Assembly in the House of Commons, an omission which had gone unnoticed in 1707 and had later led to the constitutional crisis of 1843. Ferrier's brand of analytic unionism was too uncomfortable and too eccentric to become part of the unionist mainstream.[30]

Moreover, the Scots critique of parliamentary sovereignty which had flourished briefly during the Ten Years' Conflict went into a century long hibernation, within the legal profession at least. The theories of sovereignty associated with the English jurists William Blackstone (1723–80), John Austin (1790–1859) and later, of course, Dicey would become the staples of Scottish constitutional law through to the 1950s. Insofar as there was continuing Scots dissent from the notion of parliamentary sovereignty it was, as we shall see in chapter 6, a clerical critique conveyed almost exclusively through the medium of ecclesiology and in terms of the crown rights of the Redeemer. On the other hand, Scots lawyers abandoned the language of fundamental law and Treaty rights. From the mid-nineteenth century even lawyers who were sympathetic to the high-flown theories of presbyterian ecclesiology succumbed to the view that the Treaty of Union could not constrain the sovereign will of the British parliament. A vivid example of this comes in the work of Alexander Taylor Innes (1833–1912), a leading

[30] *Ibid.*, pp. 18, 20, 29–34.

jurist, active member of the Free Church of Scotland and as such a critic of the British parliamentary betrayal of the Kirk. Nevertheless, Innes felt unable to articulate his grievances in a juridical idiom. In his *Law of creeds in Scotland* (1867) Innes catalogued various breaches of 'the international fairness and equality which the Union Treaty seemed to stipulate'. Objectionable as these were, Innes was under no illusions that there was any legal or constitutional remedy to hand. No generation could absolutely bind its successors, regardless of any commitment to irrevocableness enshrined in any agreement. Moreover, Innes asked: 'What party is there to insist on the fulfilment of the Union obligations to Scotland?' There was none, of course, for, as Innes noted, Scottish MPs at Westminster had, of course, no separate constitutional standing with regard to Scottish matters. Ultimately, Innes was in thrall to absolutist conceptions of sovereignty. 'Can the supreme power of the state be bound, absolutely and unchangeably, by *any* engagements?' he asked in vain.[31] This line of reasoning led Innes to a position on the voluntaryist wing of the Free Church. Disavowal of the Free Church's pretensions to be the true-establishment-in-waiting and, indeed, disestablishment of the Kirk itself would liberate the fractured Scots presbyterian tradition as a whole from the toils of parliamentary Erastianism. Juridical orthodoxy dictated that it was useless trying to engage with the British state, through insistence upon the fundamental rights enshrined in the Union; retreat from the state connection by way of voluntaryism was the only sensible option.

---

[31] Alexander Taylor Innes, *The law of creeds in Scotland* (Edinburgh and London, 1867), pp. 119, 125, 127.

By the late nineteenth century parliamentary sovereignty was a dominant feature of Scottish unionist culture. Aeneas Mackay (1839–1911), Professor of Constitutional Law at Edinburgh, argued in 1882 that it was not 'expedient' to 'bind for ever by any words the supreme power in the state'. Constitutional entrenchment was impractical. Mackay discerned the reality of British constitutional law: that after the lapse of 'a decent interval' since the Union of 1707, the legislature had 'discovered that the words "always" and "in all time coming" in the Act of Union meant only as long as they chose, and the evident utility of Scottish subjects the vote of a majority in the British parliament.'[32] Similarly realistic, the jurist Alexander McGrigor claimed in his tract *The British parliament* (1887) that the British parliament was 'supreme in power'.[33] The Scottish historian William Law Mathieson took the view that the framers of Union had attempted the impossible in 1707: 'Our ancestors called into being a sovereign parliament and then attempted by a mere injunction to restrain its power.' The British parliament, Mathieson believed, remained 'unfettered', for 'what the English and Scottish parliaments in 1707 declared to be unchangeable the British parliament will always be entitled to change'.[34]

---

[32] Aeneas Mackay, *A sketch of the history of Scots law* (Edinburgh?, 1882), p. 21.

[33] Alexander McGrigor, *The British parliament, its history and functions: an address delivered to the Liberal Unionist association of the College Division of Glasgow, On 28th January 1887* (Glasgow, 1887), p. 35.

[34] William Law Mathieson, *Scotland and the Union: a history of Scotland from 1695 to 1747* (Glasgow, 1905), pp. 213–14.

Curiously, a hard version of state sovereignty persisted even in the federalist unionism of F. S. Oliver (1864–1934). A Liberal Unionist with an open and creative mind, Oliver was one of the most sophisticated Scottish political theorists of the early twentieth century. Notwithstanding his commitment to the Union of 1800, Oliver's grave sense of the urgency of the Irish problem meant that he was prepared to contemplate novel solutions to it, including the reorganisation of the United Kingdom along federal lines. In addition, Oliver was also an imperial reformer, favouring a more cohesive system of governance within the British Empire. Indeed, it was this latter question which called forth one of the most incisive works by a Scot on the subject of political union, Oliver's book *Alexander Hamilton: an essay on American union* (1906). Tellingly, this exhibited some of the unusual characteristics of banal unionism. The book's ostensible subject was the transformation of the American experiment in government from a loose confederacy of states into a federal republic. Lurking behind this topic, however, was the real matter of Oliver's text, as he made clear in his extended theoretical conclusion: how might Britons draw lessons for the future consolidation of the British Empire from the American experience of state formation across a vast territory of multiple state governments? Oddly, but not untypically for a Scot of his time, Oliver's comparative approach to the study of unions barely touched upon the Anglo-Scottish Union of 1707. Nevertheless, one can pick up from stray references within the work Oliver's views on issues of sovereignty and fundamental law. The federal union of the United States was not so much a direct model for a union of the British Empire as a guide to the true essence of political union.

Nevertheless, Oliver was convinced that early twentieth-century Britain found itself in a Hamiltonian predicament: 'how may we convert a voluntary league of states, terminable upon a breath, into a firm union'. The British Empire was at present, Oliver believed, 'not a political fact, but only a phrase, an influence, or a sentiment'. The contemporary reality of imperial government was at odds with the theory of proper sovereignty and union. An intolerable situation prevailed, with a British democracy at the imperial core ruling over other democracies at the peripheries of Empire. The solution was to create a proper imperial union, without intermediate levels of imperial governance. The imperial centre needed to rule over peoples directly, not indirectly over states. 'Sovereignty', Oliver revealed, was the 'true nature of union'. The 'test of union' was the 'utter sovereignty of the central government'. Thus, true union precluded limitations on the sovereign power created by the union: 'Any political arrangement in which powers are withheld, or granted upon terms, or are subject to revision at the will of any member of the confederacy, is not a real union, but only an alliance.' There was, unsurprisingly, little scope for fundamental law in Oliver's analysis of union, and presumably in the Union which he barely mentioned.[35]

Nor did the sophisticated typology of unions set out by the constitutional jurist Arthur Berriedale Keith (1879–1944) in his *Theory of state succession* (1907) reveal more than a chink

---

[35] F. S. Oliver, *Alexander Hamilton: an essay on American union* (London, 1906), pp. 476, 481, 486. For Oliver, see D. G. Boyce and J. O. Stubbs, 'F. S. Oliver, Lord Selborne and federalism', *Journal of Imperial and Commonwealth History* 5 (1976–7), 53–81.

in the doctrine of parliamentary sovereignty. Although Keith acknowledged the Union as an enduring contract in international law, he did not consider this to be an insuperable restriction on the action of parliament: 'It is not possible to say that the terms of union between Scotland and England do not form a binding contract, though in that case both parties have really disappeared, and yet the terms of that contract are liable to be altered, and are altered from time to time by the Imperial Parliament.'[36]

Ironically, during the first half of the twentieth century the most suggestive interpretations of fundamental law were introduced into Scottish unionist culture by way of Dicey himself. *Thoughts on the Union between England and Scotland* (1920) was a work of Anglo-Scottish collaboration co-authored by Dicey and R. S. Rait (1874–1936), a Scottish constitutional historian and Principal of Glasgow University. In the course of the book Dicey and Rait attempted a nuanced reformulation of the doctrine of parliamentary sovereignty to take into account the curious arrangement of 1707, which seemed to create a reservation of apparently unalterable laws: 'The statesmen of 1707, though giving full sovereign power to the Parliament of Great Britain, clearly believed in the possibility of creating an absolutely sovereign legislature which should yet be bound by unalterable laws.' Yet the authors maintained that, whatever the statesmen of 1707 believed, entrenchment involved a logical contradiction. Nevertheless, Dicey and Rait made the marginal concession that the protected Acts of 1707,

---

[36] Arthur Berriedale Keith, *The theory of state succession* (London, 1907), p. 9.

most obviously the Act of Security for the Scottish Kirk, 'ought to be morally or constitutionally unchangeable, even by the British parliament'. In other words, such measures could not be logically unalterable; but in practice it would be recognised that to alter them involved a step so drastic that it threatened the very being of the constitution, and, in this respect would inevitably strengthen the hand of the political opposition to such a change. 'A sovereign parliament, in short, though it cannot be logically bound to abstain from changing any given law, may, by the fact that an Act when it was passed had been declared to be unchangeable, receive a warning that it cannot be changed without grave danger to the constitution of the country.'[37] Curiously, Dicey's *Introduction to the study of the law of the constitution* made clear how one slight change to the Union agreement of 1707 would indeed have enshrined the Union as the fundamental law of the United Kingdom, though without conceding his overall theory of sovereign government:

> If indeed the Act of Union had left alive the parliaments of England and of Scotland, though for one purpose only, namely to modify when necessary the Act of Union, and had conferred upon the parliament of Great Britain authority to pass any law whatever which did not infringe upon or repeal the Act of Union, then the Act of Union would have been a fundamental law unchangeable legally by the British parliament: but in this case the parliament of Great Britain would have been, not a sovereign, but a subordinate, legislature, and the ultimate sovereign body

[37] A. V. Dicey and R. S. Rait, *Thoughts on the Union between England and Scotland* (London, 1920), pp. 247, 252–4.

in the technical sense of that term, would have been the two parliaments of England and of Scotland respectively.[38]

Such Diceyan niceties were, however, lost on early twentieth-century Scottish unionists.

The basic Diceyan doctrine of unlimited parliamentary sovereignty remained the orthodox position in Scottish constitutional jurisprudence as late as the middle of the twentieth century when the standard textbook in the field for Scottish lawyers was Walter Fraser's *An outline of constitutional law*, which appeared in 1938 and was followed by a second enlarged edition in 1948. An advocate, Fraser (1911–89)[39] was also lecturer in constitutional law, first at Glasgow, and then at Edinburgh, and an uncompromising Diceyan. Fraser contended that there was 'no body of constitutional law which is sharply distinguished from ordinary law'. The legislative power of the British parliament was, therefore, 'absolute and unlimited'. The Union was no exception to this, nor indeed was the clear intent in the Act of Security that the Kirk be entrenched as a fundamental law. 'No parliament', Fraser informed entrants into the Scottish legal profession, 'can pass Acts which will be binding on its successors, although language has sometimes been used in Acts of Parliament which would suggest the contrary.' Indeed, the Act of Security had itself been amended by the 1853 legislation repealing the terms of confessional subscription for Scottish university professors.[40]

---

[38] Dicey, *Introduction*, p. 69 fn.

[39] Fraser was later raised to the judicial bench as Lord Fraser of Tullybelton.

[40] Walter Fraser, *An outline of constitutional law* (London and Edinburgh, 1938), pp. 3, 9–10.

Lord Cooper and after

A crucial turning point came in 1953 with Lord Cooper's unexpected *obiter dicta* in the case of *MacCormick* v. *Lord Advocate.* This is also known as the royal numerals case for it involved a legal challenge by the nationalist politician John MacCormick (1904–61) to the Queen's assumption of the title Queen Elizabeth II when she was clearly the first Queen Elizabeth of Great Britain. The title Queen Elizabeth II was an affront to Scots and to the principles of the Union. The Court of Session found against MacCormick's complaint on various grounds including his lack of standing to bring a case and the fact that the Queen's choice of title was not subject to legal challenge, being a matter of the royal prerogative.[41] Nevertheless, Lord Cooper (1892–1955) issued a very full opinion which reserved judgment in certain related issues and expressed a deep unease with the orthodox pieties of British constitutionalism. In particular, Cooper, who was also a distinguished legal historian of medieval Scotland, appeared to resent the way in which English juridical norms had eclipsed a distinctively Scottish constitutional tradition. Why should it be assumed – as it so clearly was – that English norms should prevail over Scottish norms in a British state which had been created *de novo* in 1707?

> The principle of the unlimited sovereignty of parliament is a distinctively English principle which has no counterpart in Scottish constitutional law. It derives its origins from Coke and Blackstone, and was widely popularised during

[41] *Session Cases 1953*, pp. 396–418.

the nineteenth century by Bagehot and Dicey, the latter having stated the doctrine in its classic form in his *Law of the Constitution.*

Why, moreover, should the English parliamentary tradition be privileged over the Scottish parliamentary tradition in a post-1707 British parliament?

> Considering that the Union legislation extinguished the Parliaments of Scotland and England and replaced them by a new Parliament, I have difficulty seeing why it should have been supposed that the new Parliament of Great Britain must inherit all the peculiar characteristics of the English Parliament but none of the Scottish Parliament, as if all that happened in 1707 was that Scottish representatives were admitted to the Parliament of England. That is not what was done.

Cooper also confronted the issue of constitutional entrenchment and the logic of the Diceyan doctrine of unlimited parliamentary sovereignty. Cooper concluded that, whatever the rights and wrongs of MacCormick's case, there were certain fundamental laws at the heart of Britain's Treaty-derived constitution which were subject to judicial review.

> The Treaty, and the associated legislation, by which the Parliament of Great Britain was brought into being as the successor of the separate Parliaments of Scotland and England, contain some clauses which expressly reserve to the Parliament of Great Britain powers of subsequent modification, and other clauses which either contain no such power or emphatically exclude subsequent alteration

by declarations that the provision shall be fundamental and unalterable in all time coming, or declarations of a like effect. I have never been able to understand how it is possible to reconcile with elementary canons of construction the adoption by the English constitutional theorists of the same attitude to these markedly different types of provisions.[42]

Cooper's dicta in *MacCormick* v. *Lord Advocate* provided a strong impetus towards a new kind of constitutional jurisprudence in Scotland, one which departed significantly from the canons of Diceyan analysis. Before 1953 it was hard for Scots to articulate their dissatisfactions with the doctrine of parliamentary sovereignty, as MacCormick himself recalled in his memoirs, *The flag in the wind* (1955): 'Even as a law student in Glasgow University studying constitutional law and history I had resented and suspected Dicey's famous doctrine of the sovereignty of Parliament, which, of course, we were taught to regard as sacrosanct.'[43]

Cooper elicited an immediate response from Kenneth Middleton (1905–95), the sheriff of Lothians and Peebles, who in 1954 published an article in Scotland's leading law journal, the *Juridical Review*, on the constitutional significance of the Union. Although Middleton endorsed Cooper's assault on Dicey, he also believed that Cooper had himself misconstrued the Union. Britain was not, Middleton argued, a creation *de novo*; rather the two pre-existing parliaments had been 'altered rather than extinguished'. Although the difference between a

---

[42] *Ibid.*, pp. 409–14, at p. 411.
[43] John MacCormick, *The flag in the wind* (London, 1955), p. 188.

'merger' of two parliaments and the 'creation' of a new parliament appeared slight, it was, Middleton insisted, 'material': the 'parallel Acts ratifying the Treaty of Union did not assert that the two Parliaments transferred their authority to a new sovereign body.' This was not what the Union actually said, which was indeed bland to the point of terseness; for 'what was enacted was that the two kingdoms should be united, so as to form one united kingdom, and be "represented by one and the same parliament"'. There was no suggestion that a British parliament was to be created 'in order to supersede' the existing parliaments. Strictly speaking, the two parliaments 'did not divest themselves of their powers by uniting on equal terms'. Of course, their powers were 'restricted' by Union, and also 'extended' by the 'wider jurisdiction conferred on the common parliament'. Nevertheless, Middleton detected crucial evidence for the continued existence of the Scots parliament within the Union. After all, despite the merger of parliaments there had been 'no breach of legal continuity following the Union'. Instead, pre-1707 Scots and English statutes continued to enjoy legal currency so long as they were not inconsistent with the Union. Somehow these statutes were held to be binding without any confirmation by the new parliament of Great Britain. Why? The only acceptable conclusion was that the Scots and English parliaments continued to exist, albeit within the merged Union parliament. Middleton speculated that this state of affairs further implied the continued legal existence of two separate nations, which in turn gave the entrenched clauses of the Union a measure of 'legal validity'. If the Scots and English nations enjoyed institutional continuity despite the Union, then the 'contractual conditions of the

Treaty of Union are capable of being relied on'. On this basis, Middleton reached the radical conclusion that the original intent of the authors of the Treaty encompassed a hypothetical right to dissolve the Union. The right of dissolution was 'an indefeasible right, however difficult to assert'. Obviously, this provision was not spelled out in the Articles of Union. The judicial review of legislation was unknown in 1707. Possibly, some Scottish convention might in extreme circumstances come into being as an expression of the will of the Scots nation to pronounce the Union 'terminated'. Yet, despite Middleton's admission that there was no constitutional machinery to compel observance of the Articles of Union, he was sure that the Union itself 'implied' some 'sanction' on a tyrannical British parliament.[44]

No longer was there a single orthodox reading of the British constitution; Cooper had let out the genie of analytic unionism. Another variant soon appeared in the work of Cooper's leading disciple, T. B. Smith. Whereas Cooper's revisionism depended on the fact that the Union was a Treaty, Smith needed to be persuaded that the Treaty was indeed a fact. In a 1957 article Smith asked whether there had ever been an Anglo-Scottish Treaty 'in the sense that that term is properly used in international law'. He answered in the affirmative, but he denied that it was to be found in the Articles of Union agreed by the two sets of Commissioners in 1706; nor was it

---

[44] K. W. B. Middleton, 'New thoughts on the Union between England and Scotland', *Juridical Review* (1954), 37–60, esp. 37–8, 53, 55, 58–60. See also K. W. B. Middleton, 'Sovereignty in theory and practice', *Juridical Review* 64 (1952), 135–62.

still extant or justiciable. The Articles of Union did not possess 'the characteristics of a treaty'; they constituted rather 'a record of negotiations'. Moreover, the Articles had been amended in the Scots parliament during the ratification process. So where was the Treaty of Union to be located? Smith argued that the substance of the Treaty was to be found in 'the complex of exchanged Acts of the two Parliaments'. This was 'a complex and unorthodox agreement', but notwithstanding 'the anomalies and *ad hoc* constitutional expedients, we seem to have a valid international treaty concluded in March 1707'. However, Smith also took the view that this Treaty was very short-lived and had expired by 1 May 1707, the day the United Kingdom came into being. Thus there was no means of redress for any possible violations of the Treaty, because after 1 May 1707 the parties to the Treaty no longer existed, and as a result 'the treaty as an obligation *iure gentium*' similarly expired. There was, however, a further wrinkle in the Union. Although neither Scotland, nor England, nor the Treaty of 1707 had any existence in public international law, the fact that the Treaty had preserved separate legal systems north and south of the border meant that Scotland and England continued to exist as 'quasi-foreign states in questions of private international law'. However, Smith detected a more profound paradox at the heart of the Union: 'This new state, though as I believe bound in constitutional law by the conditions of its own creation, could not in public international law be bound to a treaty to which it was no party.' Nevertheless, Smith, like Cooper, was 'quite unable to accept the view of those English constitutional lawyers who hold that the terms of Union have no more force than an ordinary Act of Parliament'. The Union constituted a 'fundamental law' of the British state, which trumped mere Acts of Parliament.[45]

In his book *British justice* (1961) Smith amplified some of these themes, engaging with the basic errors in constitutional theory which led to serious misunderstandings of the Union and the nature of the British state. In the first place, Smith demolished the fallacy that the Act of Union had been 'based on the legislative Act of a sovereign Parliament'. This was nonsense, Smith argued, for the 'English Act of Union as legislation has no legal status in Scotland'. However, Smith also took issue with the 'Scottish fallacy' that the Union persisted as a Treaty in international law. No Treaty obligations now existed, Smith repeated. Scots were mistaken if they hoped to understand the Union by way of international law; rather the Union provided a 'skeletal' basic constitution for the British state. The Union was the 'fundamental written constitution' of the British state, with a status greater than ordinary legislation, though no longer attaining the status of a Treaty in international law. The Union was not justiciable in international law, but it might be in domestic law. The Scottish courts had yet to accept or decline a role as 'guardians of the Constitution'; nevertheless, Smith believed that it was up to the judges to decide 'if there be laws of this country superior to ordinary legislation (as I believe, though few, there are)'.[46]

---

[45] T. B. Smith, 'The Union of 1707 as fundamental law', *Public Law* (1957), 99–121, at 100–1, 104–6, 108–9.

[46] T. B. Smith, *British justice: the Scottish contribution* (London, 1961), pp. 203–13.

Another distinctive voice in this discussion was that of Ronald King Murray (b. 1922) who, over the course of his career, wrote a series of incisive articles on the Union which exploded some central assumptions about what had actually happened in 1707. Murray attained great eminence in law and politics, but also managed to combine these activities with academic work, acting as an assistant – the equivalent of a junior lecturer – at Edinburgh University in moral philosophy between 1949 and 1952 and later in the Department of Constitutional Law. Between 1970 and 1979 he was Labour MP for Leith and served as Lord Advocate in the Labour administrations of 1974–9. As Lord Murray he went on to sit in the Court of Session between 1979 and 1995. Murray's first notable intervention in this revitalised field came in an article in *Public Law* (1958) which challenged the purported sovereignty of an Erastian British parliament. What had happened in 1707, Murray claimed, was the reciprocal re-establishment of both the Church of Scotland and Church of England through the Union. This meant that the Church of Scotland had been 'conceived as a constituent of the state rather than as a subordinate part of it'.[47]

More devastating still was Murray's comprehensive demolition of conventional constitutional wisdom in an article in the *Scots Law Times* in 1961. Here Murray argued that considerable legal and constitutional confusion had arisen from the conventional historical labels attached to the great watersheds in British state formation. The description of the achievement

---

[47] R. K. Murray, 'The constitutional position of the Church of Scotland', *Public Law* (1958), 155–62, at 158.

of 1603 as a Union of the Crowns was an obvious misnomer, Murray argued, while the familiar renderings of the deeds of 1707 as a 'Union of Parliaments' or an 'incorporating Union' created a smokescreen which prevented proper analysis of the arrangements entered into in that year. Indeed, only in 1707 had there been what might be properly described as 'an indissoluble Union of the Crowns' which emerged out of the 'temporary association' which had lasted from 1603. The accession of James VI to the throne of England had involved merely a 'personal Union'. In 1603, argued Murray, there had been 'no direct alteration of the internal law of either kingdom, except perhaps as regards the status of aliens'. But why had the Union of 1707 not been a Union of Parliaments? Murray noted that while Article I which created the new United Kingdom was 'entrenched' and Article II which ensured the Hanoverian succession was 'partly entrenched', Article III of the Union which provided for a common British parliament was 'not entrenched'. Nevertheless, a Union of the Parliaments had occurred, albeit not entrenched, though the Union of Parliaments was less significant than the Union of the Crowns, which was the real achievement of 1707:

> Firstly, from the legal standpoint the Union of the Crowns and the Union of the Parliaments both took place in 1707; and, secondly, the Union of 1707 was in law primarily a union of the crowns. The article uniting the parliaments did not unite them indissolubly nor did it even trouble to dissolve the pre-existing Parliaments of England and Scotland.

Murray challenged the realist view that 'the Act of Union . . . in substance incorporated Scotland into a Greater England which, for decency's sake, changed its name to Great Britain'. The terms of Union – whose 'true legal basis' was a 'solemn contract' enshrined in a series of Articles and Acts, not a single Act of a single parliament – 'say nothing about the incorporation of one party by the other'. Whatever happened in 1706–7, the operation of the agreement made by the sovereign states of England and Scotland must, Murray argued, work symmetrically. If the creation of Great Britain 'has made no inroads into pre-existing English institutions it can hardly have had a different effect for pre-existing Scottish institutions'. Indeed, Murray happily contemplated the 'possibility' that the 'mutual incorporation' of England and Scotland into Great Britain was 'not legally complete'. The delayed 'Union of the Crowns' of 1707 had not even extinguished 'the constituent crowns of England and Scotland'. Murray was particularly intrigued by the elevated constitutional status of Article XXIV of the Union. The entrenchment of this Article, which provided that the Scottish state regalia, namely crown, sceptre and sword of state, should remain in Scotland for all time was 'perhaps indicative of a sort of radical reversionary right of Scottish sovereignty in event of the Union breaking down'. Why else, Murray wondered, was this provision entrenched 'for all time'? The Union, it appeared, was not a 'simple unitary state'. Rather Murray speculated that a 'quasi-federal structure' had played an unacknowledged part in the original intent of the Union's founding fathers in 1706–7. The Union may have created 'a new legal person', but it did so, Murray contended, 'without wholly dissolving the legal personalities of its constituent nations'. The closest analogy was the Swedish–Norwegian real union of 1815. Although Scotland and England had been brought together under the same monarch with a single succession law constituting 'one international person', they remained 'distinct legal entities internally'. Murray concluded that the Union of 1707 'did not wholly destroy either the kingdom of England or the kingdom of Scotland as public legal entities'. Thus, although Scots found it irritating that the English had a habit of referring to Elizabeth II as the 'Queen of England', this style was, Murray argued somewhat perversely, 'not wholly wrong'. On the other hand, however, Elizabeth might also be styled quite properly as 'Queen of Scotland'.[48]

By 1980 when he published a further devastating article on the Union in the *Law Quarterly Review*, Murray was an open devolutionist. Devolution, he insisted, was not at odds with the framers' vision in 1706–7, repeating his argument that the united parliament had not been entrenched by the framers of Union. Murray continued to insist that the Union 'did not incorporate the public institutions of Scotland into those of England – it merely provided a basis upon which they could be made the same'. By extension, as 'some semblance of Scottish – and English – statehood continues to subsist' and as 'this subsistence was foreseen', then devolution was closer to the spirit of true unionism, Murray implied, than the anti-devolutionist insistence upon a unitary United Kingdom.[49]

An enormous contribution to Scottish analysis of the Union state was made by John D. B. Mitchell (1917–80), an

[48] R. K. Murray, 'The Anglo-Scottish Union', *Scots Law Times* (1961), 161–4.

[49] R. K. Murray, 'Devolution in the U.K. – a Scottish perspective', *Law Quarterly Review* 96 (1980), 35–50, at 40.

Englishman who immersed himself in the jurisprudence of his adopted land. Mitchell was educated at the London School of Economics and went on to teach law at the University of London. In 1954 he was appointed to the chair of Constitutional Law at the University of Edinburgh, the first English lawyer to hold it. While in Edinburgh, the Englishman went native. In 1964 Mitchell published a most remarkable work, *Constitutional law* (2nd edn, 1968) which advanced a Scotocentric interpretation of the British constitution, against the grain of conventional constitutional literature. In addition, Mitchell explored the possibility that the British parliament had been 'born unfree'. This was because the Union of 1707 – which was most certainly not a singular Act of the English parliament – was the foundational text of the British constitution. Although it seemed somewhat minimalist for a constituent blueprint, the Union of 1707 nevertheless provided a 'skeletal' constitutional 'framework' for the United Kingdom, albeit one which did not indicate the existence of any machinery for constitutional amendment. According to Mitchell, interpreters of the United Kingdom's constitution needed to engage with a set of hitherto neglected problems which sprang 'from the fact that its constitution is neither federal nor strictly unitary'. Similarly, historians of the British constitution had to come to terms with two distinct pre-1707 histories of British liberties. In particular, the seventeenth-century age of revolutions took rather different – though connected – forms in England and Scotland. The British constitutional lawyer had to acquire mastery not only of UK legislation and pre-1707 English legislation, but also of pre-1707 Scottish legislation. The post-1707

bicameral British parliament provided only a delusive simu-
lacrum of continuity with the pre-1707 English parliament.[50]

No longer was the old Diceyan orthodoxy the dominant mode of constitutional interpretation in Scotland. However, it had not given way to a rival orthodoxy. Rather, Scottish
constitutional law was in a state of flux and creative disor-
der. There were considerable divergences of opinion in the
ranks of the anti-Diceyans. Most obviously, there was a deep
division between those such as Cooper, Smith and Mitchell
who believed that there had been a constitutional revolution –
however conservative – in 1707, and those such as Middleton
and Murray, who argued for the shadowy continuity of the
pre-1707 Scottish constitution within the British state. As we
shall see in chapter 7, there was also a sophisticated nationalist contribution to the debate on the Union, in the work of
Sir Neil MacCormick (b. 1941), the son of John MacCormick
and variously a Member of the European Parliament for the
SNP and Regius Professor of Public Law at the University of
Edinburgh. Nationalist jurists such as MacCormick have read
into Cooper's critique of English parliamentary sovereignty
the case for an historical, if submerged, Scottish constitutional tradition of popular sovereignty.[51] Nor was Diceyan

---

[50] J. D. B. Mitchell, *Constitutional law* (1964: Edinburgh, 1968), esp. pp. 4,
19–20, 69–75, 92–8. For Mitchell's career, see M. Loughlin, 'Sitting on the
fence at Carter Bar: in praise of J. D. B. Mitchell', *Juridical Review* (1991),
135–53. St John Bates *et al.* (eds.), *In memoriam J. D. B. Mitchell* (London,
1983) focusses on Mitchell's work in European law.

[51] For Neil MacCormick's interpretation of the British constitution, see
below, chapter 7, 'Early nationalism as a form of unionism'.

interpretation a dead letter in Scottish circles. Colin Munro (b. 1949), the Professor of Constitutional Law at Edinburgh, continued to uphold the doctrine of parliamentary sovereignty. Indeed, Munro, a constitutional realist, made a compelling case for the old orthodoxy. Surely there was 'no instance of legislation being held invalid as being contrary to the Acts of Union'?[52] The orthodoxy was also enshrined in the Report of the Royal Commission on the Constitution (1973) chaired by the Scottish judge Lord Kilbrandon (1906–89). Paragraph 56 of the Report noted that '[n]o special procedures are required to enact even the most fundamental changes in the consti- tution'. Nevertheless, in a speech to the Holdsworth Club in 1975 Kilbrandon conceded that this lack of a special kind of constitutional machinery for dealing with fundamental ques- tions of the constitution did not mean that such questions had no constitutional standing. Although the Treaty of Union had become 'defunct' with the very creation of the United Kingdom on 1 May 1707, nonetheless, Kilbrandon thought it 'desirable to retain the phrase'. The alternative, he feared, was 'falling into the trap of speaking of the Act of Union, as if that were a piece of legislation of the United Kingdom parlia- ment', which it was not. Kilbrandon went further, speculating whether it was a mistake 'to accept the unlimited sovereignty of the Great Britain parliament on the precarious ground that such was always an attribute of the English parliament, even if that were not true of the Scots parliament'. Yet judicial

---

[52] Colin Munro, *Studies in constitutional law* (2nd edn, 1999: Oxford, 2005 pbk), esp. pp. 137–42.

review was ruled out. Kilbrandon conceded the possibility of a real infringement – 'delict' – of the Treaty of Union, but denied that there was any court in which such a cause was 'justiciable'.[53]

However, the elaborate, tantalising reticence of Cooper's *obiter dicta* in *MacCormick* v. *Lord Advocate* continued to exercise a hold over the Scottish bench. The Union continued to be invoked by claimants who argued that it had been breached and who sought remedies for the alleged breaches in the Scottish courts, as in *Gibson* v. *Lord Advocate* (1975) and *Robbie the Pict* v. *Hingston* (1998).[54] However, the courts have continued to reject the specific claims in these cases, without entirely excluding the possibility of judicial review of substantial parliamentary infringement of the Union. In *Gibson* v. *Lord Advocate*, Lord Keith set aside Gibson's case, but made the enigmatic declaration that the Union might indeed be a fundamental law: 'Like Lord Cooper, I prefer to reserve my opinion what the position would be if the United Kingdom Parliament passed an Act purporting to abolish the Court of Session or the Church of Scotland or to substitute English law for the whole body of Scots private law.'[55]

Notwithstanding the divisions among Scots jurists and the circumspection of the judiciary on these questions, the

---

[53] Royal Commission on the Constitution 1969–73 Volume I Report (Cmnd 5460), para. 56; Lord Kilbrandon, *A background to constitutional reform* (Holdsworth Club, Birmingham, 1975), pp. 15–16.

[54] *Gibson* v. *Lord Advocate, Session Cases 1975*, pp. 136–45, at pp. 143–4; 'Robbie the Pict v. Hingston (No.2)', *Scots Law Times* (1998), 1201–3. See also *Sillars* v. *Smith, Scots Law Times* (1982), 539–41.

[55] *Session Cases 1975*, 144.

Union of 1707 increasingly attracts the attention of public and constitutional lawyers across the United Kingdom.[56] Diceyan orthodoxies are under interrogation in England as well as in Scotland, and jurists have become aware in recent decades of various limitations on the sovereignty of parliament, including the status of the 1707 Union. There is, of course, a European dimension to these developments. Did the Treaty of Rome place limitations upon Europe's supra-national authorities analogous to those which the Treaty of Union had supposedly imposed on the British parliament?[57] Closer to home, moreover, new questions have arisen concerning the matter of Britain. Elizabeth Wicks of the Birmingham School of Law has argued that the making of the British state in 1706–7 was a highly peculiar arrangement in international law, which took place in two clear stages, a point obscured by the fact that the two stages occurred 'almost simultaneously'. The first stage involved 'two renunciations of title to the entire territories of England and Scotland', and the second saw 'a new state acquiring title over the same territory immediately thereafter'. Wicks cautions against the casual assumption that the union

---

[56] See e.g. D. J. Edwards, 'The Treaty of Union: more hints of constitutionalism', *Legal Studies* 12 (1992), 34–41; M. K. Addo and V. M. Smith, 'The relevance of historical fact to certain arguments relating to the legal significance of the Acts of Union', *Juridical Review* (1998), 37–66; N. Walker, 'Beyond the unitary conception of the United Kingdom constitution', *Public Law* (2000), 384–404; E. Wicks, 'A new constitution for a new state? The 1707 Union of England and Scotland', *Law Quarterly Review* 117 (2001), 109–26; E. Wicks, *Evolution of a constitution: eight key moments in British constitutional history* (Oxford, 2006), ch. 2.

[57] A. O'Neill, 'A tale of two constitutions: the Treaty of Union and the Treaty of Rome', *Scots Law Times* (1997), 205–12.

agreement was the basis of the British constitution, for the new state of Great Britain, she warns, was a third party. This new entity was not a party to the Treaty of Union; nor 'were the two Acts of Union passed by the English and Scottish parliaments of legal relevance in this new state. England and Scotland may have made clear their intentions of being replaced by a specific new state, but how could this bind a state which did not at the time exist?' Wicks concludes that 'the effects of the Union, such as the existence of a joint parliament and the protection of the Scottish legal system, find force in the U. K. Constitution, but the Acts of Union cannot themselves be regarded as a constitution'.[58] Michael Upton, on the other hand, has come to the conclusion that there is, strictly speaking, no single entity which might be described as the British constitution. Rather, such is the nature of the Union agreement and the separate existence of Scots and English legal systems that there are, in fact, 'two constitutions, and while their differences are probably only trivial, and can with good reason be interpreted harmoniously by the courts, they are nevertheless separate institutions'. The British constitution has legal existence only 'separately' in Scots or in English law. The 1707 Union involved 'a qualified transfer of powers by an act of delegation'. Nevertheless, Upton concedes that the emergence of a doctrine of unqualified parliamentary sovereignty came to supersede the Union agreement, and, as a result, he accepts that 'the constitution of 1707 has fallen into desuetude'.[59] However, might the tide now be running in the

---

[58] Wicks, 'New constitution', 112, 125.

[59] M. Upton, 'Marriage vows of the elephant: the constitution of 1707', *Law Quarterly Review* 105 (1989), 79–103, at 84, 91–2.

other direction? Cooper's critique of Diceyanism has recently surfaced – introduced by the Scottish law lord, Lord Hope of Craighead – in the legal deliberations of the House of Lords, though in a case where another Scots law lord, Lord Rodger of Earlsferry, studiously ignored the potential significance of the Union.[60] The status of the Union remains unresolved, but no longer is it – as it was widely assumed to be prior to 1953[61] – something of a non-question.

[60] T. Mullen, 'Reflections on Jackson v. Attorney General: questioning sovereignty', *Legal Studies* 27 (2007), 1–25, at 8–9. Nor is the equality of status the Dentists Act (1878) enjoyed with the Act of Union now so secure. See 'Thorburn v. Sunderland City Council', *Common Market Law Reports* 93 (2002), 1461–1500, at 1492, which introduced a hierarchical distinction between 'ordinary' statutes and 'constitutional' statutes.

[61] Cf. Middleton, 'New thoughts', 39: 'Dicey's *Law of the Constitution* has been for generations accepted in the schools of law in Scottish universities as an authoritative exposition of the constitution of the United Kingdom.'

4

Narratives of belonging: the history and ethnology of organic union

The presupposition of most recent commentary on the Union – including the chapters preceding this one – is that Britain was the artificial conjunction of two long-established nations with distinctive cultures, identities and traditions. These differences were accommodated within the novel asymmetric structure of a mixed-unitary state which permitted the co-existence of separate church establishments and legal systems beneath the central authority of a single crown and parliament. It is an unchallenged feature of modern scholarship that the Union was a multi-national hybrid.[1] Even if the Scots and English peoples shared a common linguistic inheritance and basic Protestantism, even if there was a whiff of inevitability about the Union of 1707, not least in the aftermath of the Union of the Crowns, nobody nowadays questions the idea that the Union necessitated the construction of a new kind of British nationhood out of somewhat disparate materials. By extension, it is generally assumed that the Scots constituted a national minority within the British multi-national state, and that the success of the Union is to be judged in terms of the sensitivity of British institutions to the needs and aspirations of the Scottish minority.

---

[1] See e.g. R. Rose, *Understanding the United Kingdom: the territorial dimension of government* (Harlow, 1982), pp. 10–11.

However, some of these assumptions sit uneasily with the theoretical literature on nationalism. In his influential book *Imagined communities* (1983) Benedict Anderson argued compellingly that all communities beyond small face-to-face groupings such as tribes and villages were imagined.[2] By Anderson's lights, Scotland is no more authentic or natural than Britain. Both need to be imagined by their constituent bodies, even if one seems less inauthentic than the other. Theorists of nationalism have also begun to refine the distinction between 'ethnic' and 'civic' nationalisms, that is between nationalisms based on a shared ethnicity and those which lack a shared ethnic denominator and are defined rather by allegiance to a common set of institutions. The distinction retains some validity, but it has become clear that 'ethnic' and 'civic' nationalisms retain their purchase among students of nationalism largely as ideal types, not as real descriptions of nationalism on the ground. Instead scholars have become aware that there are no purely 'ethnic' or 'civic' nationalisms. Purportedly ethnic nationalisms almost always contain some civic or institutional features, or embrace some measure, however slight, of polyethnicity, while civic nationalisms are almost never simon pure, but articulate some sense of shared ethnic belonging, however lukewarm. The nationhood of post-1707 Britain seems to fit snugly into the category of civic nationalism, for Britain seems quite obviously to be a multi-national entity whose unity resides in the institutions of monarchy, parliament, the armed services and, latterly, the Empire. However, it would

[2] B. Anderson, *Imagined communities* (London, 1983).

be remarkable had loyalty to Britain been entirely innocent of ethnic nationalism.

Certainly, in the days before political scientists discovered that the United Kingdom was a multi-national state, the assumption prevailed that Great Britain – at least – was an example of a successfully integrated nation state. Political scientists tended to focus upon class cleavages within an unproblematic nation which contained none of the problems associated with unstable polyethnic entities such as Yugoslavia. The British nation was taken for granted. Moreover, the roots of this assumption have largely gone unexamined, except in the special case of Ulster where it is recognised that ethnic and religious factors continue to reinforce what Ian McLean and Alistair McMillan have described as 'primordial unionism'.[3] This chapter will explore the ways in which Scottish unionist intellectuals – particularly historians and ethnologists – constructed a British ethnic nationalism. Here the focus switches from the analytic unionism – the ways in which jurists and constitutional theorists analysed the workings of the Union – to something more emotive, to organicist conceptions of the Union as a natural outgrowth of shared ethnic characteristics. In particular, this chapter will examine the ways in which Scots came to regard the Union not as a bloodless and mechanical alignment of distinct nation states but as an organic union which reunited two peoples from a common ethnic stock, the Teutonic, or Saxon, peoples of England and Lowland Scotland, as a single British nation.

[3] I. MacLean and A. McMillan, *State of the Union* (Oxford, 2005).

This idea was prefigured in some eighteenth-century writings but became very influential in the nineteenth-century. Under the influence of the new sciences of ethnology, nineteenth-century Scottish intellectuals came to view race as a more meaningful category of analysis than the artificial division of peoples into states. They argued that race operated at a much deeper level than the political structures which had ostensibly separated Britain into the kingdoms of Scotland and England. A shared Saxon ethnicity, it was contended, had provided a measure of unity between the peoples of North and South Britain long before the Unions of 1603 and 1707. The history of Britain in the centuries before 1603 was recast as the unfortunate interplay of race and politics. England and Scotland, it seemed, should have evolved into Britain, a natural political unit governing similar peoples with shared manners, customs, dialects and institutions. Instead, Edward I's premature and misguided imperialist ambitions in the 1290s had provoked the national hostility of the Scots under Wallace and later Bruce. Scots historians, as we shall see, reinterpreted the Scottish War of Independence as a civil war of sorts within British Saxondom, a conflict which had the unhappy effect of sharpening national divisions between the kindred peoples of Scotland and England. In the end, however, the Unions of 1603 and 1707 had corrected this derailment, and restored the history of Anglo-Scottish Saxondom to its normal unionist course. The implications of Teutonist ethnology and historiography were politically significant. They fostered the idea that there was no serious ethnic or cultural difference between Englishmen and Lowland Scots. This meant that most

Scots – Lowland Scots at least – did not come to think of themselves as an 'ethnic minority' within the British state. Lowland Scots never saw the need to request special rights from an alien state. There was, as they saw it, nothing ethnically alien about the dominant ethnic group within the state; indeed, they were part of it, part of the dominant ethnic majority within the Union. It was only among Scottish Highlanders – Gaelic Celts who, by the lights of nineteenth-century ethnology, were culturally, linguistically and racially distinct from the rest of Teutonic Britain – that there arose a clear sense of being an embattled ethnic minority. Indeed, under the influence of Teutonist ethnology, Lowland Scots – notwithstanding their appreciation of the picturesque local colour of Highland, and pseudo-Highland, traditions – identified themselves not as members of a 'Celtic fringe' distinct from the main fabric of British society, but as part of Britain's largely homogeneous Saxon core.

Unionist interpretations of history

The history of shared Saxon origins contributed to two different interpretations of unionist belonging: to atavistic unionism – the sense that there were deep historic commonalities which had united Britons from ancient or, at least, medieval times – and to a teleological unionism – the view that the Union was in some way predestined, notwithstanding the vicissitudes of Anglo-Scottish history. Nineteenth-century Saxonist racialism was atavistic unionism at its most compelling and strident, but there were softer strains of this idiom, dating back to the eighteenth century, which drew attention to the shared cultural, linguistic and institutional histories of medieval Scotland and England, which were not couched in racialist terms. Nor was teleological unionism necessarily couched in ethnological or racial terms. A common line of interpretation emphasised how the political and religious histories of Scotland and England had been so inextricably interwoven in the centuries before 1707 that the union had been an inevitable culmination of a shared British quest for political and religious freedoms. Most significantly, the Scottish War of Independence in this analysis had witnessed a victory not only for Scottish ideas of national independence, but had also put a stop to the despotic ambitions of the Plantagenet monarchs of England. The freedoms of the English and Scottish nations, it seemed, had been closely interlinked. In the era of the War of Independence the fates of the English and Scottish nations had both depended upon the Scots winning their freedom from a Plantagenet despotism, which, had it conquered Scotland, would have become all the more entrenched in England. Scots did not automatically think in terms of the antithesis of Saxon and Celt, of an overbearing English core which had absorbed the Celtic peripheries of the British world; rather they thought in terms of the antithesis of Saxon (including Lowland Scots) and Norman, of preserving Saxon freedoms the length of Britain from the Norman Yoke and Plantagenet despotism. In thrall to unionist ideals, nineteenth-century Scottish commentators did not disown the deeds of Wallace and Bruce – far from it – but they generally defused the nationalist potential of the Scottish War of Independence. Their interpretations were far from anglophobic, and the focus was generally on longer-term British outcomes, not on the bloodiness of Anglo-Scottish conflict in the late thirteenth and early fourteenth centuries.[4] The poet and dramatist Joanna Baillie (1762–1851) made the point that the Plantagenet despotism which the Scots had thwarted had been as much a threat to English as to Scottish freedoms: 'England as well as Scotland, under Divine Providence, may owe its liberty to [Wallace]; for, had the English crown, at so early a period, acquired such an accession of power, it would probably, like the other great crowns of Europe, have established for itself a despotism which could not have been shaken.'[5] Wallace and Bruce became unionist icons and the War of Independence the foundational moment not of an enduring Scottish independence, but of a medium-term independence which ensured in the long run that the Union eventually achieved in 1707 would be a genuine partnership of equals, not a conquest.[6] In 1859 the Scottish artist Joseph Noel Paton (1821–1901) contended that 'intelligent Englishmen' knew 'full well the sources of Britain's strength and greatness', namely that 'the independence achieved under Wallace and Bruce, the Union of Scotland with her sister kingdom, on terms satisfying to both, owes not only all its practicality, but the greater portion of its success'[7]. Many nineteenth-century Scottish

---

[4] G. Morton, *Unionist-nationalism: governing urban Scotland 1830–1860* (East Linton, 1999), p. 182.

[5] Joanna Baillie, *Poetical works* (London, 1851), p. 708.

[6] See J. Coleman, 'Unionist-nationalism in stone? The National Wallace Monument and the hazards of commemoration in Victorian Scotland', in E. J. Cowan (ed.), *The Wallace book* (Edinburgh, 2007), pp. 151–68.

[7] R. J. Morris and G. Morton, 'The remaking of Scotland: a nation within a nation, 1850–1920', in M. Lynch (ed.), *Scotland 1850–1979: society, politics and the Union* (Historical Association, 1993), pp. 16–17.

historians and writers tended – without any sacrifice of Scottish nationality – to site their interpretations of the Scottish War of Independence within a longer unionist metanarrative. Indeed, some historians identified the Scottish War of Independence as the vital point of departure which had allowed a separate Reformation to unfold in Scotland, and, had, ultimately, enabled Scots presbyterians to make their own decisive contributions to the winning of British civil and religious liberties in the Revolutions of the seventeenth century.

Several Scottish historians pointed to the vital contributions which the Scottish Reformed tradition had made to the constitutional history of Britain as a whole in the post-Reformation era. The heroic efforts of Scots Covenanters at key moments during the seventeenth century had rescued the civil and religious liberties of England and Scotland alike, which were now enshrined in the Revolution settlements of 1688–9 and the Union of 1707. Notwithstanding the differences between Anglicanism and Scots presbyterianism, Britons, it seemed, had belonged for centuries to a community of fate. Recently, Neil Forsyth and James Coleman have drawn attention to a neglected Scots presbyterian interpretation of British history within which the sixteenth and seventeenth centuries – in Scotland as much as in England – were seen as key periods in the making of the modern British constitution.[8] Free

[8] N. Forsyth, 'Presbyterian historians and the Scottish invention of British liberty', *Records of the Scottish Church History Society* 34 (2004), 91–110; J. Coleman, 'The double-life of the Scottish past: discourses of commemoration in nineteenth-century Scotland', University of Glasgow Ph.D. thesis (2005).

Church ministers such as James Dodds (1812–85) and James Aitken Wylie (1808–90) peddled a Scots-inflected Whig history which stressed that Britain's civil and religious liberties depended in good measure upon the activities of heroic Scottish Protestants from John Knox through to the Covenanting rebels of the Restoration era. In *The fifty years' struggle of the Scottish Covenanters 1638 to 1688* (new edn, 1868), which was based upon public lectures given in Edinburgh, Glasgow and Liverpool, Dodds argued that the Scottish Covenanters had played a central role in the winning of British liberties. The English parliament and the Scots presbyterian Kirk, Dodds argued, had been the embodiment of the national will of the English and Scottish peoples, respectively. Both institutions had contributed enormously to the liberal constitution now enjoyed within the Union by modern Britons, though the former tended to overshadow the latter. Dodds issued a reminder that the redoubt of the persecuted later Covenanters – the western hills of the Scottish Lowlands – were the 'glorious ramparts of British freedom'.[9] Wylie, who started his career as a minister of the Original Secession Church before he joined the Free Church in 1852, lectured at the Edinburgh Protestant Institute and authored several works on the role of the Scottish Reformed tradition within British constitutional history, including *The story of the Covenant and the services of the Covenanters to the Reformation in Christendom and the liberties of Great Britain* (1880), *The Revolution of 1688* (1888) and a published lecture on John Knox delivered at the tercentenary

---

[9] James Dodds, *The fifty years' struggle of the Scottish Covenanters 1638 to 1688* (new edn, London, 1868), esp. pp. 1–11, 354, 374–6.

of the Scottish Reformation in 1860. Wylie argued that the whig values of modern Britain, enshrined in the Revolution of 1688, were at bottom Scots presbyterian principles, whose ultimate provenance was the Scottish Reformation. John Knox, Wylie contended, had 'anticipated by one hundred and fifty years the liberties of the Revolution of 1688'. The Scots Reformation, by creating a presbyterian democracy – a genuine priesthood of all believers – had broken the shackles of feudalism and set Britain as a whole on the road to the civil and political liberties which the country now enjoyed. The compact theory of government had also taken its rise, Wylie claimed, in the Scottish Reformation. Later generations of Scots presbyterians had continued the struggle begun by Knox. The constitutional battles which had convulsed seventeenth-century Britain Wylie parsed as a clash of two great parties, 'the one had adopted the axiom of the Stuarts, and the other the foundation-doctrine of the Reformed Church of Scotland'. Moreover, it was, he argued, the swearing of the Scottish National Covenant in 1638 which had 'turned the tide in the struggle. It saved the liberties of two kingdoms.' The Revolution of 1688 was the culmination and vindication of the Scottish Reformation.[10]

Within the sphere of institutional history, a familiar tripartite scheme of narration – of shared beginnings, followed by estrangement and eventual reconciliation –

[10] James Aitken Wylie, *The story of the Covenant and the services of the Covenanters to the Reformation in Christendom and the liberties of Great Britain* (Edinburgh, 1880), esp. pp. 7–11, 29, 34; James Aitken Wylie, *The Revolution of 1688: a retrospect from John Wycliffe to William of Orange* (Edinburgh, [1888]); James Aitken Wylie, 'John Knox', in Wylie (ed.), *Ter-centenary of the Scottish Reformation* (Edinburgh, 1860), pp. 71–2, 74.

connected atavistic and teleological unionisms. For several Scottish historians writing during the eighteenth century, the Union was not only about the winning of new freedoms, but also about the securing of old freedoms and the possible restoration of lost freedoms. In the eighteenth century Scots legal and constitutional historians stressed the common features of Scots and English institutions during the Anglo-Norman, or Scoto-Norman, era of juridical history. Despite these similarities, the two systems had begun to diverge, a process accelerated by the Scottish War of Independence and the Scots connection with France, which had led to the unfortunate adoption, as some commentators saw it, of authoritarian Roman law principles, institutions and practices. The Union, however, held out the prospect of the restoration in Scots law of older Scoto-Norman forms which still survived in England, such as the civil jury. It was Anglo-Scottish divergence which was seen as abnormal, not the Union. Rather the Union was widely seen as some kind of historical corrective, at times even as a *reunion* of sorts, involving the return of British history to a more natural – and inevitable – course of development.

Of course, these strains of ethnic, atavistic, teleological and restorative unionism do not exhaust the types of argument associated with the unionist interpretation of history; nor are they necessarily representative of the most common lines of analysis advanced by Scottish historians during the centuries of unionist hegemony. Indeed, the historical case for Union was most often presented in economic terms: that Scotland had derived enormous benefit in the sectors of agriculture, trade and industry as a result of the Union with England and its empire. What was uppermost in the economic interpretation of Union was not the emotive theme of belonging, but the more practical issue of how Scotland's interests were served by the connection with England. There was a loud, harmonious and long-lasting consensus among Scottish historians that the Union had underpinned Scottish agrarian improvement, Glasgow's trading successes and the rapid industrialisation of west-central Scotland in the century after 1707. The obverse side of this account of Scottish economic history was a saga of sluggish underperformance and underdevelopment in the pre-Union era. Indeed, a negativity about Scotland's pre-1707 history as an independent state was one of the principal justifications of Union. Eighteenth- and nineteenth-century historians paid particular attention to the entrenchment of Scotland's feudal law and the power of the nation's feudal magnates in frustrating the emergence of either a prosperous yeomanry or a lively burgh culture in late medieval and early modern Scotland.[11]

In addition, Scottish historians compared what they perceived to be the stunted development of parliamentary institutions in pre-Union Scotland with the orderly development of the English constitution from medieval times through to 1688. In retrospect, few tears were shed for the loss of the old Scots parliament. Instead, Scottish historians tended to criticise various features of the Scottish legislature which, in their eyes at least, had rendered it clearly inferior to the English parliament. They drew particular attention to the undivided unicameral nature of the Scots parliament, which, they felt, had fostered an atmosphere of deference towards the

[11] C. Kidd, *Subverting Scotland's past* (Cambridge, 1993).

nobility. This in turn had stymied the emergence of a fearless and independent Scottish commons. Furthermore, the screening of the Scots parliamentary agenda by a committee known as the Lords of the Articles had proved – until its abolition at the Revolution of 1689–90 – a substantial obstacle to the Scottish legislature's control of its own business. Influenced by the theories of the seventeenth-century English political writer James Harrington,[12] eighteenth-century Scottish historians understood these weaknesses in the old Scots parliament to reflect the realities of power in a feudal society. Whereas English history presented a triumphant story of the rise of liberty and a balanced constitution alongside the decline of feudal manners and institutions, the pre-1707 history of Scotland amounted to little more, it seemed, than a history of stagnation under an oppressive feudal oligarchy. Such at least was the depressing message of William Robertson's *History of Scotland* (1759) and the sociological history pioneered by John Millar, Professor of Civil Law at Glasgow.[13]

The anti-feudalist critique of the independent Scottish past remained a dominant theme of nineteenth-century Scottish historical writing. George Chalmers in his monumental *Caledonia* (1807) celebrated the Union of 1707 as the 'freeing of the people of Scotland from their parliament' and endorsed

---

[12] James Harrington, *The commonwealth of Oceana* (1656: ed. J. G. A. Pocock, Cambridge 1992).

[13] William Robertson, *History of Scotland* (1759), in Robertson, *Works* (London, 1813), esp. pp. 257–8; John Millar, *An historical view of the English government* (1787: 4 vols., London, 1803), III, pp. 73–5.

the reformist measures of the late 1740s which furthered the goal of 'a complete Union'. Chalmers remarked that only after the abolition of heritable jurisdictions, 'when law was settled as the universal rule, and justice was equally administered', could Scotland properly be said to have become a 'moral country'.[14] In his *History of Scotland from the Union to the abolition of the heritable jurisdictions* (1828), the poet and historian John Struthers (1776–1853) showed how Scotland was 'entirely indebted to the sister kingdom' for liberating the Scottish people from 'the old feudal slavery'. According to Struthers, the reality of Scotland's so-called 'liberty or independence' before the Union had 'consisted in the nobles having the power of trampling upon the king, the barons, and upon one another as occasion offered – and the barons or lairds trampling upon their tenants or dependants so long as it was their pleasure'. 'Scottish liberty' had been merely a slogan until the completion of the Union. Indeed, Struthers claimed that until Scotland had 'received a boon from England in the breaking up of her feudal government', the texture of Scottish society in the 1740s had differed very little from the Scottish way of life of the 1540s.[15] Robert Chambers (1802–71) in his *History of Scotland* (1832) argued that it was only with the abolition of heritable jurisdictions and wardholding vassalage in the aftermath of the Jacobite rebellion of 1745–6 that the common people of Scotland became

[14] George Chalmers, *Caledonia* (London, 1807), pp. 866, 874–5.
[15] John Struthers, *The history of Scotland from the Union to the abolition of the heritable jurisdictions in 1748* (2 vols., Glasgow, 1828), I, p. xlvi; II, pp. 528–9, 619, 621.

'free citizens'. Indeed, the abolition of feudal restrictions in the late 1740s stood at the centre of a positive narrative of incorporation: that the agreement of 1707 had joined Scotland and England in a political Union, which nonetheless fell short of full incorporation. Rather, the Articles of Union had preserved in certain key articles, including Articles XVIII and XX, the powers of Scottish feudal law, and it was only the opportunity presented by the need to reconstruct post-rebellion Scotland in the late 1740s which had enabled the completion of the Union, that is the full incorporation of the Scottish commons as full members of a post-feudal British society.[16]

Throughout the eighteenth and nineteenth centuries Scottish history was generally presented as a narrative of defective state formation. Generations of Scottish historians appeared to agree that Scotland's life as an independent state had been prudently extinguished in 1707. History proved, it seemed, that an independent Scottish state was not viable, and that the euthanasia of Scottish independence in 1707 had been for the best. The unionist interpretation of history depended as much on a negative verdict on the pre-1707 Scottish past as it did on an optimistic assessment of what the Scots had achieved within the Union since 1707.

However, as this chapter shows, the historiography of Union was not simply a balance sheet which set out the history of Scotland within the Union in terms of a cold calculus of profit and loss. There was a warmth at the heart of the

---

[16] Robert Chambers, *History of Scotland* (2 vols., London, 1832), ii, pp. 225–9.

Union, which today's younger generations of Scots have almost forgotten. Warfare, as Linda Colley has argued, was one of the primary motors of British integration in the century after 1707,[17] and the sense of belonging generated by service in the likes of the Seven Years' War and the Napoleonic Wars was further reinforced in the twentieth century by the shared experiences abroad and on the home front in two World Wars. Historical narratives of heroism and self-sacrifice did much to bind Scots of all classes and regions to the idea of Britishness. Reinforcing this trend from the second quarter of the twentieth century was the British Broadcasting Corporation whose ethos was shaped in large part by an apolitical, but establishment-minded and imperialist Scots presbyterian, John Reith (1889–1971), the Corporation's General Manager from 1922 and its inspirational first Director-General from 1927 to 1938.[18]

Moreover, integration was not simply a one-way street. Keith Robbins has argued very persuasively that the bonds of British society were strengthened during the nineteenth century not by a straightforward process of anglicisation or of assimilation to a dominant English norm, but by what he terms the 'blending of Britain'.[19] Sir Walter Scott (1771–1832) played a very significant role in the blending of Britain, creating a set of highly influential myths about the British past.

---

[17] L. Colley, *Britons: forging the nation 1707–1837* (New Haven and London, 1992).

[18] I. McIntyre, *The expense of glory: a life of John Reith* (London, 1993).

[19] Keith Robbins, *Nineteenth-century Britain: integration and diversity* (1988: Oxford, 1995), p. 11.

In his English novels, such as *Ivanhoe*, Scott updated the central myths of English nation building, including the complex ethnogenesis of the English nation out of the conflict of the Anglo-Saxon people and their Norman conquerors. By the same token, an English readership also devoured Scott's Scottish novels, which – notwithstanding their deep indebtedness to the sociological insights of the Scottish Enlightenment – explained the history of Scotland in a charming and accessible way to outsiders.[20] The English cult of Scott is gently satirised in the comic romance *Scotch novel reading; or modern quackery* (1824) by the English novelist Sarah Green (fl. 1790–1825). Set in London in an English family with no Scottish connections, the novel tells the story of Alice Fennel who succumbs to the prevailing Caledonian fever; that is, a surfeit of Scotch novelists and bards – Scott and Hogg in particular – has brought on an obsession with Scottish history and literature. Alice assumes a thick Scots brogue, peppers her speech with Scots diction and dresses the part of one of Scott's Highland heroines, draped in tartan and wearing a plumed Highland cap. According to Alice's father,

---

[20] For Scott as historian, see e.g. D. Forbes, 'The rationalism of Sir Walter Scott', *Cambridge Journal* 7 (1953), 20–35; R. C. Gordon, *Under which king? A study of the Scottish Waverley novels* (Edinburgh and London, 1969); D. Daiches, 'Sir Walter Scott and history', *Études Anglaises* 24 (1971), 458–77; P. D. Garside, 'Scott and the philosophical historians', *Journal of the History of Ideas* 36 (1975), 497–512; D. Brown, *Walter Scott and the historical imagination* (London, 1979); Kidd, *Subverting Scotland's past*, pp. 256–67; M. Ragussis, 'Writing nationalist history: England, the conversion of the Jews and *Ivanhoe*', *English Literary History* 60 (1993), 181–215; F. Robertson, *Legitimate histories: Scott, Gothic and the authorities of fiction* (Oxford, 1994).

We have been now, for some years, inundated with showers of Scotch novels, thicker than the snow you now see falling; and Alice, who is now in her nineteenth year, has read them all, or rather skimmed them over... without understanding one half of what she has perused, and scarce comprehending one word of a dialect with which they abound, but which she affects to use on all occasions.

Although the novel pokes fun at Waverley mania, it is itself telling evidence of an English appropriation of the Scottish past, albeit sketchy and romanticised.[21]

Nevertheless, it is the aim of this chapter to show that beyond the awareness of shared *modern* experiences since 1707, ranging from warfare to novel-reading, there was another sense, fostered by historians and, during the nineteenth century, by ethnologists, that the Scots and the English shared much deeper roots, and possibly a primordial kinship, in the pre-Union past. British history, they reckoned, was ultimately a tale of two Englands – England itself and the 'Anglian' Scots Lowlands.

A tale of two Englands

This sense of a shared primordial past emerged in the course of the eighteenth century when Scottish historians rejected as implausible and fantastic the myths of the nation's

---

[21] Sarah Green, *Scotch Novel Reading* (3 vols., London, 1824), esp. I, pp. 4–5, 9, 11, 13–15, 43.

Gaelic origins which had hitherto dominated Scottish history and political thought. In 1729 the patient scholarship of Father Thomas Innes (1662–1744), a Scots Catholic émigré indebted to Jean Mabillon's science of diplomatic, exploded the long-standing belief that the Scottish constitution dated from 330 BC when Fergus MacFerquhard had become the king of the Dalriadic Scots of the west Highlands. From a more theoretical vantage point, the historical sociologists of the Scottish Enlightenment challenged the standard narrative model which prevailed in early modern historiography. These tended to trace long continuities in the laws and institutions of particular nations from a primeval foundational moment – an ancient constitution – to the present. Rather, Scottish sociologists pioneered the four-stage theory of progress which disaggregated universal history into a series of phases, from hunter-gathering, via herding and settled agriculture, to modern commerce. The four-stage theory exposed the inevitable discontinuities in legal and political history which anachronistic accounts of original contracts and ancient constitutions tended to conceal. Enlightenment Scotland re-established the origins of the nation's laws and institutions on a firmer set of historical foundations, in the medieval past. How absurd it had been to imagine that the mythical Gaelic constitution of 330 BC might explain Scotland's system of feudal law and by extension the Scots parliament – which was essentially the king's baron court, after all. Historians decided to abandon the murky centuries of fantasy which preceded the making of Scotland's feudal institutions in the twelfth century. The real origins of Scottish history, it turned out, were not Celtic, but

Gothic, and very similar to the Gothic polity established in England by the Normans.[22]

Such ideas had circulated since the sixteenth century within the world of Scotland's feudal jurists, but now became part of the wider currency of Scottish political and historical discourse. Eighteenth-century Scottish historians generally acknowledged that the origins of the modern British polity were to be found in the similar Anglo-Norman and Scoto-Norman institutions and laws established on both sides of the border in the eleventh and twelfth centuries. Obviously, English and Scottish laws and institutions had diverged over the centuries, not least in the aftermath of the English statute of *Quia Emptores* (1290) which had significantly modified the feudal principles of English landholding. Parliaments in England and Scotland had also developed dissimilar features, including the early advent of English bicameralism. The English common law – with its trusts and recoveries and its parallel system of equity – had come to diverge enormously from the system of law found in Scotland. But what attracted the attention of eighteenth-century Scottish commentators were not the distinctive features – Scotland's Roman law heritage, for example – which distinguished the two legal and parliamentary systems found in medieval and early modern Britain, but their shared grounding in Gothic institutions. British political and legal history had begun as a cross-border unity, and the Union of 1707 now held out the prospect that the two legal systems might reconverge in a genuinely pan-British body of

[22] Kidd, *Subverting.*

law. No longer, certainly, did Scottish historians and political pamphleteers make the claim that the Scottish constitution was of a totally distinct Gaelic provenance from the English constitution. Rather a common set of political and legal institutions had been established in eleventh- and twelfth-century Britain which provided in some measure an institutional platform for eventual political Union in 1707.[23]

During the eighteenth century there was also a philological dimension to this sense of a shared Gothic heritage. The eighteenth century witnessed a revival of Scots in the poetry of Ramsay, Fergusson and Burns, which is sometimes interpreted as a cultural reaction to the loss of parliamentary autonomy in 1707 and to the hegemony of English within the British state.[24] However, eighteenth-century Scots revivalism cannot be reduced to anglophobia or parsed as a struggle for a Lallans-based cultural nationalism, however superficially persuasive such analyses might appear. The situation was much more complex, for eighteenth-century Scots literary revivalism did not only represent an assertion of Scottish cultural autonomy either within, or against, the Union, but also supplied a history of common medieval origins. Since Scots and English traced their descent from the same family of Old English dialects, then the Union of 1707, it was argued, far from being an unnatural yoking of opposites, involved the reintegration of common cultures. Moreover, since the English language had, owing to England's more extensive commercial contacts with the

---

[23] *Ibid.*

[24] See e.g. I. Ross and S. Scobie, 'Patriotic publishing as a response to the Union', in T. I. Rae (ed.), *The Union of 1707* (Glasgow and London, 1974), pp. 94–119.

Continent, absorbed more foreign elements and had changed more significantly over the previous half millennium, then a – relatively – static Scots could reasonably boast of being a truer representative of the common ethnic and cultural origins shared by the majority population of the British mainland. A host of Scots antiquarians, lexicographers and writers celebrated medieval Scots as the primeval language of the modern British nation. In his classic novel of British reconciliation, *The expedition of Humphry Clinker* (1771), Tobias Smollett (1721–71) deployed his leading Scots character Lismahagow as a mouthpiece for the curious patriotic boast that Scots was the authentic language of Old England:

> He proceeded to explain his assertion that the English language was spoken with greater propriety in Edinburgh than in London. – He said, what was generally called the Scottish dialect was, in fact, true, genuine, old English, with a mixture of some French terms and idioms, adopted in a long intercourse betwixt the French and Scotch nations; that the modern English, from affectation and false refinement, had weakened, and even corrupted their language, by throwing out the guttural sounds, altering the pronunciation and the quantity, and disusing many words and terms of great significance. In consequence of these innovations, the works of our best poets, such as Chaucer, Spenser, and even Shakespeare, were become, in many parts, unintelligible to the nations of South-Britain, whereas the Scots, who retain the antient language, understand them without the help of a glossary.[25]

[25] Tobias Smollett, *The expedition of Humphry Clinker* (1771: Oxford, 1984 pbk), pp. 199–200.

This became a familiar feature of the late eighteenth century Scots linguistic revival. John Callander of Craigforth, for example, contended that English – owing to commercial intercourse – was a corrupt variant of an Old English original, while its sister-tongue Scots had retained its purity.[26] It became common among antiquaries and philologists to refer to old Scots as the 'Scoto-Saxon dialect'.[27]

This strain of Scots revivalism took an eccentric and offensive form in the work of John Pinkerton (1758–1826), an antiquary who combined a patriotic interest in middle Scots Scottish literature with a virulent hatred of what he saw – mistakenly – as alien Celtic elements which had been grafted on to Scotland's indigenous 'Gothic' culture. Aware of the prejudice that Scots was a mere 'dialect of the English' and that the achievement of the Makars had been built upon imitation of Chaucer, Pinkerton endowed Scots literature with a bogus ancient Pictish pedigree in his 'Essay on the origin of Scotish poetry', appended to his edition of *Ancient Scotish Poems* (1786). Scots and English, he contended, were both of ancient Scandinavian provenance, the former through the Picts from whom 'the whole inhabitants of the low and rich countries of Scotland are descended': 'the Picts coming from the north of Scandinavia, and the Saxons from the south, the languages were as nearly allied as Scotish and English'. However, as the Picts had migrated to Britain, Pinkerton argued, four or five

---

[26] John Callander, *Two ancient Scottish poems; The gaberlunzie-man and Christ's Kirk on the green* (Edinburgh, 1782), pp. 8–9.

[27] See e.g. Alexander Geddes, 'Three Scottish poems, with a previous dissertation on the Scoto-Saxon dialect', *Archaeologia Scotica* 1 (1792).

centuries before the Saxons, the Scots–Pictish tongue, though a 'sister language' of the Saxon-English was purer and less corrupt, because 'an elder daughter of the Gothic and more like the mother'.[28] Some of the foremost supporters of the Scots language were to be influenced by Pinkerton's ideas. These figures included John Jamieson (1759–1838), renowned as the compiler of the first major dictionary of Scots in 1808, James Sibbald (1745–1803), who authored a *Chronicle of Scottish poetry* (1802), and Alexander Murray (1775–1813), Professor of Oriental Languages at Edinburgh who wrote a paper on the Gothic language of the Picts.[29] Under the influence of Pinkerton, philology became confused with physical anthropology, with the Gothic and Celtic peoples of Scotland assigned to separate racial categories. Racial analysis of this sort simultaneously divided the population of Scotland into two antithetical elements – Celts and Goths – and also connected the Lowland Goths with their Saxon kin in England.

In the nineteenth century Anglo-Scottish unity became for many intellectuals an ethnological fact. For many commentators the Union of 1707 symbolised a deeper physical unity grounded in shared racial characteristics. The ethnic

[28] John Pinkerton, 'An essay on the origin of Scotish poetry', in Pinkerton (ed.), *Ancient Scotish poems* (2 vols., London, 1786), I, pp. lii–liii; John Pinkerton, *A dissertation on the origin and progress of the Scythians or Goths* (London, 1787); John Pinkerton, *An enquiry into the history of Scotland* (2 vols., London, 1789).

[29] John Jamieson, *An etymological dictionary of the Scottish language* (Edinburgh, 1808); James Sibbald, *A chronicle of Scottish poetry* (4 vols., Edinburgh, 1802); Alexander Murray, 'Observations on the history and language of the Pehts', *Archaeologia Scotica* 2 (1822), 134–53.

frontier within Britain, so the consensus ran, was not at the Anglo-Scottish border defined by the Tweed and the Solway, but within Scotland itself – the line between the Highlands and the rest of Lowland Britain. Nor did nineteenth-century Scots regard themselves as belonging to a Celtic fringe. British nationhood was a mode of expressing more fundamental realities, namely a pride in Teutonic racial origins. Or, to put this another way, there was a general recognition on both sides of the border that Lowland Scots were not ethnically alien to the English, merely a northern branch of the same race. This outlook came to dominate – and to complicate – nineteenth-century readings of the Scottish War of Independence. A chorus of nineteenth-century Scottish commentators reinterpreted the Anglo-Scottish conflicts of the late thirteenth and fourteenth centuries as a tale of two Englands. Late medieval Scotland, many Scottish historians argued, had been just as Anglian as England itself. Indeed, several historians regarded Lowland Scotland and Northumbria as the true ethnic heartland of Great Britain, the home of the most purely Anglian stock within the island.

This position was widely held, even by those who did not subscribe to a racialist interpretation of history. In his extended article 'The Union with England and Scottish nationality' (1854) David Masson (1822–1907) conceded that race was 'by no means the most important element in nationality'. Nevertheless, a measure of ethnological affiliation underpinned the success of the Union: 'the populations themselves, too, with all allowance for the Gaels in the one, and the Welsh in the other, were essentially combinable – scions of the same stock'. Indeed, Masson contended that 'the southern Scots were more akin to the northern English, than these were to the southern English; the southern Scots and the northern English being Angles and Danes, with a Norman infusion, while the southern English were Saxons with a Norman infusion'. Thus, the island of Britain, Masson argued, had long been destined to be a single state: 'By as sure a law, then, as that by which the English and Scottish kingdoms had themselves been formed out of a prior consolidation of smaller parts, were these two kingdoms, in their turn, to be consolidated into one'. The only outstanding issues related to the timing of Union and 'the mode of the consolidation'. This led Masson to argue for the unionist significance of the Scottish War of Independence. Edward I's attempt to subdue Scotland had been premature and badly handled. Masson noted 'that the purposes of history' were 'better answered by postponing the Union of the two kingdoms until such time as it could be accomplished with something like the voluntary consent of both'.[30]

James Hannay (1827–73), the editor of the *Edinburgh Courant*, complained that the accident of the Scottish War of Independence had distorted the true contours of Scotland's earlier history. The War of Independence and the 'incessant struggles' which followed had 'so isolated the Scotch from the south, that they threw back their present impressions of separation into the past and substituted for real history a series of half-true traditions'. What then was Scotland's 'real history'? The answer, unsurprisingly, was Teutonist:

[30] [David Masson], 'The Union with England and Scottish nationality', *North British Review* 21 (1854), 69–100, at pp. 69–70.

nothing can be more certain that the governing part of
Scotland – the Lowlands . . . was essentially Teutonic long
before Edward was thought of. The language is there to
speak for itself, in excellent Saxon, with a Scandinavian
admixture; while to complete the likeness between North
and South Britain, even in the thirteenth century, if
England had a Norman aristocracy by conquest, Scotland
had one by colonization.

Hannay ascribed the success of the eventual Anglo-Scottish
Union to 'the natural ethnological affinity of the populations'
of the two Teutonic kingdoms.[31]

Indeed, this racialist perspective exposed major ideo-
logical contradictions in traditional accounts of the Scottish
War of Independence, a subject which had for centuries pro-
vided the prime matter of Scottish national consciousness.
According to the jurist James Lorimer (1818–90) the Scottish
War of Independence should not obscure the deeper ethno-
logical affinities between the Teutonic peoples of North and
South Britain:

> The two nations, it is said, if two nations they can still be
> called, did not differ, at the period which our authentic
> history begins, in blood, in language, or in manners. With
> the exception of a few outlying counties, which in each
> were peopled by the earlier race, they were kindred
> offshoots from the great Teutonic stem. For a time they
> were separated by an unhappy war, which has long since
> been forgotten.

[31] James Hannay, 'The Scot at home', *Cornhill Magazine* 14 (Aug. 1866),
238–56, at 239–40.

Lorimer took the view that the ethnological difference between the Scots Lowlander and the Englishman were 'very trifling'. There were, he argued, similar Gothic and Celtic elements in both populations and in very similar proportions, except during the Viking era: yet 'the greater amount of Scandinavian blood in Scotland during the Saxon period was pretty well counterbalanced in England by the Norman Conquest, which scarcely extended to Scotland'. If one excluded Highlanders and those of Cornish or Welsh descent, Lorimer believed that a Scotsman and an Englishman 'taken at random, will very frequently be as homogeneous in blood as any two individual Scotchmen or Englishmen selected in the same manner'.[32] The prominent historian John Hill Burton (1809–81) took the view that 'the Teutonic type' was 'purer' in the Scottish Lowlands than 'in the people of England'. In the light of this ethnological truth, Hill Burton was dismissive of the pseudo-histories of Scottish independence and national distinctiveness which had deceived previous generations of Scots. 'The real history of the Scottish Lowlands' was something rather different:

> that of a people enjoying, at an early period, the same
> language and institutions as the Saxon inhabitants of
> England, and so much a portion of the general Saxon
> aggregate, that, like its other principalities, the boundaries
> changed from time to time, by absorption or disjunction;
> and Scotland was politically distinct from her neighbour
> only in never being entirely absorbed into the kingdom

---

[32] James Lorimer, 'Scottish nationality', *North British Review* 33 (1860), 57–82, at pp. 65, 70 fn.

which arose from the aggregation of the general elements of the heptarchy.

Indeed, Hill Burton claimed that in the era before the Norman Conquest Scotland might easily have become a part of Saxon England. There had been 'no more alienation between the Scot and his Northumbrian neighbour', Hill Burton insisted, 'than there had been between the Northumbrian and his neighbour of Mercia; and there might have been nothing revolting to national feeling or independent pride, had Scotland been absorbed in the united Saxon kingdom'. However, the Norman Conquest intervened between the Saxon era and the pretensions of Edward I to amalgamate the two kingdoms, and it was the Norman Yoke, Hill Burton argued, which constituted the primary difference between what would have been the natural absorption of Saxon Scotland within a Greater Saxondom and the Plantagenet invasion of Scotland:

> it was otherwise when the tyrannous Norman, after having ravaged England, laid his hand on a country which had been distinctly marked off by the conquest, and had passed through two centuries of comparative freedom in exemption from the Norman Yoke. It was the attempt to impose this yoke, that first taught Scotland to see in the kingdom of England her natural enemy.

According to Hill Burton the Scottish hero William Wallace was a 'representative and champion of the Saxon or pure Norse inhabitants of Britain, who had not yet been subjected to the southern yoke.' 'Scottish nationality', therefore, was in reality no older than the thirteenth century when the Scots found

162

themselves 'estranged from England' in language, manners and institutions, and as such a perversion of ethnology and of deeper trends in British history. Implicit in Hill Burton's analysis was a sense that the War of Scottish Independence had been a tragic blunder, which diverted British history from its natural course, namely the ultimate unification of Teutonic North and South Britons into a single ethnically homogeneous nation state. Yet in the medium term history had followed another course altogether. As a result of Anglo-Scottish hostilities, Scotland's 'Saxon institutions' had been 'gradually buried under foreign importations'. Nevertheless, Scotland's Auld Alliance with France had been artificial and, fortunately, 'superficial'. Thus, the tinges of Romanist despotism which had marked Scotland's legal system had turned out to be 'more nominal than real' and certainly no obstacle to eventual Union with England. Notwithstanding the unnatural estrangements and alliances consequent upon the Scottish War of Independence, the Scots had not, ultimately, been 'incapacitated to join their brethren of the old Saxon stock, from whom they had long been severed'.[33]

To some Scots racialists, indeed, the very idea of Scottish nationhood was ethnologically meaningless and the very name of 'Scotland' a misnomer. The historian Duncan Keith claimed of 'Scotland' that 'the very name suggests an untruth'. The term Scotland – which referred to the Gaelic Scots – did

[33] John Hill Burton, *History of Scotland from the Revolution* (2 vols., London, 1853), I, pp. 515–16, 519–20; John Hill Burton, *History of Scotland from Agricola's invasion* (7 vols., Edinburgh and London, 1867–70), I, p. 207; II, p. 278.

not reflect the country's dominant Teutonic racial characteristics. Keith lamented that 'had it not been for the unfortunate capture of William the Lion in 1174, it looked very like as if the frontier of Scotland was to be advanced to the Humber, the south of Scotland and the north of England were one in race and feeling'. At any rate, race seemed to make a mockery of the border between the supposed Scottish and English nations. Such, Keith acknowledged, was the 'close connection' during the twelfth century 'between the Norman rulers of both countries' that it 'required near to two centuries of internecine warfare to make the one English and the other Scotch'. Moreover, he confessed that, while it 'grates against our proud national feeling of independence', the 'candid mind almost regrets that some matrimonial arrangement was not effected, by which people identical in race, in feeling, and religion, should have been united under one head'.[34]

Similar views can be found in the work of Dr Ebenezer Duncan (d. 1922), physician to the Victoria Infirmary on Glasgow's South Side and president of the Sanitary Association of Scotland. Duncan not only took a keen interest in racial hygiene as an aspect of public health, but also subscribed to the Teutonist interpretation of Scottish history and to racialist theories in the sphere of craniology. Duncan contended that Scottish heads appeared to be larger and – more importantly – longer than English heads. As the Anglo-Saxon and Scandinavian racial type was known to be dolichocephalic,

---

[34] Duncan Keith, *A history of Scotland civil and ecclesiastical* (2 vols., Edinburgh, 1886), I, pp. 36, 250, 265.

the long-headedness of modern Scots provided a compelling case for the purity of the people's Teutonic ancestry. Indeed, Ebenezer Duncan asserted that the names England and Scotland were 'of no value ethnologically'. Duncan claimed that the Scots were, on the grounds of their purer Teutonic blood, racially speaking more English than the English themselves: 'it may sound paradoxical, but I believe it is true that, ethnologically, if a pure English race is to be found anywhere in Britain, which I doubt, the purest English are the Scotsmen of the south-eastern counties of Scotland, and next to them come the people of Northumberland and Durham'. Moreover, Scottish nationhood, such as it was, had been Teutonic in origin. Duncan described the five hundred years or so between the founding of the Northumbrian kingdom of Bernicia and the coming of the Flemings to Scotland as 'the formative centuries' in the making of Scottish nationhood, 'during which the larger and most populous part of Scotland was Teutonised in speech and civilisation, and the people gradually welded into a homogeneous nation'.[35]

In *The Story of the British Race* (1899) John Munro took the line that throughout the British Isles one could find ethnically mixed populations, which, regional variations notwithstanding, nonetheless contained strong affinities with one another. However, one particular group of populations stood out as characteristically Teutonic, namely the areas where more than 50 per cent of the adult male population

---

[35] Ebenezer Duncan, *The Scottish races: their ethnology, growth and distribution* (Glasgow, 1896), pp. 9–11, 13–15.

had fair complexions, light-coloured eyes and fairish, light brown or reddish hair. This pure Teutonic stock was to be found in Northumbria and the Severn Valley, Munro noted, but also – tellingly – north of the border, in Angus and the Lothians.[36]

The Teutonist interpretation of Scottish history was not only confined to the world of the intelligentsia, but also made its way into more popular media, such as school textbooks. Margaret Macarthur's popular *History of Scotland* introduced pupils to the contrasting roles of the Teutonic and the Celtic races in the Scottish past. The War of Scottish Independence, Macarthur informed pupils, had been a kind of domestic feud between English and Scottish components of the Teutonic race. Moreover, she claimed that Edward I's conquest of Scotland had produced an unlikely – and ironic – set of reactions in the two racial groups which inhabited medieval Scotland. Whereas 'the Celts in the North looked on this change in the government with apathy', the Plantagenet invasion had 'roused a spirit of defiance and opposition where resistance was least to be looked for, among the Lowlanders', who were, of course, 'the descendants of the earliest Teutonic settlers, and had remained more purely English in blood and speech than their kinsfolk on the southern side of the Border'. In other words, the Scottish War of Independence, pupils were told, had been at bottom the cause of the *true English* of Lowland Scotland who found themselves at war with the Normanised English of England. According to Macarthur, at the Battle of Bannockburn 'the Saxons of the Lowlands [had] decided their

---

[36] John Munro, *The story of the British race* (London, 1899), p. 121.

own fate and that of the Celtic people by whose name they were called, and to whose kingdom they chose to belong'.[37]

Nineteenth-century Scotland's most outspoken nationalist historian recognised the damage done to the very idea of Scottish nationhood by the Teutonic racialists. William Burns was a Glasgow solicitor, who advised coal owners and iron masters, and a prolific champion of Scottish causes, most famously the media campaign against the use of 'England' as an insulting synonym for 'Great Britain'. Burns devoted his history of the Scottish Wars of Independence to challenging the racialist theories of Scottish ethnology. Burns recognised clearly the anti-nationalist implications of Scottish Teutonism. A fixation on ethnology and racial origins at the expense of all those other elements of nationality which made nations undermined the coherence of Scottish nationhood, and a nationalist interpretation of the Scottish War of Independence would collapse under its internal contradictions:

> The simplest reader must see that one obvious effect of this Anglo-Saxon theory, especially, is to pluck out from the history of Scotland its very heart and soul, by depriving it of all logical sequence ... If it be the fact, that the people who fought the War of Independence were, after all, not in any proper sense the Scottish nation, but merely 'a portion of the general Saxon aggregate', as Mr. Burton assures us they were; if it be true, as noticed by a writer in the *North British Review*, that, 'with the exception of a few outlying counties, which in each were peopled by the earlier race,

[37] Margaret Macarthur, *History of Scotland* (3rd edn, London, 1879), pp. 1, 3–4, 42, 50.

they (the nations north and south of the Tweed) were
kindred offshoots of the great Teutonic stem, separated for
a time by an unfortunate war, which has long since been
forgotten' . . . if these are correct representations, then, the
history of our country ceases to have any meaning; the
stirring annals of her struggles for independence and
integrity, as against Romans, Angles, Danes, and
Norsemen, are of no more value than what may have been
passing in another planet, and the War of Independence
itself, in which the Anglo-Normans were repulsed,
hitherto supposed to have been a noble effort of
patriotism, was an unfortunate blunder, or, at best, a
splendid specimen of wrongheadedness.

Burns took particular exception to what he termed 'the theory of displacement'. Although there were some variants in
the theory, Burns succinctly defined the broad thrust of this
new and dangerous historiographical consensus. It taught
that 'the descendants of the native Celtic-speaking races' of
dark-age Scotland had been 'almost entirely "pushed out" of
the Lowlands, and "cooped up" within the Highlands, by
a new Teutonic-speaking population', consisting of Angles,
Scandinavians, some hybrid Anglo-Danes and some Norman-
French adventurers. A compelling vision of Scottish nationhood required, as Burns perceived, a narrative of ethnogenesis
distinct from that of Scotland's partners in Union.[38]

Yet many late nineteenth-century commentators subscribed to the view that British Saxondom – Lowland Scots

---

[38] William Burns, *Scottish War of Independence* (2 vols., Glasgow, 1874), I,
pp. 16–17, 276–7.

as well as English – shared a common ethnic provenance. In this light it was the tardiness of Union, not Union itself, which demanded explanation. The advocate G. W. T. Omond (1846–1929) opened his *Early history of the Scottish Union question* (1897) by posing the question as it was then commonly understood: 'The races which inhabited the northern parts of England and the southern parts of Scotland were descended from a common stock and spoke a common language. But for centuries the problem of uniting them baffled the best-laid plans of kings and statesmen.'[39]

The last of the line

The twentieth century witnessed a retreat from scientific racialism in most areas of intellectual enquiry. In line with this development, ethnological interpretations were gradually filtered out of the academic mainstream of Scottish history. Other features of historical analysis also went into decline. The central features of Scottish unionist historiography – including the narratives of economic underperformance, failed state formation and defective constitutional development – yielded to a more sensitive approach to history, which no longer judged pre-1707 Scottish history directly against an English yardstick. The unconcerted demolition work of Herbert Butterfield and Lewis Namier on the English whig interpretation of history – and by extension on English self-regard – had eventual repercussions on Scottish historical writing. Nationalist

[39] G. W. T. Omond, *The early history of the Scottish Union question* (Edinburgh, 1897), p. 9.

interpretations were in the ascendant in Scottish historiography, certainly from the 1960s onwards. Nevertheless, there was a prominent exception to the general trend. The ethnological interpretation of the North British past – shorn, of course, of its more offensive features – persisted into the last quarter of the twentieth century at the very heart of the Scottish historical establishment. Indeed, the last of this line was Gordon Donaldson (1913–93), Professor of Scottish History at the University of Edinburgh and Her Majesty's Historiographer in Scotland. A fierce critic of Scottish nationalism and of the claims of the Highlands to special treatment, whether in politics or history, Donaldson readily identified himself with Teutonic Scotland. As an adopted Shetlander, he felt a special attachment to one particular aspect of Scotland's Teutonic past, to the Norse heritage of the northern isles. While the generality of Scots who wished to dress the part of a patriot opted for kilts, trews and other forms of tartanry, Donaldson acquired a Viking costume.[40] This Viking manqué was himself profoundly patriotic, not least in defending his academic turf from the errors of English historians, but saw no reason to conclude that Scottish patriotism was incompatible either with support for the Union or even with the anglicisation of Scotland. Unionism and anglicisation were, he insisted, part of the warp and woof of Scottish history. In 'Foundations of Anglo-Scottish union' (1961) Donaldson claimed that if Edward I's scheme to marry his heir the future Edward II to the Maid of Norway had not been dashed

---

[40] J. Kirk, *Her Majesty's historiographer: Gordon Donaldson 1913–1993* (Edinburgh, 1996), p. 72, for Donaldson's acquisition of 'a Norse costume and spurious horned helmet'.

by the latter's death at sea in 1290, then not only would a union have taken place between England and Scotland, but 'Scottish nationality would never have developed.' The Scottish War of Independence, it seemed, was something of an aberration. Similarly, during the sixteenth century, Donaldson argued, the Scottish state had been 'consciously Anglo-Saxon'. Moreover, the Reformations of England and Scotland nurtured a vernacular Protestantism within which Anglo-Scottish affinities were pronounced. Union, Donaldson concluded, had been 'in the making' for 'centuries' before the political unions of 1603 and 1707 – which, in themselves, constituted only 'two incidents in the long process creating a united nation'. In another essay entitled 'The anglicisation of Scotland' Donaldson argued that these connections went much deeper still. Indeed, he insisted that within Scotland's long history the roots of anglicisation went as deep as those of Gaelicisation. Anglicisation was neither inauthentic nor foreign to the experience of nationhood:

> Anglicisation of the country we now call Scotland started in the sixth century, almost contemporaneously with the beginning of its Scotticisation or Hibernicisation, for Angles settled in what is now south-east Scotland within less than a century of the arrival in Argyll of Irish 'Scots'. Scots and Angles alike expanded at the expense of the earlier inhabitants, the Picts and Britons.

Throughout his career Donaldson, like other members of his generation, continued to employ the old categories of 'race' and 'blood', which had been such a feature of historical discourse between 1800 and 1945. These fuelled his Teutonist interpretation of history, the final version of which is to be found in

171

Donaldson's popular survey *Scotland: the shaping of a nation*, first published in 1974, with further editions in 1980 and 1993:

> In view of the lack of an obvious frontier between north and south Britain, the existence of physical barriers within Scotland, the differences of race and language among its people, the contrast between Highlands and Lowlands and the affinities between the Lowlands and England, it is remarkable that a separate state, with its frontier at the Tweed and the Solway, ever came into existence and preserved its identity.

It seemed obvious to Donaldson, as it had to a long tradition of Scottish historians, that, by contrast with the accidental hybrid of Scottish nationality, British nationhood expressed an underlying ethnic unity.[41]

[41] G. Donaldson, 'The anglicisation of Scotland', in Donaldson, *Scotland's history: approaches and reflections* (ed. J. Kirk, Edinburgh, 1995), p. 118; G. Donaldson, 'Foundations of Anglo-Scottish union', in Donaldson, *Scottish Church History* (Edinburgh, 1985), pp. 138, 142, 163; G. Donaldson, *Scotland: the shaping of a nation* (1974: Nairn, 1993), p. 23.

5

From assimilationist jurisprudence to legal nationalism

Jurisprudence constitutes one of the most important branches of unionist political thought in Scotland over the past three centuries. In chapter 3 we have already examined how Scots jurists parsed the particular problem of sovereignty within the field of constitutional law. This chapter takes a broader approach to Scots juridical thought within the Union, not only exploring constitutional questions regarding the status of Scots law, but also investigating the depth of commitment felt by Scots lawyers to the preservation of Scottish legal distinctiveness, attitudes to legal reform, including programmes to anglicise Scots law, interpretations of Scottish and British legal history, and the relationship of Scottish legal culture more generally to the politics of Union.

Although jurisprudence might seem at first sight to be a somewhat arcane branch of political thought, the unusual status of Scots law within the Union of 1707 means that the subject deserves special treatment. Articles XVIII, XIX and XX of Union appeared to guarantee the preservation of a Scottish legal system within the Union. Yet this was no more than a fragile semi-autonomy. Public law was a matter for the new British state, but Scots private law was to be preserved in its entirety. There was no attempt to define public or private law or to clarify the grey areas between them. The Union agreement was also silent on the question of whether Scots legal appeals might be brought to the British House of Lords from the supreme courts of Scotland, whether from the Court of Session in civil cases or the High Court of Justiciary in criminal trials. Article XVIII did permit parliamentary intervention in Scots private law where change might be for 'the evident utility of the subject', though without setting out the constitutional machinery for testing such utility, however evident it might be. In effect, Scots law was subject rather to the legislative oversight of a British parliament, the vast majority of whose members were wholly unfamiliar with Scots law.

As a result of the provisions for Scots law laid out in the Union agreement, there has been a widespread assumption that, following the loss of the Scottish parliament in 1707, the Scots legal system – alongside the established Church of Scotland – functioned as a mainstay of Scottish national identity in the centuries following the Union. This casual equation of Scots law and national identity has encouraged a further assumption that Scots law became a seedbed of Scottish nationalism. The need to defend a precarious Scots legal distinctiveness from the legislative or appellate encroachments of Westminster, so the argument runs, fostered a nationalist outlook among Scottish jurists, culminating in the legal nationalism which has flourished since the middle of the twentieth century.[1] In addition, a notion prevails that from the Union onwards Scottish jurists were not only aware that their legal system was different from England's and needed to be protected,

---

[1] For a critical examination of the phenomenon of Scots legal nationalism, see I. D. Willock, 'The Scottish legal heritage revisited', in J. P. Grant (ed.), *Independence and devolution: the legal implications for Scotland* (Edinburgh, 1976), pp. 1–14.

but also that in his *Institutions of the law of Scotland* (1681) James Dalrymple, Lord Stair (1619–95) had endowed Scots law with a philosophical coherence which was manifestly wanting in the abject jumble of precedents which made up the English common law.[2] Scots jurisprudence, it is believed, was celebrated as an intellectual triumph, not least as Stair's pioneering work was continued by his successors in the institutional tradition of Scots jurisprudence – Erskine, Bankton and Bell. The common law was surely seen as a muddled inferior by comparison with the pellucid system of institutional jurisprudence. Scots jurists displayed an attachment to principle rather than precedent. Thus, the admission of alien English precedents into Scots law, it was held, would not only have served to undermine the native spirit of the law, but would also have weakened its philosophical rigour. Scots law became, therefore, in the absence of a legislature in Edinburgh, a focus for national aspirations, while the vaunted quality of its jurisprudence made the Scots legal tradition a vital source of national pride; or so it is widely believed.

These received ideas possess a great deal of plausibility, at least from a superficial inspection of the available evidence. However, closer analysis reveals a history not only more complex and ambiguous than the accepted story, but one which at certain points diverges dramatically from the conventional narrative. In particular, as we shall see, legal culture has been predominantly unionist, not only during the banal unionism of the period between about 1750 and 1950, but even during the

---

[2] Cf. N. MacCormick, 'Stair as analytical jurist', in D. Walker (ed.), *Stair tercentenary studies* (Stair Society, Edinburgh, 1981), pp. 187–99.

ascent of Scots legal nationalism in the second half of the twentieth century. Scots legal nationalism did not pose a challenge to political unionism. As will become clear, legal nationalism was largely a unionist project, overlapping only at the margins with political nationalism. Properly parsed, legal nationalism was at most a kind of cultural nationalism which co-existed happily with loyalty to the British state, and in one of the most influential cases, as we shall see, drew its prime motivation from a frustrated Scots-British imperialism. Nor can one detect many traces of Scots legal nationalism before the second half of the twentieth century, though nineteenth-century Scots jurists, as will become evident, had been exposed to the sorts of arguments that might be used to construct such an ideology, without, it seems, experiencing any temptation to deploy these on behalf of Scots law. The eighteenth century provides an even more unexpected story, that of a legal culture intent not on the maintenance of Scots law within the Union, but rather displaying an openness to the reform of Scots law inspired by external examples, especially those drawn from England. Modernisation mattered more to eighteenth-century Scots jurists than the preservation of traditional Scots legal forms and institutions in aspic as symbols of an historic nationhood. Anglicisation and assimilation, it transpires, were the surprising hallmarks of eighteenth-century Scottish legal culture.

Yet emulation of England was not a consistent feature of Scots jurisprudence after the eighteenth century; nor indeed was it the whole of the story during the eighteenth century. The chapter will explore long-standing tensions within Scottish legal culture between inward-looking defences of Scottish particularism, on the one hand, and, on the other, cosmopolitan aspirations to identify with larger supra-national bodies of law. These supra-national entities have included the civil law world and the family of hybrid 'mixed systems' of law which partake of both Roman and common law elements, as well as the laws of the British Empire and the European Community. Eighteenth-century Scots did not think of their legal system as impeccably Scottish in pedigree and character; rather they acknowledged that they participated – by way of their share in the pan-European inheritance of civil, canon and feudal law – in a supra-national *ius commune*. This common heritage of legal learning constituted the common basis for legal practice across much of Europe, though, over time, the reification of local variants in customs, decisions and proce-dures saw individual jurisdictions become differentiated into distinct bodies of national law. As late as the mid-eighteenth century Scots jurists still thought of the Roman law as the common law of Scotland. Moreover, the authority of Scots law rested not on any sense that it reflected the will of the Scottish nation, but in the recognition that it manifested, under local conditions, the universal truths of the law of nature. Scots jurists also acknowledged that other legal systems bore the imprint of natural law; as such they were worthy of imitation in areas where Scots law was found wanting. By the same token, twentieth-century legal nationalism did not only arise from a defensive anxiety for the purity of Scots law within the Union state, but also drew upon the ambition that a wider stage might be found on which Scots lawyers might flaunt their distinctive-ness from the alien common law tradition. This can be seen most obviously in the work of T. B. Smith, a frustrated imperi-alist who complained that Scots law had become parochial and inward-looking when it might properly since 1707 have become the law of the British Empire. Smith found an alternative outlet for his imperialist energies, forging international connections between Scots law and kindred forms of jurisprudence within the far-flung family of 'mixed' legal systems, which included South Africa, Quebec, Ceylon (as it then was) and Louisiana. The Anglo-Scottish relationship, it transpires, provides but a limited explanation of a multi-faceted phenomenon which is inadequately described by the term 'legal nationalism'.

Assimilation and Enlightenment

Legal nationalism had no purchase on eighteenth-century Scottish jurisprudence. Not only was the concept unknown to eighteenth-century lawyers, but the particular circumstances of the Scottish legal profession provided scant encouragement for parochial defensiveness, regardless of the fact of Union. In large part this was because Scots legal education was not yet a domestic affair. Early modern Scots had been drawn – in the absence of established legal curricula in the Scottish universities – to study law in the French universities during the sixteenth century, and more recently in the Dutch universities, especially Leiden and Utrecht. Many Scots continued to study law at the Dutch universities until about the middle of the eighteenth century. Indeed, the first steps towards consolidating the study of law in the Scottish universities advanced in a decidedly cosmopolitan manner. In 1707, for example, Edinburgh University established a Professorship of Public Law and the Law of Nature and Nations. Further chairs followed at Edinburgh, a chair of Civil Law, by which was meant Roman law, in 1709 and only in 1722 a chair of Scots Law. The order in which these professorships were established accurately reflected contemporary priorities. Indeed, not until 1750 did Scots law become a necessary element in the training of a Scottish lawyer. Arguably, Scots law played only a very minor role in determining entry to the legal profession. Entrance to the legal profession was by way of the civil law, that is Roman law, a subject to which aspirant Scots advocates were exposed in the Dutch universities. Only in 1692 did an alternative method of entry to the Faculty of Advocates present itself by way of an examination in Scots law. In 1724 the Dean of Faculty recommended that entry should depend on an examination in Scots law. After some discussion, the proposal fell by the wayside, and a further push was needed to make an examination in Scots law a formal requirement for advocates, which it became from 1750.[3]

Thus, although the Scottish legal system had been preserved in Articles XVIII, XIX and XX of the Treaty of Union, the distinctiveness and semi-autonomy enjoyed by Scots law did not constitute bulwarks of Scottish nationhood within the new British state. Eighteenth-century Scots lawyers – many of whom were trained in Leiden and Utrecht in the civil law – did not treat the status of Scots law in a narrowly positivist or nationalist idiom. Contemporary projections of Scots law as a national system of law were set within the context of the wider

---

[3] *Minute book of the Faculty of Advocates I 1661–1712* ed. J. A. Pinkerton (Stair Society, Edinburgh, 1976), pp. 115–16; *Minute book of the Faculty of Advocates II 1713–1750* ed. J. A. Pinkerton (Stair Society, Edinburgh, 1980), pp. 72–5, 77, 79, 85, 115–16, 232, 239, 241.

law of nature and nations from which national laws derived their ultimate authority. For example, the jurisprudence of Stair had involved an attempt to systematise the various components of Scots law – customs, decisions and statutes; feudal, canon and civil law – and to relate the whole to the law of God as revealed to man in scripture and a universal law of nature which was made manifest to man through the faculty of reason.[4] This outlook is epitomised by the claim of the Scottish judge Lord Cullen that anyone 'who has the Common and Scotch law, may soon acquire that of any disciplined country. Reason (whence it proceeds) is every where the same; though uttered and applied by different signs, of words and forms.'[5] Scots jurists acknowledged that other legal systems bore the imprint of natural law; as such they were worthy of imitation in areas where Scots law was found wanting.

The principles of the law of nature and nations inculcated an open-minded pluralism in Scots lawyers far removed from either legal chauvinism or anxious defensiveness. Education abroad and exposure to the supra-national legacies of the civil law, Romano-canonical law and feudal law reinforced such attitudes. That Scots law enjoyed a precarious existence within the Union at the mercy of an English-dominated legislature was something which struck their twentieth-century successors very forcibly; but it made little impression on eighteenth-century Scots jurists. The Union did very little to

---

[4] James Dalrymple, *The institutions of the law of Scotland deduced from its originals and collated with the civil, canon and feudal laws; and with the customs of neighbouring nations* (Edinburgh, 1681), 'Common principles of law'.

[5] Francis Grant, *Law, religion and education considered* (1715), I, 'Law', p. 97.

dent the outward-looking openness of Scots jurisprudence. For instance, eighteenth-century Scots jurists complacently accepted the appellate jurisdiction of the House of Lords, despite the fact that the Treaty of Union was silent on the subject of such appeals. From the outset of the new united state, the British House of Lords responded to appeals from the Scottish courts by bringing them within its jurisdiction, beginning with *Rosebery* v. *Inglis* in 1708. The question of appellate jurisdiction only became a controversial issue when it became entangled with religion in the Greenshields case of 1710–11. Here it was the religious dimension of the issue which was controversial, not the juridical role of the House of Lords in overturning a Scottish decision. For much of the eighteenth century the British House of Lords exercised appellate juris-diction over both civil and criminal causes from the Court of Session and the High Court of Justiciary in the absence of any significant disquiet on the part of Scottish lawyers and judges.[6]

Examined at close quarters, in fact, eighteenth-century Scottish legal culture presents a very different picture from the familiar image of Scots law as a crucial buttress of post-Union Scottish identity. If anything, the reverse is true. Scottish legal commentators of the eighteenth century did, as it hap-pens, spend considerable time comparing and contrasting the laws of Scotland and England; but they did so largely to point up failings in the *Scottish* legal system. A chorus of judges,

---

[6] A. J. Maclean, 'The 1707 Union: Scots law and the House of Lords', in A. Kiralfy and H. MacQueen (eds.), *New perspectives in Scottish legal history* (London, 1984), pp. 50–75; A. J. MacLean, 'The House of Lords and appeals from the High Court of Justiciary, 1707–1887', *Juridical Review* (1985), 192–226.

professors and pamphleteers sang the same song: that Scots law was backward by comparison with that of England; that Scots law was too deeply imbued with feudal principles; that the forms and institutions of Scots law were inappropriate to the needs of an emerging commercial society, or indeed for the growing market in livestock and agricultural produce; and that feudal practices were both intrinsically authoritarian and, as anachronisms in a market society, dysfunctionally oppressive.[7] What mattered most to eighteenth-century Scots jurists, it turns out, was not the much-vaunted philosophical coherence of Scots law, but more practical concerns to uphold the core values of liberty and property and to find the correct legal infrastructure which might enable processes of agrarian improvement and commercial development. Scots legal patriotism did exist but its aims were the modernisation of the Scottish economy and the liberation of the Scottish people from the shackles of the feudal law, not the preservation of Scots law as a feudal museum piece.

Moreover, was England's legal system really so different from Scotland's? Although the contrast between Scotland's civilian jurisprudence and the English common law has become a staple of modern Scottish legal thought, this was less obvious to eighteenth-century jurists. Indeed, one of the most pronounced features of eighteenth-century Scottish legal history was an emphasis on the shared origins of both legal systems in the reception of feudal institutions during the Norman era. Although the Normans had not conquered Scotland, Scoto-Norman law had borrowed from its

[7] C. Kidd, *Subverting Scotland's past* (Cambridge, 1993).

Anglo-Norman cousin. 'When one dives into the antiquities of Scotland and England', wrote Lord Kames in his *Essays on British antiquities* (1747), 'it will appear that we borrowed all our laws and customs from the English. No sooner is a statute enacted in England, but, upon the first opportunity, it is introduced into Scotland; so that our oldest statutes are mere copies of theirs.'[8] Kames's *Essays on British antiquities*, his *Historical law tracts* (1758) and Sir John Dalrymple's *Essay towards a general history of feudal property in Great Britain* (1757) explored the common Anglo-Norman origins of legal institutions on both sides of the border and went on to track their subsequent divergence. According to Kames in his *Historical law tracts*, 'the whole island originally was governed by the same law'. This meant that Britain provided fascinating matter for comparative legal analysis. The laws of England and Scotland, so Kames contended, 'have such resemblance, as to bear a comparison almost in every branch; and they so far differ, as to illustrate each other by their opposition'.[9] Dalrymple took a similar line: 'The progress of these laws, however little attended to, is in both countries uniform and regular, advances by the same steps, goes in almost the same direction, and when the laws separate from each other, there is a degree of similarity even in the very separations.'[10] However, the comparison did not show Scotland in a good light. England's legal system was

---

[8] Henry Home, Lord Kames, *Essays upon several subjects concerning British antiquities* (Edinburgh, 1747), p. 4.

[9] Henry Home, Lord Kames, *Historical law tracts* (2 vols., Edinburgh, 1758), I, pp. xiii–xiv.

[10] John Dalrymple, *Essay towards a general history of feudal property in Great Britain* (1757), p. v.

far in advance of Scotland's. Scotland was much slower – by centuries – in its departure from the harsh rigidities of the feudal system. Dalrymple noted that '[i]n the declensions of almost every part of the feudal system, the English have gone before us; at the distance sometimes of one, and sometimes of many centuries, we follow.'[11] Kames perceived that the feudal law remained a key part of the law of Scotland, whereas in England it had been 'reduced to a shadow'.[12] Although a judge of the Court of Session, Kames hoped that the divergent legal systems of England and Scotland might be reunited in a common British legal system. Indeed, he lamented the 'unhappy circumstance that different parts of the same kingdom should be governed by different laws'.[13] Such a reunion would not, of course, be on the basis of their shared feudal origins, but on a jurisprudence more appropriate to the needs of a commercial age.[14]

But some elements from this distant past were worth recovering. In the 1780s some Scots jurists argued that centuries of Anglo-Scottish estrangement since the Norman era had seen the loss of the civil jury in Scotland, overturned by obnoxious Romanist practices introduced from France in the sixteenth century, and that the Union provided the opportunity for its restoration in Scotland, not only as a public benefit, but also in order to ensure civic equality among the people of North and South Britain.

---

[11] *Ibid.*, p. 332. [12] Kames, *Historical law tracts*, I, p. viii. [13] *Ibid.*, I, p. xiii.
[14] See e.g. D. Lieberman, 'The legal needs of a commercial society: the jurisprudence of Lord Kames', in L. Hont and M. Ignatieff (eds.), *Wealth and virtue: the shaping of political economy in the Scottish Enlightenment* (Cambridge, 1983), pp. 203–34.

The principal concern of Enlightenment jurisprudence was not with national differences between the legal systems of Scotland and England, or indeed between these two systems as representatives of distinctive idioms of civilian and common law approaches to the law; rather its primary concern was with the responsiveness of legal systems, such as Scots law, to social and economic change. Generally speaking, most Scots jurists during the age of Enlightenment evaluated legal systems in terms of social progress. Indeed, the famous four-stage, or stadial account of mankind's progress was rooted in the native tradition of natural jurisprudence derived from Grotius and Pufendorf. The stadial analysis of mankind's progress from the hunter-gatherer stage via pastoral life and then settled agriculture to commercial society tends to strike modern observers as an anticipation of the Marxist theory of history. Certainly, it seems to assign a primary role in historical explanation to a society's economic underpinnings. However, as Knud Haakonssen has shown, the social theory of the Scottish Enlightenment was not fixated on the economic base of a society, but rather – examining the past through the lens of natural jurisprudence – upon the forms of property found in a particular society.[15] The four-stage theory was, more aptly, a story of progress from a world without private property – whether the common ownership imagined by Grotius or the state of negative dominion more plausibly hypothesised by Pufendorf – to ownership of herds of cattle and other moveables, then to real estate and finally to money and bills of exchange, the symbolic forms

[15] K. Haakonssen, *The science of a legislator: the natural jurisprudence of David Hume and Adam Smith* (Cambridge, 1981).

of property upon which commerce depended. The mechanisms of social change were complex, and progress was not reducible to monocausal explanation. Instead, Scottish social theorists conjectured how changes in manners, the economy, laws, institutions and culture might move as an ensemble, if not absolutely in tandem. However, they also speculated how institutional or legal bottlenecks might retard underlying patterns of social and economic change. Scotland was a case in point. Jurisprudence underwrote stadial analysis; but equally, stadial analysis was the yardstick by which Scots jurisprudence was found sorely wanting. Scots law, its native jurists argued, was not in the vanguard of progress; indeed Scotland's feudal law was stunting the growth of the Scottish economy and restricting the freedom of its people.

Given these agenda, it is unsurprising that jurists worried less about the gradual anglicisation of the Scots law, than about the law's sensitivity to the transition between agrarian and commercial society. Far from championing the characteristic feudal features of Scots law as a badge of nationhood, eighteenth-century Scots jurists denounced these as relics of a barbaric past whose abolition was long overdue. Eighteenth-century Scottish jurists eschewed reaction. There was no point in preserving a distinctive legal heritage, if in so doing one merely perpetuated archaism. Rather Enlightenment Scotland tempered a theoretical interest in jurisprudence with a very practical approach to the ways in which the law might enhance the freedom of the individual or contribute to prosperity. Thus, although the feudal institutions and forms of Scots law were expressly guaranteed by Article XX of the Union, Scots jurists generally welcomed the anti-feudalist thrust of the legal reforms which followed the failed Jacobite rising of 1745–6. Two major acts which went through the Westminster parliament in 1747 abolished, respectively, wardholding vassalage and heritable jurisdictions – the private franchise courts of the Scottish nobility and gentry – in an attempt to eradicate the conditions which had encouraged rebellion in Scotland. While some Scots jurists found fault with various technical aspects of the Heritable Jurisdictions Bill, there was no opposition in principle to this apparent encroachment on Scottish legal privileges. Far from denouncing the Heritable Jurisdictions Act as a gross infringement of Article XX of the Union, which appeared to protect Scottish feudal particularities from the Westminster legislature, Scots jurists tended to welcome the reform as 'completing the Union'. There was a recognition that the Union itself was something of a compromised half-way house, in which Article XX's protection of feudal privileges appeased the sectional interests of the Scottish nobility. Thus the abolition of heritable jurisdictions was widely perceived within Scotland as a liberating measure which established a proper equality between the prosperous post-feudal commons of England and their downtrodden Scottish counterparts. Until then the Scottish commons had remained thirled to an outdated system of feudal vassalage and had held such liberties as they possessed at the precarious whim of baronial courts. Moreover, the legislation did away completely with a particular type of heritable jurisdiction, the powerful regality courts, which had the capacity to withdraw cases from other jurisdictions, even from the king's courts, when the parties were subjects of the regality. The demise of heritable jurisdictions amounted not so much to an assault on Scots law as the opportunity for a national system of law to flourish in Scotland unchecked by the partial interests of feudal barons and their baillies. All things considered, the infringement of a flagrantly defective Article of Union was a small price to pay for the liberation of the Scottish commons from the petty tyranny of overmighty subjects.

Most pamphleteers welcomed heritable jurisdiction reform, in hyperbolic fashion, as the ending of a system of oppression, which had left many Scots in a position 'worse than Egyptian slavery'. Jurists were more careful, but in the end no less decisive, in their analyses. In his *Institute of the laws of Scotland* Lord Bankton, who had at first been suspicious of the campaign to abolish heritable jurisdictions, rejoiced that those Scots who were formerly subject to heritable jurisdictions were now 'put upon the same foot of liberty and independency with the other people of Britain'. Similarly, George Wallace in *A system of the principles of the law of Scotland* (1760) celebrated the anti-feudal reforms of 1747–8 as the release of the Scottish commons from petty local authoritarianism: 'oppressive jurisdictions which subjects had possessed, were resumed to the crown; servile tenures were abolished; and tyrannical principles were banished from the law'.[16] Tobias Smollett, writing in the persona of Matt Bramble, a character in his epistolary novel *Humphry Clinker* (1771), recorded of the Scottish Highlanders that 'their slavish tenures are all dissolved by act of parliament; so that they are at present as free and independent of their chiefs as the law can make them'.[17] 1747 became a

---

[16] Kidd, *Subverting*, pp. 158–60; George Wallace, *A system of the principles of the law of Scotland* (Edinburgh, 1760), p. xix.

[17] Tobias Smollett, *Humphry Clinker* (1771: Harmondsworth, 1967), p. 292.

canonical date in Scottish whig jurisprudence and historiography, a moment which marked the completion of the Union, when its promises of liberty and equality were extended across the border to an impoverished and enslaved Scottish commons. As a result, Scots historians wildly exaggerated the sufferings of the Scottish rural population in the decades and centuries before heritable jurisdictions reform and the abolition of wardholding vassalage. Indeed, the anti-feudalist legacy of Enlightenment jurisprudence would persist well into the nineteenth century, and would remain a central feature of the standard interpretation of the nation's legal past. Anti-feudalist attitudes were reinforced by a long-running campaign to amend and eventually abolish the Scots system of entails, or tailzies, an issue which was first aired during the 1760s and was only finally settled with the Rutherfurd Act of 1848.[18]

Feudal excesses were not the only perceived defects of the Scots legal heritage. Historians drew attention to the failures of the Court of Session and High Court of Justiciary during the Restoration era, when the law courts had become engines of royal oppression. The Scottish whig interpretation of history demonised late seventeenth-century judges as the abject tools of absolute monarchy. Far from being a bulwark against tyranny, Scots law had facilitated the persecution of presbyterians and helped to stifle political opposition. Nor were Scots political commentators entirely certain that the

---

[18] N. T. Phillipson, 'Nationalism and ideology', in J. N. Wolfe (ed.), *Government and nationalism in Scotland* (Edinburgh, 1969); N. T. Phillipson, *The Scottish whigs and the reform of the Court of Session 1785–1830* (Stair Society, Edinburgh, 1990); A. W. B. Simpson, 'Entails and perpetuities', *Juridical Review* (1979), 1–20.

potential for judicial tyranny had been eradicated from the Scots legal system. In particular, they worried that the ill-defined law-making powers of the Court of Session, its *nobile officium*, was an affront to constitutional government and the rule of law.

Nineteenth-century jurisprudence

The ideological status of Scots law did not change dramatically in the course of the nineteenth century. The thirty-year period from 1785 to 1815 witnessed a sustained campaign to extend the benefits of civil jury to Scotland, while the issue of tailzies rumbled on, as we have seen, till the middle of the nineteenth century. The wider question surrounding the propriety of Scotland's feudalist heritage for an increasingly urban, commercial and industrial Scotland remained a stock feature of political and juridical debate throughout the nineteenth century. While a conservative jurist such as Sir Walter Scott saw the importance of inherited legal forms as a bastion against the utilitarian or rationalist insensitivities of radical reform, he also subscribed to theories of legal evolution, and shed no tears for the passing of the more oppressive and anachronistic features of the Scottish feudal law. Modernisation remained central to early nineteenth-century Scottish jurisprudence, albeit with some awareness that the very existence of a Scots legal system set limits to the assimilation of Scots and English law. George Joseph Bell (1770–1843), who established the principles of Scottish commercial law, is representative of this balanced approach. Bell took an outward-looking stance to the problems of commercial jurisprudence. After all, the law merchant was 'part of the law of nations, grounded upon the principles of natural equity'. Nevertheless Bell took the view that 'much caution' was 'to be observed in the adopting of English judgments as authorities in Scotland'. His objection was not to the anglicisation of Scots law per se, but to the *degree* of anglicisation, being frightened 'lest the purity of this part of jurisprudence, and the integrity of our own system of law, should be impaired by too indiscriminate a use of English authorities'.[19]

The post-Enlightenment continuities in Scottish juridical discourse sit very oddly indeed with one of the other marked features of nineteenth-century Scots jurisprudence, namely the apparent interest in the new theories of legal nationalism propounded on the Continent. Nineteenth-century Scots jurists displayed a very keen receptivity to the philosophy of legal nationalism articulated by the German historical school of jurisprudence, whose leading proponents were Gustav Hugo (1764–1844) and Friedrich Karl von Savigny (1779–1861). Savigny, in particular, posited the existence of an organic connection between customary law and the character of a people; though, ironically, he devoted his own career to excavating the original Roman essence of the civilian tradition from the Germanic topsoil which had covered it during the middle ages. Nevertheless, other jurists in the German world applied Savigny's approach to their own traditions, and developed an organicist German legal history.

[19] G. J. Bell, *Commentaries on the law of Scotland and on the principles of mercantile jurisprudence* (Edinburgh, 1810), 'Preface'.

Scottish jurists proved responsive to the insights of the German historical school.[20] In 1826 John Reddie (d. 1851) published *Historical notices of the Roman law, and of the recent progress of its study in Germany*,[21] and Elias Cathcart, who had been a candidate for the chair of Civil Law at Edinburgh in 1826, published his translation of the first volume of Savigny's *History of the Roman law during the middle ages* at Edinburgh in 1829.[22] In addition, the Reverend W. Gardiner, an episcopal clergyman based in Edinburgh, had produced an English translation of Hugo's German version of Gibbon's chapter on Roman law, which was published at Edinburgh in 1823.[23] From the early nineteenth century Scots lawyers – or at least the more intellectually adventurous among them – were also attracted by the German universities, a trend which peaked in the second half of the nineteenth century. Between 1850 and 1899 forty-one (that is 8 per cent) out of 512 intrants to the Faculty of Advocates attended German universities. While this figure is not particularly large, it conceals the fact that over the course of the nineteenth century those who did experience a

---

[20] J. Cairns, 'The influence of the German historical school in nineteenth-century Edinburgh', *Syracuse Journal of International Law and Commerce* 20 (1994), 191–203. See also C. Harvie, 'Legalism, myth and national identity in Scotland in the imperial epoch', *Cencrastus* no. 26 (1987), 35–41.

[21] John Reddie, *Historical notices of the Roman law, and of the recent progress of its study in Germany* (Edinburgh, 1826).

[22] C. von Savigny, *The history of the Roman law during the middle ages*, I (transl. E. Cathcart, Edinburgh, 1829).

[23] W. Gardiner (transl.), *Survey of the Roman, or civil law; an extract from Gibbon's Decline and Fall, with notes, by Professor Hugo of Gottingen* (Edinburgh, 1823).

German education tended to be among the academic leaders of the profession, including eight university professors, among them John Dove Wilson, John Kirkpatrick, James Lorimer, Aeneas Mackay, James Muirhead and John Rankine. Lorimer and Muirhead were among Savigny's most enthusiastic admirers in Scotland.[24]

In his edition of Savigny's *Private international law*, published in Edinburgh in 1869, William Guthrie, a Scots advocate, set out the wider significance of Savigny's work on the relationship between law and nationhood. He informed his readers that it was 'the fundamental principle' of Savigny's philosophy that 'law grows with the life of the nation, and is inseparable from it'. Indeed, he noted that 'Savigny places the origin of law, properly so called, in the consciousness of nations'. Guthrie went on to summarise Savigny's argument that law is 'in a state of perpetual growth' and that 'the main and most influential condition of this growth is its generation within a community held together by a common spirit and common traditions'. It was 'the character and whole outward circumstances of the nation in which it springs up', moreover, which 'determine in a very great degree the nature and peculiarities of each system of law'. The message could not have been clearer.[25]

In the mid-nineteenth century one can detect intimations of legal nationalism. A few jurists demonstrated their

---

[24] A. Rodger, 'Scottish advocates in the nineteenth century: the German connection', *Law Quarterly Review* 110 (1994), 563–91, at 563–5.

[25] William Guthrie, 'Introduction', Savigny, *Private international law: a treatise on the conflict of laws* (transl. W. Guthrie, Edinburgh, 1869), pp. xxxv–xxxvi.

appreciation of Scots law as a reflection of the spirit of the Scottish people. George Moir, a Professor of Law at Edinburgh, defended the purity of Scots law in terms reminiscent of Savigny's jurisprudence. In *The appellate jurisdiction: Scotch appeals* (1851) Moir was concerned to uphold the systemic coherence of Scots law from English interference. In particular, Moir stressed the organic nature of Scots law; it was well suited to the 'habits and character' of the Scots people 'among whom it has grown up for centuries'. Would its 'integrity' be preserved or 'undermined and supplanted' by English principles? It all depended, Moir believed, on the composition of the 'court of last resort'. The House of Lords dealt with Scottish appeals by way of a panel of English judges whose knowledge of the law of Scotland was extremely scanty. They were unlikely to be well disposed to a system with which they were unfamiliar; and whatever sympathy they might possibly harbour for Scots law was surely misplaced. Moir worried about the long-term future of Scots law: 'We think we see the ancient fabric of our law already beginning to undergo this process of transition, its outlines wavering, growing dim, passing into other forms, till it reappears at length in a shape in which scarcely a trace of the original edifice is to be detected.' In particular Moir feared that Scots might exchange their 'simple feudal system for the mysteries of freehold and copyhold, of fines and recoveries'.[26]

But how representative was Moir of mid-nineteenth-century Scots legal opinion? In spite of the very close

---

[26] [George Moir], *The appellate jurisdiction: Scotch appeals* (Edinburgh, 1851), pp. 3–4, 8.

connections which prevailed between Scottish and German jurisprudence during the nineteenth century – and the undoubted Scottish fascination with Savigny's ideas – these did not immediately lead to the formation of a body of Scottish legal nationalism. The undoubted influence of Savigny on nineteenth-century jurisprudence did nothing to quell well-established anxieties about the utility of the domestic system of feudal law. In turn this inhibited the emergence of a body of Scots legal nationalism.

More representative of mid-nineteenth-century legal attitudes than legal nationalism were the anti-feudalist and anglicising tendencies of the Glasgow Law Amendment Society, which, despite its title was something of a national cause; its campaigns during the early 1850s enjoyed the support of over thirty newspapers across Scotland as well as numerous chambers of commerce.[27] As Alan Rodger has noted, the nineteenth-century Scots business and mercantile communities were composed of 'practical men rather than romantic supporters of a native legal system of whose doctrines they would be entirely ignorant'.[28] The Society's platform amounted to legal nationalism turned on its head, for it argued that Scots law was inappropriate for Scottish society. As one proponent of Law Amendment argued, 'the fitness of the Scotch laws to the Scotch people has scarcely ever been less than at present'. What mattered was not the intrinsic features of Scots law but

---

[27] I. G. C. Hutchison, *A political history of Scotland 1832–1924* (Edinburgh, 1986), pp. 93–5.

[28] A. Rodger, 'The codification of commercial law in Victorian Britain', *Law Quarterly Review* 108 (1992), 570–90, at 572.

their adaptability to the needs of the people they supposedly served:

> The conviction is rapidly spreading that our laws and judicial establishments are not adapted to the requirements of the people, nor consistent with the advancement of the age. What was suitable to the nation in its early condition of rudeness and poverty, is found to meet but imperfectly the wants of society in a high and progressive state of development.[29]

The Society favoured wholesale reform of Scots law to bring it more closely into line with English law, in the interests of commerce and industry. Where the law of England was 'not objectionable in principle', it would 'probably be found expedient to give to it the preference, especially in mercantile affairs'.[30] Specifically, the Glasgow Law Amendment Society favoured the overhaul of the sheriff court system, the abolition of written pleadings in cases involving sums of less than fifty pounds, the need to harmonise Scots and English systems of mercantile law and the need to reform failings in the Scots law of bankruptcy. The formulation of a Common Commercial Code in 1862 for the German Confederation provided another prompt towards the assimilation of Scots and English commercial law. Savigny's organicism was not the only

[29] A Scotch Lawyer, *The amendment of the law* (reprinted from the *North British Daily Mail*; Edinburgh, 1853), pp. 1, 5.

[30] *Report of the committee, appointed at a preliminary meeting, to consider and report on the proper constitution of a Law Amendment Society in Glasgow, in connection with the London Society for promoting the amendment of the law* (Glasgow, 1851), p. 11.

inspiration to reach Scotland from the nineteenth-century German world.

The views of the mercantile community were reflected in the jurisprudence of the Scots professoriate. Dove Wilson favoured the assimilation of the systems of commercial law in Great Britain to underpin a uniform system of commercial law for the British Empire. In his inaugural lecture of 1867, James Roberton (1821–89), the Professor of Conveyancing at Glasgow University, dwelt on Scotland's troublesome feudal inheritance. '[I]f we were taking possession of a new country', he mused, 'we should never dream of establishing the feudal system. We cannot forget, however, that we are an old country.' Therefore, the *tabula rasa*, Roberton conceded, was not an option. However, within three years a frustrated Roberton had become more radical in his approach to the feudal law, and the *tabula rasa* was indeed an option. By 1870 Roberton declared himself to be on a 'crusade' against the feudal system: 'now I am satisfied that nothing short of a total abolition of the present system ought to be the aim of every one'. Scotland enjoyed prosperity 'in spite' of its feudal system. Roberton favoured wholesale reforms designed to 'sweep away a system fitted only for the earlier or darker periods of our history, and forming at present one of the greatest blots upon the jurisprudence of our country'.[31]

Feudal law also played an important role in shaping interpretations of Scottish legal history. Aeneas Mackay,

---

[31] James Roberton, *Introductory lecture delivered on 7th November, 1867* (Glasgow, [1867]), pp. 17–18; James Roberton, *Proposed abolition of the feudal system: an address delivered to the Glasgow Legal and Speculative Society, on 11th February, 1870* (Glasgow, 1870), pp. 18, 27–8.

the Professor of Constitutional Law at Edinburgh from 1874, argued that the heritable jurisdictions had been a 'parody of justice'.

> Their effect had been to exclude the powers of the King's courts and the impartial administration of justice throughout large districts of Scotland, both in civil and criminal law to a variable extent, according to the measure of the grants of regality or barony; so that an apparent paradox has a certain amount of truth, that Scotland never possessed one law until it had ceased to be an independent state.

The creation and consolidation of a national Scots legal system had taken place after 1747 – within the Union. Indeed, as late as 1882 Mackay could still contemplate a future union of the laws: 'when the time comes for the union of the laws, many principles and some parts of Scottish jurisprudence will pass into the future British code'.[32] Indeed, in his *Comparative principles of the laws of England and Scotland* (1903) J. W. Brodie-Innes maintained the original identity of English and Scots law and noted a tendency towards their reconciliation.[33]

Legal nationalism

Scots legal nationalism took its rise only in the twentieth century, and to a large extent during the second half of the

---

[32] Aeneas Mackay, *A sketch of the history of Scots law* ([Edinburgh?], 1882), pp. 17, 22–3.

[33] J. W. Brodie-Innes, *Comparative principles of the laws of England and Scotland* (Edinburgh and London, 1903), p. 4.

twentieth century. Moreover, its inspiration was less directly from the organicist jurisprudence of Savigny than it was from the novel idea, coined around the end of the nineteenth century, that there existed a family of mixed legal systems which partook of both the civilian and common law traditions. The notion of a third family of legal systems can be found in the work of Frederick Parker Walton (1858–1948),[34] a Scots lawyer who gained some eminence as a jurist in different parts of the British Empire. Walton taught Roman law at Glasgow University, and then became Professor of Roman Law at McGill University in Montreal. As well as being a member of the Scottish bar, Walton was a member of the Quebec bar, and became aware of the similarities between the Anglo-civilian mixed character of both provincial systems. Walton, who prefigured the imperial strain of Scottish legal nationalism which was later openly articulated by T. B. Smith, later went on to become Director of the Khedival School of Law in Egypt.[35] The idea of mixed legal systems also surfaced in the 1920s in the work of the French comparativist Henri Levy Ullman, whose seminal lecture on this topic promptly appeared in translation in Scotland's leading law journal, the *Juridical Review*. According to Levy Ullman, the mixed legal systems suggested 'a picture of what will be some day the law of the civilised nations'.

---

[34] F. P. Walton, 'The civil law and the common law in Canada', *Juridical Review* (1899), 282–301.

[35] K. G. C. Reid, 'The idea of mixed legal systems', *Tulane Law Review* 78 (2003), 5–40, at 8.

Mixed jurisprudence was the destiny of the Anglo-American and civilian worlds.[36]

The inter-war era witnessed the first glimmerings of legal nationalism proper in Scotland. The Stair Society, a body devoted to the recovery of Scotland's distinctive legal history, was founded in 1934.[37] The 'Proposals' behind its formation described Scotland's legal system as 'its most distinctive national heritage'. The *Introduction to the law of Scotland* (2nd edn, 1933) published by William Murray Gloag, Professor of Law at the University of Glasgow, and Robert Candlish Henderson, Professor of Scots Law at Edinburgh, opened with a belligerent rebuttal of the 'presumption' that statutes were generally applicable throughout Great Britain and Northern Ireland. Gloag and Henderson noted that this was not true of any amendments to statutes in which Scotland was 'expressly excluded' or even where a statute was 'expressed in technical terms of English law without an interpretation clause giving the equivalents in the law of Scotland'. Moreover, they insisted that pre-1707 English statutes were of 'no authority in Scotland' unless their application had been extended to Scotland by a later Act, as was the case with the law of high treason.[38] In the late 1930s Lord Normand began to express worries about

---

[36] H. Levy-Ullmann (transl. F. P. Walton), 'The law of Scotland', *Juridical Review* (1925), 370–91.

[37] An earlier call to study Scotland's legal heritage had been somewhat antiquarian in character and had few immediate consequences: see e.g. John Inglis, Lord Glencorse (1810–91), *The historical study of law* (Edinburgh, 1863).

[38] W. M. Gloag and R. C. Henderson, *Introduction to the Law of Scotland* (2nd edn, Edinburgh, 1933), pp. 1–2.

the depressing future of Scots law as a debased form of English law.

The principal figures in the construction of Scots legal nationalism were Lord Cooper of Culross, who rose to become Lord President of the Court of Session, Sir Thomas (T. B.) Smith, who was Professor of Law at Aberdeen between 1949 and then at Edinburgh, Andrew Dewar Gibb (1893–1973) who was Regius Professor of Law at Glasgow University from 1934 to 1958, and his successor David Walker (b. 1920), Regius Professor of Scots Law at Glasgow between 1958 and 1990 and author of *The Scottish legal system* (1959).[39] These figures did not comprise a coherent school of legal nationalism, either in politics or juridical method, though sometimes the dominant strain of legal nationalism in Scotland is described as the Cooper–Smith ideology.[40]

Scots legal nationalism was – and is – a quite distinct phenomenon from political nationalism.[41] Only occasionally do the two distinct strains of ideology coincide in the thought of a particular individual, such as Gibb. More commonly,

---

[39] Walker had strong views on legal education. See D. M. Walker, 'Legal studies in the Scottish universities', *Juridical Review* (1957), 21–41 and 151–79. In spite of – or perhaps because of – these views, his work does not appear to have given rise to a school of jurists comparable to the Cooper–Smith school.

[40] See esp. H. MacQueen, 'Two Toms and an ideology for Scots law: T. B. Smith and Lord Cooper of Culross', in E. Reid and D. L. Carey Miller (eds.), *A mixed legal system in transition: T. B. Smith and the progress of Scots law* (Edinburgh, 2005),

[41] For a typology of legal nationalisms, see G. L. Gretton, 'The rational and the national: Thomas Brown Smith', in Reid and Carey Miller (eds.), *A mixed legal system*, pp. 32–3.

however, the leading lights of legal nationalism have not been nationalist in their politics. Indeed, Cooper, the acknowledged founding father of Scots legal nationalism, was a Unionist in his politics. Cooper stood for parliament as a Unionist, winning election in 1935 and served the National Government as Solicitor-General for Scotland, and later as Lord Advocate.[42] Gibb too stood as a Unionist candidate before his partial reinvention as a nationalist politician.[43] Legal nationalists on the whole tended to be conservative and anti-collectivist – including the political nationalist, Gibb – and Smith, in particular, was strangely attracted to the legal systems of South Africa and Louisiana, notwithstanding the illiberal politics found there during the 1950s and 1960s.

Legal nationalism, moreover, has assumed various different forms, only one of which is connected to political nationalism. Moreover, for the legal nationalists – who valued custom, judicial decisions and legal principles more than legislation – there were ironic benefits in the parliamentary Union of 1707. The lack of a Scottish parliament not only ensured a higher profile for the Scottish legal heritage, but it also protected the purity of Scots law from the legislative interference of a parliament in Edinburgh. An active Scottish parliament might indeed have distorted the nation's legal heritage. There was, indeed, something to be said for the remoteness of Scots law from Westminster. On the other hand, some legal nationalists

---

[42] MacQueen, 'Two Toms', p. 47.

[43] L. Farmer, 'Under the shadow of Parliament House', in L. Farmer and S. Veitch (eds.), *The state of Scots law* (Edinburgh, 2001), pp. 151–64, at p. 155.

did argue that a Scottish parliament (though not necessarily Scottish independence) was required to superintend the Scottish legal system. Another group focussed less intently on the legislature than on the appellate system. It was the House of Lords, in its judicial capacity as the highest court of appeal in the United Kingdom, which was central to the preservation of Scots law. Furthermore, a frustrated imperialism lies behind the cosmopolitan strain of legal nationalism associated with Smith. Even the outright nationalist, Gibb, was far from being a Little Scotlander, and indeed shared some of Smith's imperialism. Gibb's opposition to surreptitious 'Law from over the Border' in the form of insensitive appellate decisions by the House of Lords was tempered by the forlorn hope that Scots law might have become the law of the British Empire, a theme which surfaces in Gibb's *Scottish Empire*.[44] Smith's championship of a wider civilian tradition and a quasi-imperial family of mixed Anglo-civilian systems has been described as a form of 'neo-civilian irredentism'.[45] On the other hand, others acknowledged the role of the civil law in the Scottish legal heritage, but did not perceive it as a defining characteristic of Scottish jurisprudence. Walker, for example, was a non-civilian legal nationalist, and a concern for the civil law component in Scots law was far from the forefront of his defence of the Scottish legal system.

---

[44] Andrew Dewar Gibb, *The shadow on Parliament House: has Scots law a future?* (Edinburgh, 1932); Andrew Dewar Gibb, *Law from over the border* (Edinburgh, 1950); Andrew Dewar Gibb, *Scottish Empire* (London, 1937), p. 312.

[45] N. R. Whitty, 'The civilian tradition and debates on Scots Law: part II', *Tydskrif vir die Suid-Afrikaanse Reg* (1996), 442–57, at 445.

Legal nationalists did not – on the whole – assign a negative role to the Union of 1707 in their interpretations of Scottish history. Indeed, it is an article of faith among them that the golden age of Scottish jurisprudence took place largely within the Union. Cooper famously divided Scotland's juridical history into a series of phases: a Scoto-Norman phase; a dark age between about 1350 and 1650; a golden age of Scottish jurisprudence between 1681 and about 1800; and the onset of a distorting anglicisation since about 1820.[46] The golden age of Scottish jurisprudence which began a couple of decades before the Union of 1707 was stifled neither by its passage nor indeed by the first century or so of co-existence with English law within the British state. Anglicisation was a bad thing, of course, but it long post-dated the Union and was not ascribed directly to the Union itself.

Nevertheless, Smith argued that notwithstanding – indeed because of – the Union the two legal systems of Scotland and England were 'quasi-foreign' in the sphere of justice. Indeed, the two legal systems were rooted in contrasting approaches to legal problems: 'The Scottish legal system has its basis upon philosophical principles and is deductive; the English system, which is inductive, is a product of empiricism and precedent.'[47] Insofar as such an entity as 'British law' existed, it existed – almost invisibly indeed as a sort of

---

[46] T. M. Cooper, *Selected papers 1922–1954* (Edinburgh and London, 1957), 'Some classics of Scottish legal literature' (1929), pp. 39–52; 'The Scottish legal tradition' (1949), pp. 172–200; 'The dark age of Scottish legal history, 1350–1650' (1951), pp. 219–36.

[47] T. B. Smith, 'Severalty of administration of justice in the United Kingdom', *Juridical Review* 56 (1949), 151–71, at 167–8.

non-entity in conventional juridical wisdom – as the fundamental law of the British constitution. Smith contended that
'[t]he Union of 1707 did not create "British law" except perhaps in that very field where practically all English lawyers and
many Scottish lawyers have most clearly failed to perceive it – at
the very heart of the constitution itself'.[48] Smith regretted that
since 1707 English law had 'usually tended to prevail' in matters concerning the constitution; if only, he mused, the capital
and the new British parliament had moved to Berwick-on-
Tweed, 'the minds of the members might have been awakened
to the true position'.[49] Although Smith maintained that Scots
law and English law were of equal status within the Union,
it was difficult to dislodge the common assumption among
English jurists that English law was British law and that the
pre-1707 English law was applicable across the United Kingdom. In exposing this fallacy, Smith drew attention to the
curious case of Prince Ernst of Hanover, whose naturalisation
as a 'British' subject was based upon a pre-Union English law.
Was Prince Ernst's naturalisation effective in Scotland? Smith
thought not.[50] Instead, Smith argued that the English common
law mind had failed to notice, far less acknowledge, the plural
strands of British justice, what he termed its 'severalty'.

Smith was appalled at the reduced status of Scots law
within Britain and its Empire – *de facto*, he believed, though

---

[48] T. B. Smith, *British justice: the Scottish contribution* (London, 1961), p.
203.
[49] T. B. Smith, 'British justice: a Jacobean phantasma', *Scots Law Times*
(4 June 1982), 157–64, at 163.
[50] Smith, *British Justice*, p. 25.

not properly *de iure* – as a 'tolerated local jurisdiction'.[51] Scots law, Smith insisted, would have provided a more robust platform for the laws of Britain's colonies and Empire than the law of England: 'At the time of the Union . . . the private law of Scotland as stated by Stair and Mackenzie was much fitter for export to the Commonwealth beyond the seas than the English common law.'[52] On what constitutional basis, asked Smith, was English law preferred to Scots law after 1707 as the law of the supposedly British Empire? There was, it turned out, no justification for this preference, other than the raw might of English power within the British state. On similar grounds Smith complained that British military law was, in effect, English law: 'the Scottish soldier when he puts on his kilt so to speak puts off the protection which his national jurisprudence would afford him, were he to be tried by a Scottish court'. Smith did not reject the imperial pretensions of the English common law because he was anti-imperialist. Smith was himself a pronounced legal imperialist, and wished rather to carve out an imperial role for Scots law on the global stage. Scots law had not become the law of the British Empire, as Smith believed it ought to have become. Instead it had been cheated out of its rightful destiny. Smith found a substitute for Empire in the group of mixed legal systems found in former zones of Dutch and French influence which came into contact with the English common law tradition through later absorption within the British Empire or

---

[51] T. B. Smith, 'Pretensions of English law as "imperial law"', 'Constitutional Law', *Stair Memorial Encyclopedia*, v (Edinburgh, 1987), para 711 at p. 379.

[52] T. B. Smith, *A short commentary on the law of Scotland* (Edinburgh, 1962), p. 61.

within the world of Anglo-American law. His career involved a quest for a new supra-national destiny for Scots law at the centre of another empire. Smith aspired to create a Scottish legal empire, no longer one based upon the British Empire, but one in which Scots law was the leader of an association of the world's mixed legal systems.

The term legal nationalism does not do justice to the scope of Smith's ambitions, for his mission was a global one. He wished to preserve the civilian element not only in Scots law but in the worldwide family of mixed jurisdictions. The empire of mixed systems might become the equal of the recognised 'empires' of law. As Smith himself noted, the Code Napoleon had been exported to thirty-six states and adopted in thirty-five others, while Anglo-American common law was the law of a third of the world's population.[53] To this end, Smith promoted connections with Scotland's 'neighbours in law', who were quite different from Scotland's 'next door neighbours'.[54] Scots jurists should forget about English models, and learn instead from the mixed legal systems of Quebec, South Africa, Louisiana, Ceylon and Mauritius. Smith practised what he preached, holding visiting posts at Tulane, in Louisiana (1957–8), Cape Town (1958), Witwatersrand (1958) and Louisiana State (1972), and also lectured at McGill, in Quebec (1963). He wrote for law journals in South Africa and Louisiana, and modelled the Scottish Universities Law Institute, which

[53] T. B. Smith, 'Legal imperialism and legal parochialism', *Juridical Review* (1965), 39–57, at 41.
[54] T. B. Smith, 'Unification of law in Britain: problems of coordination', *Juridical Review* (1967), 97–126, at 98.

he helped establish in 1960, on the Louisiana State Law Institute.[55] Smith was also sympathetic to the civilian side in the '*bellum juridicum*' waged in South African legal circles during the 1950s and 1960s between the purists (who wished to defend the civilian element in their legal system from common law encroachments) and their 'pollutionist' adversaries.[56] Smith had no time for what he termed the 'common law cuckoo' in the civilian nest.[57] Anglo-American legal principles were also vividly described as 'strange gods' whose worship he hoped to expel from the purified mixed jurisdictions.[58]

Smith was neither a parochial nationalist, nor a diehard opponent of change. Rather he promoted a dynamic and cosmopolitan Scots jurisprudence, in touch with the best practice of the civilian and mixed traditions, and prepared to update Scots law to meet the challenges of the modern world. 'If English lawyers have tended in the past towards the vice of self-satisfied imperialism', Smith noted, 'the parochialism which has infected Scottish legal thinking is even more to be deplored.'[59] In a revealing article, 'Legal imperialism and legal parochialism', Smith expressed a keen resentment for 'the

---

[55] Reid, 'Idea of mixed legal systems', 11–13.

[56] G. A. Mulligan, 'Bellum Juridicum (3): Purists, pollutionists and pragmatists', *South African Law Journal* 69 (1952), 25–32; [Proculus], 'Bellum Juridicum: two approaches to South African Law, *South African Law Journal* 68 (1951), 306–13.

[57] T. B. Smith, 'The common law cuckoo', in Smith, *Studies critical and comparative* (Edinburgh, 1962).

[58] T. B. Smith, 'Strange gods: the crisis of Scots law as a civilian system', in Smith, *Studies*.

[59] Smith, 'Unification', 100–1.

pseudo-comparative law that looks on English law as the sole alternative fount of legal wisdom, or preens itself when an isolated doctrine of Scots law wins a skirmish over its English counterpart'.[60] Parochialism in Scots law marched arm-in-arm with deference to English norms. Scots jurisprudence needed to be revitalised by a genuine strain of comparative law which looked beyond London for its comparisons. The prospect of the United Kingdom's joining the European Community held out a special allure. Scots law was destined to be a bridge between the civilian systems of the European Community and the common law world. Indeed, here it is worth noting that Smith's imperial vision for Scots law mutated through three overlapping forms: the wistful regret that Scots law was not the law of the British Empire, and, he realised, never would be; the attempt to create a Scots-led legal empire in the family of mixed systems from Quebec to Ceylon; and the vision that Scots law might play the leading role in the formation of a new *ius commune*, the law of the European Community. Smith articulated a brand of Scots-British imperialism far removed from the 'self-satisfied imperialism' of the English legal tradition. Moreover, Smith openly espoused legal union, though not within Britain per se or 'a London-dominated juristic empire'.[61] Whereas the 'unification of British law without regard to regional unification' with the civilian systems of Europe was anathema to Smith, the prospect of a new Anglo-civilian *ius commune* was an enticing one.[62]

---

[60] Smith, 'Legal imperialism', 45.   [61] Smith, 'Unification', 109.
[62] *Ibid.*, 108.

Legal nationalism was, of course, far removed from the assimilationist jurisprudence of the Enlightenment, but the supra-national and imperialist affinities of legal nationalism aligned it more closely with political unionism than with nationalist theories of Scottish independence. Legal association with England within a broad European framework of reconciliation and assimilation was far from incompatible with legal nationalism. Indeed, Scottish jurisprudence within the Union had never been suffocatingly thrawn and defensive. Feudalist and civilian perspectives had encouraged outward-looking and comparativist approaches to the law, and cosmopolitanism had flourished even within the superficially inhospitable environment of legal nationalism. For the most part, Scots legal nationalist jurisprudence was a brand of unionist political thought, albeit less obviously so than the anglicising jurisprudence of the Scottish Enlightenment.

6

The two kingdoms and the ecclesiology of Union

In 1707 Protestantism and the English language – regardless of local variants in churchmanship and dialect – were the lowest common denominators of British nationhood. In *Britons: forging the nation, 1707–1837* (1992) – one of the most influential history books in our times – Linda Colley argued that a shared Protestantism provided the principal bonds of Anglo-Scottish integration during the first 130 years of Union. She drew particular attention to the ways in which this core Protestantism found negative expression as anti-Catholicism, a strain of insular xenophobia which segued easily into francophobia. Britons, Colley argued, discovered a common purpose in a century or so of intermittent warfare against France, the principal national representative of militant Roman Catholic Otherness. Colley had much less to say about Protestantism as an affirmation of Anglo-Scottish belonging. This is unsurprising, for in many ways Protestant religion was the grit in the Union, not its glue. Colley ends her survey of British integration in 1837 – the year of William IV's death, an event which brought Queen Victoria to the throne and severed the British connection with the Electorate of Hanover, which passed in the male line. Yet 1837 also fell part way through the Ten Years' Conflict of 1834–43, a tense religious battle between the presbyterian Church of Scotland, which asserted its spiritual authority independent of the state, and an Erastian British parliament, which quashed these pretensions, though only at the cost of the defection of around two-fifths of the clergy of the established Kirk, who withdrew at the Disruption of 1843 into the Free Church of Scotland. The differences between Scots presbyterianism and Anglicanism were not so substantial that they threatened the continuation of the Union, but nor were they so trivial that they could be easily melted into a common British Protestantism. In particular, Scots presbyterians and Anglicans held divergent views on church–state relations. This led to a series of cross-border debates between eminent Anglican and presbyterian controversialists on questions of religious establishment. The need to conserve the distinctive features of a properly constituted presbyterian Kirk within an Erastian British state ensured that Scottish unionist political thought was at its most articulate in the sphere of ecclesiology.

Unionist ecclesiology is not reducible to a single interpretation of the constitutional status of the Scots Kirk within the British state; rather it was a fertile field which generated more ideological ingenuity and creativity than any other branch of constitutional discourse, and covered a very wide range of positions. At the assimilationist extreme – and highly atypical of mainstream Scots presbyterian opinion at any period within the Union – was the sermon *A United Church for the British Empire* delivered by the Reverend James Cooper (1846–1922), Professor of Ecclesiastical History at the University of Glasgow, at Forres in 1902. A leading force in the Scottish Church Society, a pressure group at the 'high' end of the Kirk which promoted the ideal of catholicity, Cooper was optimistic that ecumenical initiatives were moving in tandem with the trend towards imperial unity. There was contact between Scots presbyterians and episcopalians, and Anglicans were beginning to show interest in the idea of lay eldership and to express misgivings about prelatical and lordly conceptions of episcopacy. Cooper declared that 'God is reading, in the glory of our United Empire, a lesson to the British Churches. He is showing us what a good thing it would be to have a United Church – a United Reformed Church – for the British Empire!' Cooper himself had strong ties to the north-east of Scotland, and it is possible to discern the influence of Morayshire episcopalianism in his comprehensive ecumenism.[1] Yet, notwithstanding Cooper's influence within the presbyterian Kirk, of which he would become Moderator in 1917, this plea for an ecclesiastical unity which might match the political unity of the British state and Empire was a rarity within the Scots presbyterian tradition,[2] and, as such, frankly, quasi-utopian in its hopes for presbyterian–Anglican reconciliation. Allegiance to the British state was not predicated upon religious unanimity, and neither church establishment openly aspired to create

---

[1] James Cooper, *A United Church for the British Empire* (Forres, 1902), p. 12; D. M. Murray, *Rebuilding the Kirk: presbyterian reunion in Scotland 1909–1929* (Edinburgh, 2000), pp. 247–8.

[2] Another exception was the ecumenical proposal of 1957 for bishops-in-presbytery and full communion with the Church of England, which provoked a controversy stoked by the Beaverbrook press. See *Relations between the Anglican and presbyterian churches: being a joint report presented by representatives of the Church of England, Church of Scotland, the episcopal church in Scotland, the presbyterian Church of England, Jan. 1957* (Edinburgh, 1957), esp. pp. 21–6; T. Gallagher, 'The press and Protestant culture: a case study of the *Scottish Daily Express*', in G. Walker and T. Gallagher (eds.), *Sermons and battle hymns: Protestant popular culture in modern Scotland* (Edinburgh, 1990), pp. 193–212, esp. pp. 194–8.

a Church of Britain. Instead, a degree of religious friction between the presbyterian and Anglican establishments persisted throughout the Union, occasionally rising to a high level of intensity, but never threatening the political stability of the British state. At certain points Scots presbyterian defensiveness escalated into a full-blown critique of the ecclesiastical dimensions of the British state, but never developed into political nationalism. In 1871 the Reverend James Begg, a leading Free Churchman, published *A violation of the Treaty of Union the main origin of our ecclesiastical divisions and other evils*. This pamphlet stands in stark contrast, of course, to the ecumenical and assimilationist Protestantism imagined by Cooper. Yet, it is important to note that Begg does not blame the Union per se for Scotland's religious ills; rather he ascribes these to infringements of the Union.[3]

Most Scots presbyterians agreed that the Union entrenched the privileges and status of the Church of Scotland free from Erastian parliamentary interference and, indeed, often invoked the Union of 1707 to signal their legitimate differences in ecclesiology from the dominant Anglican tradition. The Union was a shibboleth for the Scots presbyterian mainstream, however much presbyterians might complain about Erastian usurpations on the Kirk's freedoms. Yet the Scots presbyterian community was a fragmented one. It contained beyond the confines of the Kirk itself other groups, including the Reformed Presbyterians and the Seceders, who

---

[3] James Begg, *A violation of the Treaty of Union the main origin of our ecclesiastical divisions and other evils* (Edinburgh, 1871).

openly challenged the legitimacy of the Union of 1707; nevertheless even these branches of the presbyterian tradition remained unionist in principle. This is because Reformed Presbyterians and Seceders were anti-Unionist unionists – unionists who favoured a close association with England on the terms of the Solemn League and Covenant of 1643, which would have established presbyterian church government throughout the British Isles, not the misbegotten compromised Union of 1707, whereby Anglican and presbyterian establishments co-existed within the British state.

Until the 1920s religion was unquestionably the central issue of division between Scots and English within the Union. During the first two centuries of Union Scots, as we have seen, lapsed into the complacencies of banal unionism and, for the most part, expressed contentment with the overtly political features of the Anglo-Scottish relationship. However, the tranquillising effects of banal unionism did not extend to the sphere of religion. Here Scots were much more exercised about the nature of the Union, the way it operated in practice and the consequences for the Scots presbyterian tradition. A relaxed acceptance of the political and economic benefits of the Union was accompanied by a large measure of Scots presbyterian disenchantment with the ecclesiastical aspects of Union. Is it reasonable to describe this as a combination of political unionism and religious nationalism? Religious nationalism does not quite capture the nature of Scots presbyterian disillusionment with the British state. At bottom, for Scots presbyterians the vexing problem of the two kingdoms was not the relationship of the kingdoms of Scotland and England, but the relationship of the spiritual kingdom and the temporal kingdom. Scots presbyterians subscribed to the doctrine of the two kingdoms, that the spiritual kingdom ruled by Christ was not subordinate to the temporal kingdom. Anglo-Scottish differences merely happened to overlie and confuse a more basic and universal problem of the proper relationship which should pertain between the spiritual realm of the church – Christ's kingdom – and the temporal authority of the state. The Kirk was doctrinally anti-Erastian. Therefore, an Erastian British state posed a major dilemma for – otherwise unionist – Scots presbyterians committed to a tradition of ecclesiology which valued a clear demarcation between the parallel sovereignties of the spiritual and temporal realms. When Scots presbyterians challenged the authority of the British state in ecclesiastical matters, they did so not on behalf of the Scottish kirk and nation per se, but to defend the crown rights of the Redeemer, the sovereignty of Christ Himself over the spiritual kingdom. By the same token, commentators have sometimes treated the General Assembly of the Church of Scotland, a national body which functions as its chief court and legislature, as if it were a surrogate parliament for the Scots nation within the Union; but, again, this interpretation involves a reductive assimilation of the ecclesiological to the political.

The doctrine of the two kingdoms was set out in the Westminster Confession of the Faith, the credal standard of the Church of Scotland, to which all ministers were required to subscribe in full. Indeed, it was one of the core principles of the Westminster Confession, and suffused various parts of the document. In particular, Chapter 23 of the Westminster

Confession dealt with the legitimate authority of the 'Civil
Magistrate' with regard to the church: 'The civil magistrate
may not assume to himself the administration of the word
and sacraments, or the powers of the keys of the kingdom of
heaven: yet he hath authority, and it is his duty, to take order,
that unity and peace be preserved in the church.' Although the
two kingdoms were separate jurisdictions, there were some
points of contact between them. Clearly, the civil authorities
were not expected to abridge the church's authority within
its own sphere, though – somewhat ambiguously, perhaps –
the magistrate nevertheless had external duties towards the
good order of the church establishment. Chapter 25 'Of the
church' made it clear, however, that temporal authority over
the church was strictly forbidden: 'There is no other head of the
church but the Lord Jesus Christ.' Erastianism, therefore, was
an abomination, an illegitimate usurpation of Christ's powers. Chapter 30 'Of church censures' explained how authority
over the church was delegated from Christ to his ministers,
and did not descend in any way from the state: 'The Lord
Jesus, as king and head of his church, hath therein appointed a
government in the hands of church-officers, distinct from the
civil magistrate. To these officers the keys of the kingdom of
heaven are committed.' Chapter 31, 'Of synods and councils'
conceded that the temporal authority might lawfully summon
synods, but pointed out that if the civil authorities were 'open
enemies to the church', then ministers themselves had the right
by virtue of their office to meet together in assemblies without
the requirement of any civil sanction. Nevertheless, the separation of the spiritual and temporal realms constrained the

church as well as the civil authorities, for the business of synods was exclusively ecclesiastical and clerics were enjoined 'not to intermeddle with civil affairs'.[4]

The Treaty of Union complemented the principles of two kingdom ecclesiology, for the Act for Securing the Kirk of Scotland appeared to put the Kirk beyond the reach of the new British parliament. There was a crucial asymmetry in the British polity. Whereas the Church of England was a creature of sixteenth-century statute, literally the church by law established, the privileges of the Church of Scotland – as Scots understood them – were fundamental preconditions of the Union and themselves constitutive of the British parliament. Arguably, the privileges of the Church of England were also constitutive of the British state, though this did not feature in Anglican argument; equally, the Kirk was the creation of the pre-Union Scots parliament, though Scots presbyterians tended to focus on their entrenched rights embodied in the Union agreement. To complicate matters further, Anglicanism was by no means reducible to Erastianism. There was a prominent strain of Anglicanism which insisted on the apostolic independence of the Church of England from Erastian pretensions, but this did not play a central role in

---

[4] There are numerous editions of the Confession, formally *The Confession of faith agreed upon by the assembly of divines at Westminster: examined and approved, anno 1647, by the General Assembly of the Church of Scotland; and ratified by Acts of Parliament 1649 and 1690*. The edition in my possession – a gift from my late and much-missed colleague, John McCaffrey – is contained within *The subordinate standards, and other authoritative documents of the Free Church of Scotland* (London, 1858), pp. 15–123, esp. pp. 98–101, 117–20.

presbyterian understandings of the Anglican Other, at least until William Gladstone launched an anti-Erastian critique of Thomas Chalmers's Scots presbyterian theory of establishment during the late 1830s. However, misunderstanding certainly worked in both directions, and many of the tensions in Anglo-Scottish church–state relations during the first century and a half of Union stemmed directly from an Anglican failure to engage empathetically with either the general principles of Scots presbyterian ecclesiology or with the Scots presbyterian interpretation of the Kirk's status within the Union.

Union, Secession and Disruption

At the time of the Union the fears of the anti-incorporationists were largely articulated in terms of anxieties about the future security of the Scots presbyterian Kirk without the safeguard of a domestic legislature in Scotland. Federalists took the view that an incorporating Union left the Kirk hanging on the whims of an Anglican-dominated parliament, and that even the Act for Securing the Kirk of Scotland was a mere parchment guarantee, which a sovereign parliament might overturn whenever it so wished. As this was the compelling core of the federalist case against incorporation, some perceptive Scots incorporationists saw the need to highlight the special place of the Kirk within the Union state. The Kirk, it was argued, was – along with the Hanoverian monarchy – the most entrenched institution of the British state. This, at least, was how presbyterian incorporationists understood the Union; on the other hand, it is telling that those incorporationists who were most relaxed about the prospect of an untrammelled British parliamentary sovereignty were Erastians from episcopalian backgrounds, such as William Seton of Pitmedden and the Earl of Cromarty. Among presbyterian incorporationists the most elaborate case for the Kirk's status within the Union was advanced by Francis Grant, one of Scotland's leading jurists, who would be elevated to the Court of Session as Lord Cullen in 1709. Grant was also active as a presbyterian layman in the Scottish movement for the reformation of manners. In *The patriot resolved* (1707) Grant argued that the presbyterian Kirk was entrenched within the foundations of the British constitution. The Act for Securing the Kirk of Scotland was, he contended, 'not in the case of a mutable law'. Far from being a 'simple law', it was in the nature of a 'contract; not supervenient, but fundamental to the new constitution'. The very fact that the Church of Scotland was now untouchable – as indeed was the Church of England – meant that politicians and clerics would no longer be tempted to agitate for its amendment or destruction: 'we see abroad, when they despair of gaining the subversion of one another's constitution, what calm there is even betwixt Protestants and Papists, Lutherans and Calvinists' in Switzerland and parts of Germany.[5] Similarly, Sir John Clerk of Penicuik argued that as a fundamental element of the Union agreement the Kirk was now more secure than when it depended on the votes of the old Scots parliament, a body not unswayed by corruption. No longer did the Kirk rest on an Act of the Scots parliament,

---

[5] Francis Grant, *The patriot resolved* (Edinburgh, 1707), pp. 12–18.

which that body was capable of amending or repealing; now it was integral to the British constitution.[6]

Nevertheless, whatever confidence Scots presbyterians had in the kirk's security was soon dashed. The imposition of lay patronage on the Scots Kirk in 1712 by a Tory administration in flagrant contravention of the Union brought sharply into focus Anglo-Scottish divergences on questions of sovereignty, including its ecclesiological dimension. The affront of patronage would persist as a major Scottish grievance throughout the eighteenth century, provoking two secessions from the Scottish church. As a result, many Scots presbyterians – especially among those who defected from the establishment, but even, on occasions, among the ranks of the supposed trimmers and temporisers[7] who remained within the Kirk – advanced strict constructionist criticisms of Anglican and Erastian perversions of the Union. Indeed, for much of the eighteenth century the Kirk would present an annual protest against patronage to the British government.

It was the external relations of presbyterianism with the state, not the internal issues of theology and worship, which largely dictated the relentless process of fragmentation that progressively undermined Scots presbyterian unity between the Revolution of 1689–90 and the Disruption of 1843. Even at the Revolution there were Covenanting Presbyterians who

---

[6] John Clerk, *A letter to a friend giving an account of how the Treaty of Union has been received here* (Edinburgh, 1706), pp. 8–9.

[7] For the trimmers and temporisers, see C. Kidd, 'Constructing a civil religion: Scots presbyterians and the eighteenth-century British state', in J. Kirk (ed.), *The Scottish churches and the Union parliament, 1707–1999* (Scottish Church History Society, Edinburgh, 2001), 1–21.

found themselves unable to join the re-established presbyterian Kirk because the new regime had not been founded on the basis of the Covenants of 1638 and 1643. These Covenanters came to be known as the 'anti-government' party because their alienation from the Kirk establishment was at bottom a critique of the uncovenanted nature of Scotland's Revolution settlement. The Union of 1707 – a union which did not follow the hallowed blueprint for Anglo-Scottish association set out in the Solemn League and Covenant of 1643 – further enraged the Covenanters. The fact that the Union of 1707 was a pluralist arrangement recognising the distinct presbyterian and episcopalian establishments of Scotland and England flew in the face of Covenanting pledges to implement presbyterian government throughout the British realms. Moreover, the new British parliament was a standing affront to Covenanting sensibilities. The presence of a bench of bishops in the House of Lords involved a clear breach of the doctrine of the two kingdoms, by which church and state should each be free to govern its own realm – spiritual or temporal – without interference from the other. For Covenanters the achievement of 1707 had broken the sacred agreement of 1643.[8] The Covenanters renewed the Covenants in 1712 in large part as a means of registering their protest that the Union of 1707 had united 'these covenanted lands' in terms directly contradictory to the divine and enduring pledges recorded in the Solemn League and Covenant. Those who renewed the Covenants in 1712

---

[8] C. Kidd, 'Conditional Britons: the Scots Covenanting tradition and the eighteenth-century British state', *English Historical Review* 117 (2002), 1147–76.

lamented that 'the nations formerly cemented in peace and love in conjunction with truth and righteousness, [had] broken these bonds and united themselves upon another footing, by the late sinful incorporating union'.[9] This remained a bone of Covenanting contention with the new British state. In 1761 the Reformed Presbyterians – as the Covenanters were known after 1743 – issued a Testimony which reiterated 'the covenanted interest of Christ in these lands', claiming that the Union of 1707 was 'founded upon an open violation of all the articles of the Solemn League and Covenant still binding upon the nations'.[10]

The Seceders, who left the Kirk in 1733 over the question of patronage, adopted a similar stance of anti-Unionist unionism. In 1732 the General Assembly of the Church of Scotland passed an Act anent Calls, which tidied up the procedure involved in appointing a minister where the patron had, by not appointing his own candidate within a six-month window from the demise or departure of the previous incumbent, allowed his right of patronage to lapse. Whereas some presbyteries had, in these circumstances, effectively allowed congregations the right to elect their own choice of minister, the Act anent Calls tightened up procedures and confined the powers of election to heritors and elders. To some traditionalists this

---

[9] *The National Covenant and Solemn League and Covenant with the acknowledgement of sins and engagement to duties; as they were renewed at Douglas, July 24th 1712* (1712), 'Preface', pp. 5, 36; 'A solemn acknowledgement of publick sins, and breaches of the National Covenant and Solemn League and Covenant', pp. 26, 31, 37, 53, 62.

[10] *Act, declaration and testimony, for the whole of our covenanted reformation* (1761), pp. 5, 89.

was an affront to the democratic principles of presbyterianism. For stating this publicly, the Reverend Ebenezer Erskine (1680–1754) of Stirling was disciplined, which provoked his secession along with several of his followers in the ministry. In December 1733 they organised themselves as the Associate Presbytery.[11] The Seceders adopted some Covenanting principles, though stood at some remove from the militant dissent of the Covenanters from the Hanoverian state.[12] Nevertheless, when the Seceders prepared to renew the Covenants in December 1742, they complained that Scotland had been 'incorporated with our neighbours in England, upon terms opposite unto, and inconsistent with, our covenant-union with them'. The Union of 1707, the Seceders declared, fell short of 'covenant-union'.[13]

The Secession itself soon split asunder. A further schism, the Breach of 1747, was a consequence of the burgess oath. This required that burgesses in the towns of Edinburgh, Glasgow and Perth take an anti-Popish oath professing 'the true religion presently professed within this realm, and authorized by the laws thereof', an oath which seemed to some Seceders to imply an acknowledgement of the established church. This led to a schism-within-a-schism and the formation of rival Burgher and Anti-Burgher strands of presbyterian dissent.

---

[11] A. L. Drummond and J. Bulloch, *The Scottish church 1688–1843* (Edinburgh, 1973), pp. 40–4.

[12] Kidd, 'Conditional Britons'.

[13] *Act of the associate presbytery for renewing the National Covenant of Scotland, and the Solemn League and Covenant of our three nations in a way and manner agreeable to our present situation and circumstances in this period* (Glasgow, 1759 edn), p. 26.

However, it should be stressed that all of the dissident groups mentioned so far, the Covenanters (or Reformed Presbyterians), the Burghers and the Anti-Burghers, all subscribed to the establishment principle, rejected the very idea of voluntaryism and dissented only as a strategic necessity, their ultimate goal being the renovation of the Kirk establishment on their terms. Although these groups detected certain theological backslidings within the establishment, what primarily determined their estrangement from the Kirk was the connection of the church with a defective state, one moreover which interfered illegitimately with the spiritual realm. A spectacularly outspoken critique of the British state came from the professor of divinity among the Anti-Burghers, the Reverend Archibald Bruce of Whitburn (1748–1816). In his *Historico-politico-ecclesiastical dissertation on the supremacy of the civil powers in matters of religion* (1802) Bruce denounced the English Reformation as a flawed experiment, in which the Papacy had not been abolished, but rather its powers had been transferred instead to the English monarchy. The English crown, thenceforth, had enjoyed a monstrous prerogative in ecclesiastical matters which derived from this timid and botched transition to caesaropapism. Whereas the full-blown Reformation of the Scots had ushered in civil and religious rights, in England it had augmented the powers of the crown through the creation of an 'English *pontifex maximus*'. Bruce had no fears about expressing himself in this way or about sounding disloyal. Allegiance to the British state, it appeared, could be disaggregated into a general demand on all subjects and a reserved sphere in which Scots presbyterians were able to vent their rejection of the state's Anglican features. Bruce explained that the absolute security given to Scots presbyterians as a condition of Union meant that any Scots presbyterian was at full liberty to denounce those aspects of the royal prerogative which were purely Anglican, such as the royal supremacy over the Church of England. Indeed, he went further, arguing that in this respect the law of treason did not encompass disloyalty to the monarchy when such disloyalty proceeded from sound Scots presbyterian principles. Bruce bore fantastical witness to the incompatibility of Scots presbyterian and Anglican conceptions of the British state.[14]

The Second Secession – or Relief Church – began in 1752 with the deposition of the Reverend Thomas Gillespie (1708–74) from the Kirk for his refusal to participate in the induction of an unpopular presentee over the express wish of the congregation. In 1761, together with another minister, Thomas Colier, Gillespie formed the Presbytery of Relief, 'for the relief of Christians oppressed in their Christian privileges'. Although patronage was again the issue which provoked another breakaway from the Kirk, this Second Secession diverged significantly from the first, being a voluntaryist schism from the church. By 1800 it is estimated that around a fifth of the Scottish population belonged to one of the several presbyterian churches which had splintered from the establishment.[15]

---

[14] Archibald Bruce, *Reflections on freedom of writing* (1794), pp. 6–9, 80–1, 94–105; Bruce, *An historico-politico-ecclesiastical dissertation on the supremacy of civil powers in matters of religion, particularly the ecclesiastical supremacy annexed to the British crown* (Edinburgh, 1802), pp. ix –xi, 87–8, 148–51.

[15] A. Herron, *Kirk by divine right* (Edinburgh, 1985), pp. 65–6.

Over time the voluntaryism of the Relief Church seeped into the old Secession. In the last decade of the eighteenth century the inspiration of a 'New Licht' in matters of ecclesiology encouraged a number of Seceders to question the continuing relevance of the Covenants, the authority of the magistrate in matters of religion, and, indeed, the need to maintain an establishmentarian ecclesiology. By 1806 the Secession had further fragmented into New Licht Burghers, Auld Licht Burghers, New Licht Anti-Burghers, and Auld Licht Anti-Burghers, with the more numerous New Lichts advocating voluntaryist disengagement from political questions while a rump of Auld Lichts – including, however, articulate figures such as Bruce and the Reverend Thomas McCrie (1772–1835) – continued to insist upon a traditional conception of church–state relations.[16]

Notwithstanding the convulsions throughout the Presbyterian community wrought by questions of church–state relations, the Scottish judiciary had not yet succumbed to an Erastian doctrine of full parliamentary sovereignty. In *Minister of Prestonkirk* v. *Earl of Wemyss* (1808) Lord Justice-Clerk Charles Hope (1763–1851) issued a judgment which dwelt on the fears of Scots at the time of Union towards a decidedly hostile Church of England:

> Accordingly, actuated by that jealousy, our ancestors, at the Union, provided that the regulations applicable to our national church should be absolutely irrevocable, and that the Parliament of Great Britain should have no power to

---

[16] *Ibid.*, pp. 78–83.

alter or repeal those provisions. An attempt to do so (such were the precautions then observed) would amount to a dissolution of the Union, and the consequences might be dreadful. Resistance on the part of Scotland could hardly be termed rebellion.[17]

However, over the next three decades the legal position hardened, and, ironically, it was Hope and his son, members of one of Scotland's foremost legal dynasties, who would articulate the most uncompromising position on the sovereignty of parliament in the years which preceded the Disruption of 1843.

The issue of church–state relations and the question of parliamentary sovereignty came to a head within the establishment during the Ten Years' Conflict of 1834–43. This crisis took its rise from the initiatives of reformist Scots presbyterian Evangelicals – inspired by Thomas Chalmers – who, in the wake of British parliamentary reform in 1832, decided to embark on an overhaul of the Kirk, beginning with the Veto Act of 1834, passed as an Act of the General Assembly of 1834, which introduced a congregational veto into the workings of lay patronage. To what extent could this Act passed by an ecclesiastical legislature reform the workings of an Act passed by the British parliament in 1712? Was the General Assembly of the Kirk an integral part of the British constitution created by the fundamental law of the Treaty of 1707, and sovereign in

---

[17] Lord Justice-Clerk Hope, 'Opinion in case of Minister of Prestonkirk v Heritors Feb. 1808', in John Connell, *A treatise on the law of Scotland respecting tithes, and the stipends of parochial clergy* (3 vols., Edinburgh, 1815), III, p. 320.

its own spiritual sphere? Or was the General Assembly a mere synod, subordinate to crown-in-parliament, the only legitimate organ of lawmaking in the United Kingdom? The dispute brought into collision Anglican-inflected and Scots-inflected conceptions of the British constitution, the nature of the British state and the location (if any single place, wondered Scots presbyterians) of sovereignty within it.[18]

However, the Ten Years' Conflict was not simply a conflict between a Scottish Kirk and an Anglo-British parliament. Rather the Scots presbyterian Kirk was internally divided. At its extremes stood the – so-called – Moderate Party, composed of legalists who understood the constitutional realities of British parliamentary sovereignty, and the Non-Intrusionist Party, a body of Evangelicals who championed both the crown rights of Christ over his church and their rights under the Treaty of 1707. The Reverend George Cook (1772–1845), the leader of the Moderates, accepted the logic of parliamentary sovereignty, arguing that it was 'impossible that society can exist if one legislature be not supreme'.[19] The Moderates' Non-Intrusionist opponents saw no reason to retreat either from the theory of co-ordinate sovereignty which underpinned the doctrine of the two kingdoms or from the claim that the protections afforded the Kirk in the Treaty of Union placed constitutional limits on the operation of parliamentary sovereignty. The

---

[18] For the constitutional significance of the Ten Years' Conflict, see M. Fry, 'The Disruption and the Union', in S. J. Brown and M. Fry (eds.), *Scotland in the age of the Disruption* (Edinburgh, 1993), pp. 31–43.

[19] *Auchterarder case: revised speeches of George Cook DD and Robert Whigham, Esq, in the General Assembly on Wednesday May 22, 1839* (Edinburgh, 1839), p. 6.

Reverend William Cunningham (1805–61) – who became the Free Church Professor of Theology, then Church History, after the Disruption – argued that the Moderate theory of church–state relations was incompatible with the Westminster Confession of Faith.[20]

The long and far from inevitable road to Disruption began in 1834 when the General Assembly's Veto Act was immediately put to the test in Auchterarder where the congregational veto was exercised against the patron's appointee, Robert Young. The rejected nominee, having exhausted his right of appeal in the church courts when the General Assembly upheld the veto, then took his case, on the advice of John Hope (1794–1858), the Dean of the Faculty of Advocates and Moderate elder, to the civil courts. In March 1838 the Court of Session delivered its judgment by a vote of eight to five in Young's favour, and found the Veto Act to be *ultra vires*. The majority on the bench articulated a doctrine of parliamentary sovereignty unencumbered by refinements or qualifications regarding the special constitutional status of the Kirk. Lord President Hope (Charles Hope, the former Lord Justice-Clerk and father of John Hope) ruled that throughout Scottish history – Catholic and Protestant – the legislature had 'vindicated its authority over the Church'. Parliament, he went on, was 'the temporal head of the Church, from whose acts, and from whose acts alone, it exists as the national church, and from

---

[20] William Cunningham, *The objects, nature and standard of ecclesiastical authority* (Edinburgh, 1840); *Three letters of Dr. Cunningham and Dr. Bryce on the circa sacra power of the civil magistrate* (Edinburgh, 1843).

which alone it derives all its powers'. Indeed, Hope found the claim that Christ was head of the church in any practical legislative or judicial sense to be an 'absurdity'.[21] So much for the doctrine of the two kingdoms; so much, indeed, for the Treaty of Union.

The General Assembly appealed the Auchterarder decision to the House of Lords, looking for a judgment which would clarify the respective jurisdictions of the civil and ecclesiastical realms, and their courts. In 1839 the House of Lords confirmed the judgment of the Court of Session. The conflict had escalated. As other cases regarding the Veto Act wound their way through the civil courts, they threw into further relief the conflict of civil and spiritual right, not least in the Strathbogie case where the members of the Presbytery of Strathbogie were immediately confronted by the dilemma of whether to follow the law of the land as interpreted by the civil courts or the orders of the Evangelical-dominated General Assembly. However, no longer was there simply a clash of jurisdictions within Scotland; the judgment of the House of Lords and the failure of the British parliament to address the Kirk's grievances brought Anglo-Scottish tensions more clearly into focus. The General Assembly of 1842 issued the Claim of Right, a defiant declaration of spiritual independence from the temporal realm. Drawn up by the evangelical lawyer Alexander Dunlop (1798–1870),[22] the Claim of Right asserted that the privileges of

---

[21] 'Lord President's speech', in C. Robertson (ed.), *Report of the Auchterarder case* (2 vols., Edinburgh, 1838), II, pp. 1–20, at pp. 3, 10.

[22] S. J. Brown, *The national churches of England, Ireland and Scotland 1801–46* (Oxford, 2004), p. 353.

the Kirk were 'secured by antecedent stipulation' and 'inserted in the Treaty of Union, as an unalterable and fundamental condition thereof', and as such were 'reserved from the cognizance and power of the federal legislature created by the said Treaty'. Non-Intrusionist Kirkmen saw themselves as vindicating both the crown rights of Christ over his church and their rights under the Treaty of 1707. Thus the civil courts were in manifest 'breach of the Treaty of Union' and had 'usurped the power of the keys'.[23] In March 1843 the House of Commons debated a petition from the Kirk for consideration of its Claim of Right, but decided to reject the petition. Left without room for manoeuvre within the bonds of an oppressive establishment, the otherwise establishmentarian Non-Intrusionists withdrew from the Kirk in May 1843 at the Disruption to set up the Free Church of Scotland – free, that is, of the British state connection.

Notwithstanding their differences, all of the parties within the Kirk – even those who left it at the Disruption – were committed to the establishment principle. The question of religious establishments was at the heart of contemporary political as well as ecclesiastical debate. The passage of Catholic Emancipation in 1829 raised concerns about the status of the established churches in a Britain which had surrendered some of the apparatus of the Protestant confessional state. In Scotland, the growth of the New Licht churches in

---

[23] 'Claim, declaration and protest anent the encroachments of the Court of Session', in *The principal acts of the General Assembly of the Church of Scotland, convened at Edinburgh, May 19, 1842* (Edinburgh, 1842), pp. 35–48, esp. at pp. 46–7.

the urban Lowlands and their merger as the United Secession in 1820 gave these voluntaryists the confidence to mount a critique of the Kirk establishment. In 1829, the Reverend Andrew Marshall (1779–1854), the United Secession minister at Kirkintilloch, published an anti-establishmentarian sermon *Ecclesiastical establishments considered*,[24] which went through various editions and spawned a major controversy over the establishment principle. Within the Kirk, the Chalmersite programme of Church Extension was an attempt to reinvigorate the establishment: not only to tackle the social, moral and political problems associated with the impoverished, godless, urbanised proletariat of the new industrial Scotland but also to see off the threat of the voluntaries, in competition for the souls of the needy. Chalmers had already set out his evangelical vision of a revitalised territorial parish ministry in *The Christian and civic economy of large towns* (1819–26). In the celebrated *Lectures on the establishment and extension of national churches* (1838), which Chalmers delivered in London, he tackled the specific question of establishments.[25] These lectures, in turn, provoked a renewed phase of Anglican–presbyterian disputation, led in this instance by the anti-Erastian Anglican and then High Tory politician, William Ewart Gladstone, who published *The state in its relations with the church* in 1838. Gladstone admired Chalmers's defence of the establishment

---

[24] Andrew Marshall, *Ecclesiastical establishments considered* (Glasgow, 1829).

[25] Thomas Chalmers, *Lectures on the establishment and extension of national churches: delivered in London, from April 25 to May 12, 1838* (Glasgow, 1838).

principle and the doctrine of the two kingdoms, a robust episcopal version of which had always had its champions within the Anglican tradition. Ironically, the very fact of his High Anglican Churchmanship enabled Gladstone to empathise with the view that the Union had been intended as a 'compact', by which presbyterians 'meant to retain their full power of acting for their church'. Nevertheless, Gladstone could not accept Chalmers's rejection of apostolical succession as the defining basis of establishment.[26] National and confessional differences cut across a shared anti-Erastian ecclesiology.

Within Scotland, on the other hand, there was another important point of contact between Moderates and Non-Intrusionists which is sometimes forgotten, namely a fundamental political loyalty to the Union, notwithstanding any qualms about how the British constitution appeared, at least to Non-Intrusionists, to disadvantage the cause of the Kirk. There were political limits to the Non-Intrusionists' estrangement from the British state, and the Ten Years' Conflict was, to all intents and purposes, an intra-Unionist debate. Although there was a distinct flavour of religious nationalism to the anti-Erastian case, the Disruption of the Kirk in 1843 was contained within the Union and did not involve any overt political nationalism. Rather the domestic dispute within the Church of Scotland pitted two-kingdom unionists (Non-Intrusionists who believed that the authorities of the spiritual kingdom and the temporal kingdom ran in parallel) against Erastian unionists (Moderates who took the view that the authority of the

[26] W. E. Gladstone, *The state in its relations with the church* (London, 1838), esp. pp. 243–4.

Kirk was subordinate to the ultimate authority of the British parliament, the Union notwithstanding).

Why had it taken until 1843 for the Non-Intrusionists within the Kirk to perceive the Erastian nature of the British state? The 'Protest and Act of Separation' of those who withdrew from the Kirk in 1843 maintained that it was the confidence of Chalmers and his followers in the Union of 1707, and its fundamental grounding in the Act for Securing the Kirk of Scotland, which had sustained their adherence to the established church:

> notwithstanding the decrees as to matters spiritual and ecclesiastical of the civil courts, because we could not see that the state had required submission thereto as a condition of the establishment; but, on the contrary, were satisfied that the state, by the Acts of the Parliament of Scotland, for ever and unalterably secured to this nation by the Treaty of Union, had repudiated any power in the civil courts to pronounce such decrees, we are now constrained to acknowledge it to be the mind and will of the state, as recently declared, that such submission should and does form a condition of the establishment.[27]

It was not the running sore of patronage, but the escalating constitutional issues of the Ten Years' Conflict which had opened the eyes of those who would now quit the Kirk to the true terms of the establishment under which the Church of

[27] 'Protest and Act of Separation given in by certain ministers and elders, who withdrew from the Assembly on the 18th of May 1843', in *The principal acts of the General Assembly of the Church of Scotland, convened at Edinburgh, May 18 1843* (Edinburgh, 1843), p. 21.

Scotland had languished. As we saw in chapter 3, J. F. Ferrier's novel interpretation of a three-chambered British parliament – within which the General Assembly was co-equal in status with the other Houses of Commons and Lords – came too late, and was too fantastical, to resolve the questions of ecclesiology and church–state relations which became so bitter and divisive during the Ten Years' Conflict.[28] Nor did compromise seem to be at hand. The abolition in 1853 of compulsory subscription to the Westminster Confession of Faith for holders of chairs in the Scottish universities in non-divinity subjects was, it seemed, another clear breach of the safeguards for the Kirk's privileges supposedly protected by the Union.[29]

Compromise?

Compromise only came in the 1870s, a decade which nevertheless witnessed a renewal of cross-border misunderstanding and public controversy, this time not only between presbyterians and Anglicans, but also between presbyterians and the leadership of English Catholicism. In lectures delivered at Edinburgh in 1872, Arthur Penrhyn Stanley (1815–81), the Anglican Dean of Westminster and a former Professor of Ecclesiastical History at Oxford, tried to wean the Scots off Hildebrandism, the high Roman Catholic pretension, supposedly translated into the presbyterian doctrine of

---

[28] J. F. Ferrier, *Observations on church and state suggested by the Duke of Argyll's essay on the ecclesiastical history of Scotland* (Edinburgh and London, 1848).

[29] 16 and 17 Vict. c. 89.

the two kingdoms, that the Church was supreme in every issue which it deemed to be its own. Instead, Stanley identified a more acceptably statist brand of ecclesiology at the heart of the Scottish Reformed tradition. Erastianism, Stanley argued, was an under-appreciated theme of the Scottish Reformation. Knox's original Confession had contained 'nothing on the independence of the church', while both this document and the later Westminster Confession had been 'made binding on the Scottish Church by Act of Parliament'.[30] Stanley's remarks provoked outrage from the Reverend Robert Rainy (1826–1906), one of the leading figures in the Free Kirk. In particular, Rainy argued that Stanley had failed to discern the world of nuance that existed between Hildebrandism and Erastianism. In order to avoid Hildebrandism, it was not necessary to 'flee into the arms of Erastianism'. According to Rainy, the 'essence of Hildebrandism' was the view that 'the Church's decision ought to bind the state's conscience, and so decide the state's action'. Though seemingly 'unintelligible' to the English, presbyterian ecclesiology, on the other hand, was neither Hildebrandine nor Erastian, for presbyterians recognised the duty of the state 'to regulate its own action in its own sphere' without any ecclesiastical meddling in the legitimate jurisdiction of the temporal power. It was episcopacy – not presbyterianism – which was a step away from 'Popery', Rainy contended; that was why, an apparently common Protestantism notwithstanding, Scots presbyterians continued – more than two centuries

---

[30] Arthur Stanley, *Lectures on the history of the Church of Scotland* (London, 1872), p. 100.

after the anti-Anglican revolt of the Covenanters in 1638 – to be wary of Anglican imperialism.[31]

A further round of controversy was initiated by Henry Manning, the Roman Catholic Archbishop of Westminster, with the publication of his pamphlet *Caesarism and ultramontanism* in 1873. In the ensuing debate over his work Manning published an article in the April issue *Contemporary Review* which charged the Scots Kirk and the Free Kirk with ultramontane principles.[32] This in turn provoked an indignant reply in the July issue from Alexander Taylor Innes, a Free Kirk layman and eminent jurist, entitled 'Ultramontanism and the Free Kirk of Scotland'. Here Innes explained that it was an egregious error on Manning's part to misconstrue presbyterian ecclesiology as ultramontane. Rather the presbyterian doctrine of the two kingdoms eschewed the supremacist fallacies of both 'Caesarism' (Innes's term for Erastianism) and ultramontanism, and advocated instead a theory of 'coordinate jurisdiction' in which both church and state enjoyed 'mutual independence'. The Scots presbyterian theory of church–state relations, according to Innes, dictated that 'there is no supremacy of the one power over the other, and no subordination of the one under the other; that each has its own separate sphere: that in that sphere each is independent and supreme'. Innes insisted that Scots presbyterians – contrary to the popular misconception which still reigned in England, and now being peddled

---

[31] Robert Rainy, *Three lectures on the Church of Scotland* (Edinburgh, 1872), pp. 43–5.
[32] Henry Manning, 'Ultramontanism and Christianity', *Contemporary Review* 23 (1874), 683–702, at 699–701.

by Roman Catholics to serve their own ends – abjured ultra-montanist aspirations for the church to reign supreme over the state.[33]

However, by 1874 Anglican–presbyterian rapprochement seemed a likely prospect. The British government's repeal of the Patronage Act in 1874 appeared to offer a resolution of the Scottish church question, and to hold out the prospect that now the Free Church might reunite with the Kirk establishment. In this vein, the 8th Duke of Argyll (1823–1900), one of Scotland's leading intellectual figures as well as a prominent politician, promptly published *The Patronage Act of 1874 all that was asked in 1843* (1874), which went through several editions. However, Alexander Taylor Innes responded in *The Scotch law of establishment* (1875) that the repeal of patronage in 1874 had done nothing to alter the status of the Kirk establishment. Indeed, the abolition of patronage was a convenient means of evading the larger question of church–state relations. The Patronage Act (1874) had not erased the body of judicial decisions between 1834 and 1843 which had strangled the Kirk's autonomy, nor the laws and decisions on which these rested – all of which were still binding. Innes perceived that the Church of Scotland remains 'absolutely dependent on the state, and bound morally and legally by anything the state may choose to do'. How could Free Churchmen re-enter the establishment on these terms? Instead, Innes pronounced himself in favour of the constitutional liberation of the Kirk from its toils, what

---

[33] A. Taylor Innes, 'Ultramontanism and the Free Kirk of Scotland', *Contemporary Review* 24 (1874), 254–68.

he called 'ecclesiastical Home Rule'.[34] What did this mean in practice? In a public lecture at St George's Free Church, Edinburgh, in 1877, Innes formulated a new scheme of ecclesiology which sidestepped the thorny problem of establishment, for within the United Kingdom establishment inevitably implied subordination to a state which, it seemed, would never cast off its Erastian pretensions. Innes's alternative was to replace the formal constrictions of establishment with the more informal state 'recognition' of the church. Disestablishment was, of course, a less ambiguous alternative, but the history of Scotland's relations with England served as a warning that Scots needed to stop short of the wholesale disestablishment of presbyterianism, at least within the vexing environment of an Anglican-cum-Erastian state. Scots presbyterians had to 'insist upon retaining the statutory and parliamentary guarantees which at present secure on this side of the border against the establishment of the Church Episcopal'. Aware that voluntaryists would not like this exception to the principle of full disestablishment, Innes described his vision as a 'negative establishment' rather than a proper establishment. It was in essence a mere 'precaution': far from being the 'establishment of a Church; it is securing us, the people of Scotland, against the establishment of a Church'. In particular, it involved the 'right' of the Scots – however voluntaryist their domestic arrangements – 'to be secured against too powerful neighbours'.[35]

---

[34] A. Taylor Innes, *The Scotch law of establishment* (Edinburgh, 1875), pp. 67–8.

[35] A. Taylor Innes, 'Church and state in the present day', in R. Rainy, Lord Moncrieff and A. Taylor Innes, *Three lectures delivered in St. George's*

Innes's was the most sophisticated position in a Free Church which was now divided between constitutionalists, led by Begg, who wished to retain the aspiration – however unrealistic in practice – towards the establishment principle, and the party of disestablishment under Rainy. Contemporaries within the various presbyterian denominations debated the merits and consequences of disestablishment. However, there was broad agreement that this was not simply an ecclesiastical question but one which touched upon the Treaty of Union and the constitution of the Union state. It was a matter for Scotland as a whole to decide, urged James Mackinnon, Professor of Church History at Edinburgh and leading expert on the Union of 1707, not for ecclesiastics or even parliamentarians to decide on their own: 'Words could not be more decisive and positive than the terms of the treaty in this respect.'[36] Nevertheless the campaign for disestablishment failed to make headway, in large part because church defence became a rallying cry for Scottish Conservatives. A further complication arose from the divisions besetting the Free Church, which experienced a schism in 1892 when the Free Presbyterians withdrew over the terms of subscription to the Westminster Confession of Faith and another in 1900 when the union of the voluntaryist majority of the Free Church with the United Presbyterians (themselves a fusion in 1847 of the United Secession and the Relief) was rejected by a minority within the Free Church. Remaining

Free Church in Edinburgh, November 1877 (Edinburgh, London and New York, 1878), pp. 170, 195, 202–8.

[36] James Mackinnon, The Union of England and Scotland (London, 1896), p. 511.

true to the original establishment principles of the Free Church, this minority boycotted the union and were deposed. Nevertheless, in the Free Church case the Wee Frees sued successfully through the civil courts – all the way up to the House of Lords in 1904 – for the entire property and endowments of the Free Church. In the end an Erastian parliament had to intervene – in flagrant disregard of both two-kingdom and voluntaryist principles – appointing a commission to divide the property on an equitable basis.[37]

The Church of Scotland Act (1921)

The abolition of patronage in 1874 had failed to solve the question of church–state relations within the United Kingdom, and the failure of the disestablishment campaign and the absurdities of the Free Church case had only compounded matters. Nevertheless, a degree of closure came in 1921 with a kind of concordat between church and state. The Church of Scotland issued Articles Declaratory in 1921, which were then embodied in an Act of Parliament, the Church of Scotland Act, 1921, which gave them legal effect. The Articles Declaratory defined the Church of Scotland as a national church independent of the British state, which, in turn, paved the way for the reunion of the national Kirk establishment with the United Free Church in 1929. The Church of Scotland Act 1921 acknowledged the national status of the Kirk which was enshrined in

---

[37] F. Lyall, *Of presbyters and kings: church and state in the law of Scotland* (Aberdeen, 1980), p. 67.

Article III of the Articles Declaratory: 'As a national Church representative of the Christian Faith of the Scottish people it acknowledges its distinctive call and duty to bring the ordinances of religion to the people in every parish of Scotland through a territorial ministry.' The incorporation of Article IV of the Articles Declaratory in the Church of Scotland Act 1921 further complicated the constitutional status of the Kirk, for it appeared to be explicit state recognition of the doctrine of the two kingdoms, the very logic of which ran against the grain of the prevailing constitutional theory of parliamentary sovereignty:

> This Church, as part of the Universal Church wherein the Lord Jesus Christ has appointed a government in the hands of Church office-bearers, receives from him, its divine king and head, and from him alone, the right and power subject to no civil authority to legislate, and to adjudicate finally, in all matters of doctrine, worship, government, and discipline in the Church, including the right to determine all questions concerning membership and office in the Church, the constitution and membership of its courts, and the mode of election of its office-bearers, and to define the boundaries of the spheres of labour of its ministers and other office-bearers. Recognition by civil authority of the separate and independent government and jurisdiction of this church in matters spiritual, in whatever manner such recognition be expressed, does not in any way affect the character of this government and jurisdiction as derived from the Divine Head of the Church alone, or give to the civil authority any right of interference with the

proceedings or judgments of the church within the sphere of its spiritual government and jurisdiction.[38]

How could the British parliament acknowledge an exclusive jurisdiction within the United Kingdom yet beyond the scope of its own authority? Nevertheless, hard as it was to comprehend, given the dominance of parliamentary sovereignty in contemporary constitutional law, the British state seemed to be withdrawing any pretension to transgress the Kirk-defined boundary between the temporal and spiritual realms within Scotland. Surely, here at last after two centuries of intermittent wrangling, the 1921 Act had settled the constitutional status of the Kirk once and for all, and very much in the Kirk's favour. A further Act was passed in 1925 – the Church of Scotland (Property and Endowments) Act – which dealt with the Kirk's property and finances, and also affirmed its right to create new parishes without civil approval. These Acts of 1921 and 1925 made possible the reunion with the United Free Church in 1929.

Alas, the Church of Scotland Act, 1921, raised further constitutional problems. In particular, the Act declared that all statutes and laws insofar as they were inconsistent with the Articles Declaratory of 1921 were thereby repealed or of no effect. However, the Act did not specify which measures it had repealed. This vagueness opened the Scots presbyterian equivalent of Pandora's box, for it created a degree of uncertainty whether the 1921 Act superseded the supposedly

---

[38] The Articles Declaratory are set out in D. Murray, *Freedom to reform: the Articles Declaratory of the Church of Scotland 1921* (Edinburgh, 1993), 'Appendix I', pp. 142–5.

unalterable Act for Securing the Kirk of Scotland of 1706–7. In other words, the Kirk had got what it thought it wanted in 1921, but at the possible cost of tampering with the Kirk's security as guaranteed under the Treaty of Union. If this were so, did the Act of 1921 then perversely weaken the protections enjoyed by the Kirk? Or, indeed, was the 1921 Act itself an illegal trespass by the United Kingdom parliament on the sole matter which – possibly – lay beyond the remit of an otherwise unconstrained parliamentary sovereignty? Indeed, which measure was more deeply entrenched in the British constitution – the Act for Securing the Kirk of Scotland of 1706–7 or the Church of Scotland Act 1921? Or was the 1921 Act quite different in character from the Act of 1707, the 1921 Act being in the nature of a concordat which merely clarified in law the pre-existing relationship of Kirk and state?

Moreover, the Articles Declaratory gave rise to another devastating uncertainty, namely was the Kirk still an established church? After all, the Articles needed to be ambiguous on this point, as they allowed a reunion between an established church and the voluntaryist United Free Church, without any apparent sacrifice of ecclesiological principle on either side. Thus, the Articles pointedly omitted the language of establishment, and instead spoke of the Kirk as a national church. In addition, the insistence of the Articles on the Kirk's autonomy from the civil power made it clear that the Kirk did not owe its existence as a national church to the civil power: it was not, in other words, a kirk by law established. On the other hand, the very fact that the Kirk was recognised in an Act of Parliament appeared to confer upon it the status of an officially recognised established church. There was in time to be considerable disagreement among Scottish churchmen, lawyers and constitutional theorists on these points, though given the desire at the time by the mainstream of the Kirk to find an acceptable foundation for church reunion, some of these issues would not go fully explored until the 1970s. Nevertheless, there was some anxiety about what was implied in the Articles at the time of their formulation and passage. At one extreme of the Kirk was the National Church Defence Association, an establishmentarian pressure group within the Kirk which was set up in 1919 out of concern about the voluntaryist drift of the Articles as they took shape. The National Church Defence Association cared less about the cause of denominational reunion than to uphold the existing status of the Kirk. In particular, its members expressed some worries that the tendency of the Articles was the demotion of the Kirk to the status of a voluntary sect. After all, as the National Church Defence Association noted, the Church of Scotland would, under the Articles, enjoy an unchecked claim to complete spiritual freedom. One of its members, J. Hay Thorburn, took the view that the Articles Declaratory turned the General Assembly of the Kirk into a kind of 'pope'. Gordon Mitchell of Killearn, one of the Association's secretaries, argued that the Articles Declaratory constituted a 'chimerical compromise' between establishment and disestablishment, that they sent the Kirk on the slippery downward slope towards voluntaryism and that the ensuing Church of Scotland (Property and Endowments) Bill was in flagrant violation of the Treaty of Union.[39]

---

[39] Murray, *Rebuilding the Kirk*, pp. 142, 246–7, 258–9.

In *Ballantyne* v. *Presbytery of Wigtown* (1936), also known as the Kirkmabreck case, the Court of Session set out its view on the constitutionality of the 1921 Act. Here the parishioners of Kirkmabreck, a parish which was to be merged with a former United Free congregation at Creetown, argued that their congregational right to elect a minister, guaranteed under the 1874 Act which abolished patronage, was still operative, notwithstanding the 1921 Act. The Court begged to differ. Indeed, Lord Justice-Clerk Aitchison declared that if the matter fell within the scope of the Articles Declaratory, then it was not within the jurisdiction of the temporal courts, 'and neither the statute, nor the common law, nor previous judicial decision, whether upon statute or common law, can avail to bring the matter within the jurisdiction of the civil authority'.[40]

However, the courts continued to regard the Union of 1707 rather than the 1921 concordat as the defining landmark in church–state relations, and, possibly, a fundamental law which might in certain extreme circumstances constrain the full exercise of parliamentary sovereignty. Both Lord Cooper in *MacCormick* v. *Lord Advocate* (1953) and Lord Keith in *Gibson* v. *Lord Advocate* (1975) reserved opinion on what the question would be if the UK parliament passed an Act purporting to abolish the Church of Scotland.

Nevertheless, constitutional commentators and experts in ecclesiology found the new post-1921 position of the Kirk somewhat perplexing, and were far from unanimous on the question of whether the Kirk remained an established church or not – the latter, of course, in possible breach of the

---

[40] Quoted in Lyall, *Of presbyters and kings*, p. 72.

Treaty of Union. In answer to the question of whether the reunited Church of Scotland was established or disestablished, John H. S. Burleigh (1894–1985), Professor of Ecclesiastical History at Edinburgh University, took the view that it was 'neither, or perhaps that the question had little significance'. Establishment was an 'outmoded' or 'meaningless' concept, though he insisted that the Kirk was a national church.[41] On the other hand, Sir Thomas Taylor, a jurist and elder of the Kirk, took the view that the Church of Scotland under the 1921 Act was that rare bird 'a church that is both established and free'.[42]

Similarly, Ronald King Murray, the constitutional theorist and future judge of the Court of Session, was confident that the Church of Scotland was established. In 1958 Murray published an article in *Public Law* which challenged the assumption of some English constitutional lawyers that the Church of Scotland was not an established church by the same lights as the Church of England establishment. Murray dismissed this interpretation as a kind of Anglican chauvinism. For a start, he contended, at the Union of 1707 the Churches of England and Scotland had both been reciprocally re-established. In addition, the Church of Scotland Act, 1921, had further enhanced the status of the Kirk, because '[b]y this remarkable statute' the British parliament had conceded the 'legislative sovereignty' which the General Assembly of the Kirk

[41] J. H. S. Burleigh, *A church history of Scotland* (Oxford, 1960), pp. 404–5.
[42] T. M. Taylor, 'Church and state in Scotland', *Juridical Review* (1957), 121–37, at 137.

had claimed in the spiritual realm, and surrendered the notion of absolute parliamentary omnicompetence, given the open acknowledgement that 'there is at least one respect in which the United Kingdom Parliament is not sovereign'. Murray found this last concession a compelling mark of establishment: 'what established church', he wondered, 'could ask for a greater measure of state association than to share with the civil authority the legislative power of the state?' Of course, Murray observed, the Church of Scotland was indeed free of the state, but this did not necessarily, as some commentators assumed, make it a free church. Indeed, if anything, the Church of Scotland was more robustly established than the Church of England. This was because the Church of England, unlike the Church of Scotland, was 'subordinate to the state', with the monarch as its supreme head, and 'subject to the direct control of the executive and legislature'. Those constitutional lawyers who thought that the Church of Scotland was not established had been misled by the peculiarities of the asymmetrical dual establishment of religion which prevailed in the United Kingdom, certainly since 1921. The Church of Scotland's establishment did indeed differ in certain crucial respects from the Church of England establishment, but this did not make the Kirk's standing any less of an establishment. Most obviously, whereas the Church of England was represented in parliament by way of the bishops who sat in the House of Lords, the Church of Scotland, 'as befits its claim to share the legislative function of the state in its own right with the civil authority, has no direct representation in parliament such as that enjoyed by the Church of England; on the other hand, its legislative sovereignty in ecclesiastical matters has been confirmed by the United Kingdom legislature'.[43]

Francis Lyall, Professor of Public Law at Aberdeen University and active Churchman who served as a Commissioner to the General Assembly of the Church of Scotland, believed that it was, perhaps, misguided to push the 'logic' of the 1921 settlement too far. After all, the Articles Declaratory were at bottom a 'compromise', designed to reconcile the logically irreconcilable ecclesiologies of the Church of Scotland establishment, whose defenders had since the 1880s fought to see off the disestablishmentarian threat, and the voluntaryism of the United Free Church. Lyall concluded that 'establishment of sorts was retained' in the 1921 settlement, though not one which drew 'odious' distinctions between the position of the 'national Church' and the non-established denominations. However, Lyall was keenly aware that another ambiguity lay at the core of the 1921 arrangement. The relationship between the 1921 Act and the Treaty of Union was particularly murky. If it were accepted, argued Lyall, that 'a true interpretation of the Act is to over-set the pre-1707 legislation', then there were reasonable grounds on which to argue that the 1921 legislation was '*ultra vires* of the United Kingdom Parliament', as it was at least arguable that the church settlement of 1707 was entrenched in the Treaty and therefore beyond the scope of parliamentary repeal.[44] The eminent jurist T. B. Smith, also an elder of the Kirk, similarly found the 1921 Act to be a masterpiece

---

[43] R. K. Murray, 'The constitutional position of the Church of Scotland', *Public Law* (1958), 155–62.

[44] Lyall, *Of presbyters and kings*, pp. 68, 78, 83.

of ambiguity. Indeed, Smith thought the 1921 Act defective in that it contained a general repeal clause but failed to provide a schedule of the measures which it purported to repeal.

There was, however, no consensus on the status of the Kirk, even among its own leading constitutional interpreters. The Very Reverend James Weatherhead (b. 1931), the Principal Clerk of the General Assembly of the Church of Scotland from 1985 to 1996, took the opposite view from Lyall on the issue of establishment, arguing that the Kirk was not in fact established, or at least had not been established since the Acts of 1921 and 1925. The constitutional settlement of the 1920s had enormous significance for the Kirk, as it appeared to give the Church of Scotland the freedom to reform itself unencumbered by the need to gain parliamentary approval for such changes to what was Scotland's national church:

> While, in terms of its own constitution, the Church of Scotland was recognised as the national Church in Scotland, it was no longer properly described as 'by law established', because the law had now explicitly recognised that the Church was established by the Lord Jesus Christ. This means that, while the 1707 Act may still be regarded as law protecting the Church from state interference, and is in this sense reinforced by the 1921 Act, it cannot be construed as preventing the Church from modifying its own constitution without reference to the state, in terms of the Articles.

The recognition of the divine authority of the church's claim to spiritual autonomy meant that the Kirk was fully independent of the state. Furthermore, Weatherhead argued that the very terms of the 1921 Act rendered it a special kind of measure, superior to run-of-the-mill statutes and constitutionally entrenched. As parliament had recognised 'an area where its writ does not run', the 1921 Act amounted to a 'legislative recognition of a limitation on the sovereignty of parliament', and, as such, 'arguably', as a 'fundamental law which cannot be amended by ordinary legislation'.[45]

In a similar vein, Douglas Murray of the University of Glasgow, an expert on church–state relations in twentieth-century Scotland, argued that the term 'established church' would be 'quite inappropriate to describe the continuing relationship between church and state as set out in the Articles'. However, Murray went on to deny that just because the Kirk was not established that, therefore, it was disestablished. Rather, he took the view that the status of the Church of Scotland could best be described by an alternative form of language which eschewed the thorny question of establishment, arguing that the Kirk was rather 'national and free'. The Kirk, he maintained, 'is not established by the state, but it is a national church with a national obligation'.[46]

Colin Munro, Professor of Constitutional Law at Edinburgh University and a convinced proponent of parliamentary sovereignty, has identified several peculiarities in the 1921 Act. It was particularly 'unusual' that the terms of the Act provided that it take effect 'only on condition that the Church's General

---

[45] James Weatherhead, *The constitution and laws of the Church of Scotland* (Edinburgh, 1997), pp. 15, 17.

[46] Murray, *Rebuilding the Kirk*, p. 280; Murray, *Freedom to reform*, p. 4.

Assembly adopted the declaratory Articles'. It was not so much a parliamentary 'conferment' of a constitution upon the church as a 'recognition by the state of a concordat which allowed that the Church had its own sphere of jurisdiction'. Given these oddities in the 1921 Act, Munro understood why some members of the Kirk, who acknowledged that the pre-1921 Kirk was indeed established, nevertheless preferred to speak only of the post-1921 Kirk as the 'national Church'. But here was the crux, it seemed. Munro argued that if it were accepted – as it generally was – that the pre-1921 Kirk was established, then one could only argue that the post-1921 Kirk was not if one read the 1921 Act as 'a disestablishing measure'. Yet, the 1921 Act did not advertise itself as a law to disestablish the Kirk, and was difficult to interpret as such, except by oblique implication. The 1921 Act had left Scotland, Munro argued, with a '"lighter" form of establishment' and experienced less 'entanglement' with the state than the Church of England – which was, of course, represented in the House of Lords. Nevertheless, the Kirk enjoyed 'official recognition' and the courts of the Church of Scotland were acknowledged in law as courts of the realm, so it would be misleading to equate the Kirk with other non-established denominations as a kind of voluntary association. Therefore, making due allowance for the various curiosities and ambiguities in the constitutional position of the Church of Scotland, Munro reasoned, the Kirk must be a religious establishment, however attenuated.[47]

[47] C. R. Munro, 'Does Scotland have an established church?', *Ecclesiastical Law Journal* 4 (1997), 639–45, at 644–5.

Yet a thorny issue remained. Did the Articles entitle the Kirk to revise matters of doctrine and worship without reference to parliament? This was not so clear, for Article III of 1921 claimed that the church was 'in historical continuity with the Church of Scotland which was reformed in 1560, whose liberties were ratified in 1592, and for whose security provision was made in the Treaty of Union of 1707'. Did this mean that the Kirk was yoked – whether it liked it or not – to the dogmas of the Scottish Reformation and the Westminster Confession of Faith, or was the Kirk free to liberalise its standards in the light of ongoing Biblical research and theological understanding? Such constitutional niceties held significant implications for the ministers of the Kirk and their national flock. For practising Christians, error – say, for example, the unyielding and perhaps uncharitable Calvinism of a bygone era – possessed no right, certainly not at the heart of the church's articles of belief. On the other hand, how much scope did the Articles Declaratory give the Kirk to depart from the faith of its forebears? In the late 1970s and early 1980s the Kirk tied itself in knots over the status which the concordat of 1921 had conferred upon its Confession.[48] The Kirk's involvement, especially since the 1970s, in the campaign for Scottish devolution within the framework of the United Kingdom – and not without misgivings at both nationalist and unionist extremes of the ministry – has tended to obscure the puzzle surrounding the Kirk's own constitutional status.[49]

[48] Murray, *Freedom to reform*, esp. ch. 6.
[49] See J. H. Proctor, 'The Church of Scotland and the struggle for a Scottish Assembly', *Journal of Church and State* 25 (1983), 523–43.

An unresolved mystery

The constitutional status of the Kirk within the Union remains one of deep ambiguity. Is the Kirk establishment constitutive of the state, as appears to be the case under the – presumably – unamended Union agreement ratified in 1707, or an established church subordinate to the state – whatever parliament might say at any given time – according to the uncompromising logic of parliamentary sovereignty, or a free, national non-established church autonomous from the state on the basis of the concordat of 1921? Not only are constitutional experts unable to agree on the nature of the Kirk's status and whether it is in fact established, they – and even the judiciary[50] – are also unable to reach any firm conclusions about whether an otherwise sovereign parliament is able to legislate on matters pertaining to the Kirk. Yet, the fact that the Kirk enjoys a uniquely favoured constitutional status within the Union seems incontrovertible. As some constitutional commentators have noticed, Section 4 (2) of the Regency Act (1937), reaffirmed in subsequent Regency legislation, grants an incoming Regent full royal powers, with two exceptions. Under the Regency Act a Regent is unable to assent to a bill which changes the order of succession, for obvious reasons; less predictably a Regent is unable to give the royal assent to a bill which alters the Act of Security of the Church of Scotland (1707).[51] However, this presupposes that this Act

---

[50] *MacCormick* v. *Lord Advocate* (1953); *Gibson* v. *Lord Advocate* (1975).

[51] J. D. B. Mitchell, *Constitutional law* (1964: Edinburgh, 1968), p. 170; 1 Edw. 8 and 12 Geo. 6, c. 16, 4 (2). For the relationship between the

of 1707 has a special constitutional status, greater than the Act of 1921, which is not mentioned in the Regency Act. Moreover, it leaves open, as Lyall noted, the question of whether under normal circumstances a reigning monarch might legitimately assent to a bill which alters the Act of Security of the Church of Scotland.[52] A further complication has arisen very recently from the House of Lords' decision in the Helen Percy case. Percy, an associate minister of a parish in Angus, had been dismissed in 1997 after it emerged that she had had an affair with a Kirk elder. In 2005 the House of Lords ruled on an appeal from the Court of Session (which had upheld the Kirk's autonomy under the concordat) that, notwithstanding the 1921 Act, ministerial appointments within the Kirk were not beyond the jurisdiction of the civil courts and employment tribunals insofar as such appointments constituted contracts of employment.[53] Notwithstanding this further wrinkle, the status of the Kirk remains the most mysterious of several black holes in Britain's uncodified constitution.

> monarchy and the Church of Scotland, see V. Bogdanor, *The monarchy and the constitution* (1995: Oxford, 1997 pbk), pp. 233–8.
>
> [52] Lyall, *Of presbyters and kings*, p. 80.
>
> [53] *Percy (AP)* v. *Church of Scotland Board of National Mission* (2005) UKHL 73 (on appeal from 2001 SC 757); F. Lyall, 'Church ministers as employees: Percy v Church of Scotland Board of National Mission', *Edinburgh Law Review* 10 (2006), 446–52.

7

Early nationalism as a form of unionism

Outsiders must sometimes find the nomenclature of British politics confusing. It does seem peculiar that the champions of home rule for Northern Ireland at Stormont have tended to be described as Unionists, while the proponents of a similar measure of devolution for Scotland have generally been known as nationalists. An exception to the normal practice is Alvin Jackson's insightful book *Home rule: an Irish history 1800–2000* (2003), which aligns Irish nationalists with their Unionist opponents by way of a narrative which runs smoothly and subversively from nineteenth-century agitation for home rule to its ironic twentieth-century realisation in the Stormont statelet. Jackson's extended study of home rule also illuminates what he describes as 'a centrist tradition in modern Irish political history – a tradition that has sought to accommodate Irish nationalism with the British state' and to 'reconcile' unionist and nationalist commitments within frameworks of devolved government.[1]

Might there be a similar tale to be told about Scottish home rule? Have Scottish unionists and nationalists always belonged to discrete and impermeable ideological traditions? Did the substantive elements of their respective programmes accurately reflect the antithetical labels which they bore? Or

[1] A. Jackson, *Home rule: an Irish history 1800–2000* (2003: London, 2004 pbk), p. 376.

257

have political labels obscured as much as they have revealed about the core values of supposed unionists and nationalists? This chapter will explore the peculiarities of political labelling. It seems that there may have been a narrower division between the supposed extremes of unionism and nationalism than conventional historiography normally allows and this chapter will identify significant points of contact. Similarly, it will interrogate the assumption of a profound contrast in the mood music which accompanied the ideologies of unionism and nationalism.

Given the vast differences in the political cultures of Northern Ireland and Scotland, it is unclear whether there are any major insights to be gained from further pursuit of the initial comparison between Ulster Unionism and Scottish nationalism. However, the superficial resemblance between these 'unionist' and 'nationalist' home rule projects provides a point of departure for a closer and more sceptical analysis of the substance of Scottish nationalist political argument. How far have historians neglected a unionist dimension within the Scottish nationalist tradition? To what extent did unionists and nationalists share some of the same arguments, rhetorical strategies and tropes? Indeed, is it appropriate to parse home rule programmes as nationalisms when they were so heavily freighted with commitments to wider British and imperial loyalties? Is there not a case for examining devolutionary ideologies of this sort as manifestations of a self-confident unionist culture whose understanding of the Anglo-Scottish union at least was far from monolithic? In turn consideration of these issues prompts further questions about historical method. Have Scottish historians been in a state of denial about the strong British loyalties evident within the Scottish home rule tradition, or simply confused by the nationalist label into missing the unionist elements which co-existed with more obvious nationalist sentiments within the home rule tradition?

The lack of a serious nationalist threat to the Union until the last quarter of the twentieth century meant that unionists generally took the Union for granted. The prevalence of this kind of 'banal unionism' in unionist circles created – as we saw in the first chapter – an odd vacuum in Scottish political discourse: that the central feature of the Scottish political land-scape rarely attracted the attention of unionist commentators. However, there is a fundamental asymmetry in unionist and nationalist responses to the Union. While Scottish unionists traditionally paid much less attention to the Anglo-Scottish Union of 1707 than they did to the Union of 1800 with Ireland, the same has not been true of Scottish nationalists. Indeed, it is nationalists (or so-called nationalists) rather than unionists who have over the last century and a half paid most attention to the Union of 1707. Scottish nationalists, unlike unionists, have taken the Union seriously. Of course, nationalists have criticised the Union as an unwanted imposition on the Scottish nation – a one-sided agreement imposed on the Scottish people by the English who corrupted the spineless and self-interested elite who dominated Scotland's pre-democratic legislature. The Union, nationalists have argued, is illegitimate and oppressive, and as such demands to be taken seriously. Nevertheless, the Union has not simply been an object of nationalist criticism. British constitutional interpretation is one of the more unusual genres of Scottish nationalist litera-ture. Not only have nationalists – most notably the eminent jurist Sir Neil MacCormick – made a major contribution to the political and legal theory of Union, but the Union has even functioned as a watchword of nationalist invocation.[2] Indeed several nationalists have invoked the Union as the constitutive Treaty and fundamental constitution of the United Kingdom, and launched grievances and claims on behalf of the Scottish people on the basis of the rights for Scotland guaranteed within the Articles of Union. Whereas in the middle of the twentieth century, most unionists were Diceyans, brought up on the doctrine of the unlimited sovereignty of the British parliament and thus, by extension, on the idea of constitutional flexibility, it was Scottish nationalists who insisted – pedantically and, perhaps, hypocritically – that the Union be preserved in aspic. As late as 1968, Winnie Ewing who won the Hamilton constituency for the Scottish National Party in a by-election in 1967 asked 'How is it that the Treaty of Utrecht of 1713 which gave Britain the use of Gibraltar, must be maintained in its entirety; whereas the Treaty of Union of six years earlier between England and Scotland could be violated?'[3] While some nationalists have rejected the Union outright, others have, in effect, acted as strict constructionists of the Union, using its provisions as a stick with which to beat the English for their

---

[2] Neil MacCormick, *Questioning sovereignty* (Oxford, 1999); Neil MacCormick, 'Does the United Kingdom have a constitution? Reflections on MacCormick v. Lord Advocate', *Northern Ireland Legal Quarterly* 29 (1978), 1–20; Neil MacCormick, 'The English constitution, the British state and the Scottish anomaly', *Proceedings of the British Academy* 101 (1998), 289–306.

[3] Winnie Ewing, *Stop the world: the autobiography of Winnie Ewing* (Edinburgh, 2004), p. 67.

arrogance and insensitivity towards their Scottish partners-in-Union. Nor are these positions mutually exclusive, and nationalists have often combined criticism of the Union with its strict construction, defending Scottish interests with whatever arguments were at hand. However, the prevalence of strict constructionism in nationalist argument also yields a deeper insight into Scottish nationalist politics: that for much of the modern era the immediate object of nationalist agitation has not been the winning of independence for Scotland – a distant and, seemingly, unattainable goal – but to win self-respect for Scotland as a nation within the Union, to put a stop to the wholesale anglicisation of Scottish life and to obtain a greater measure of autonomy for Scotland within Britain and its Empire.

The more closely one examines the platforms, positions and manifesto commitments of the various 'nationalist' groupings and parties in Scottish politics between the 1850s and the 1960s, the more obvious it becomes that, for most of its history prior to its emergence as a serious and consistent vote-winning organisation in the 1970s, modern Scottish nationalism has had as its primary aim not Scottish independence per se but a greater autonomy for Scotland within a looser association of the British peoples; in other words, the goal has been revision – possibly substantial revision – of the Anglo-Scottish Union, but not its total destruction. This aspiration has – as we shall see – taken various forms: self-government for Scotland in the domestic field within a decentralised British state, which nevertheless retained sovereign powers in the fields of foreign affairs and defence; home rule for Scotland as part of a series of constitutional reforms within the British Empire; dominion status for Scotland within the

Empire or Commonwealth; a 'real' or personal union with England, meaning in effect a restored Union of the Crowns; and autonomy for Scotland as a mother nation of the Empire, alongside England. Indeed, while some early Scottish nationalists were anti-imperialist, and aligned their hopes for Scottish freedom with the antipathies of other nations – including the Irish – to English imperialism, many Scottish nationalists took the Britishness of the British Empire as seriously as they took Scottish Treaty rights within the Union, and insisted upon home rule for Scotland less as an end in itself than as a means for Scotland to play a more active role in a reinvigorated British Empire. Much of the discourse of Scottish nationalism between the 1880s and 1930s has as its focus the role of Scotland within the running of the British Empire. While nationalists saw full political incorporation with England of the sort achieved in 1707 as an unwanted burden, they did not reject either the earlier Union of the Crowns of 1603 or the British Empire as impediments to the full realisation of Scottish nationhood. Indeed, the monarchy went relatively unchallenged within the mainstream of Scottish nationalism, and even nationalists recognised a common and – properly – British monarchy as a keystone of a continuing Anglo-Scottish connection. On the other hand, the Union of 1707 – unlike the Empire or the British monarchy – was apparently an obstacle to a more effective union or association of the British peoples within a devolved empire. It is in this sense that it seems reasonable to refer to the run of early Scottish nationalists as unionists. Several of the celebrated pioneers of the Scottish nationalist cause might be more aptly depicted as reforming unionists or imperialists.

Nor should this occasion much surprise, for the early stirrings of Scottish nationalism occurred within a unionist culture, indeed an imperialist culture, and, as a result, the early forms of Scottish nationalism bore the inflections of the dominant unionism. There was a narrower line between unionism and nationalism than most Scottish historians and political scientists have hitherto imagined, though there are some conspicuous exceptions, most notably Richard Finlay who has explored the imperialist obsessions of inter-war nationalism[4] and James Mitchell who has been sensitive to the role of non-nationalist groupings in forwarding the nationalist project. As Mitchell reminds us, the nationalist parties and pressure groups have not been the sole carriers of nationalist politics in Scotland; rather, elements of the nationalist case have been promoted, at different times, by each of the mainstream parties of the Union, even the Conservatives, who played the nationalist card against centralising socialism in the late 1940s and consistently espoused measures of non-legislative or administrative devolution.[5] Whereas unionists were – as we have seen in earlier chapters – concerned to defend elements of nationhood preserved in the Union, nationalists were concerned to preserve Scotland's national dignity and autonomy within the framework of some form of Anglo-Scottish association. At the extremes of unionism and nationalism were scatterings of highly marginal and unrepresentative figures who

---

[4] R. Finlay, 'For or against? Scottish nationalists and the British Empire, 1919–1939', *Scottish Historical Review* 71 (1992), 184–206.

[5] J. Mitchell, *Strategies for self-government: the campaigns for a Scottish parliament* (Edinburgh, 1996).

championed wholesale integration of Scotland within a centralised and homogenised Greater English state or the complete severance of the Anglo-Scottish connection, but between these extremes there was a moderate continuum which encompassed both unionist and nationalist positions in varying degrees and combinations. The hybridity of the middle ground in Scottish political culture has been overlooked by a Scottish historiographical tradition which has tended to assign nationalists and unionists to separate pigeonholes. Scottish historians have emphasised the differences between moderate nationalists and unionists in lieu of teasing out the nuances of a range of constitutional proposals and solutions which emerged from the extensive middle ground of Scottish politics. Here, although most of the spectrum was occupied by the dominant unionist tradition and only one end by the minority nationalists, unionists and nationalists nevertheless subscribed to a set of shared values about the importance of the monarchy, the empire and the Anglo-Scottish connection as well as the need to defend Scottish institutions and interests within the Union. Unionists and nationalists alike resented English indifference, chauvinism and the assumption that Scotland was a mere province within an English empire. Yet the clarity of the grand narratives of Scottish historiography has worked to obscure the rich interplay of unionism and nationalism in Scottish political thought during the second half of the nineteenth and the first half of the twentieth century.

Indeed, the main narrative within the history of Scottish nationalism has not only been teleological – identifying early manifestations of strict constructionism and home rule politics as pioneering forerunners of today's Scottish National Party – it has also focussed attention on a supposed organisational lineage which leads from the National Association for the Vindication of Scottish Rights or perhaps later the Scottish Home Rule Association, by way of the Young Scots Society, the National Party of Scotland, the Scottish Self-Government Party to the Scottish National Party. Rather than each organisation being interpreted in the light of its own political statements, the assumption has prevailed that these bodies constituted a seamless apostolic succession of nationalist groupings. Genealogical imperatives have discouraged proper analysis of the arguments and proposals of early nationalist organisations on their own terms and in their immediate historical context. Here the history of political thought – an undeveloped area of modern Scottish historiography – has much to contribute to the recovery of the particularities of past political arguments and in tracing the significant differences which existed – not least in their forgotten unionisms – both among the earliest nationalist organisations and between them and later manifestations of Scottish nationalism.[6]

On the other hand, the hardening of unionist and nationalist ideologies in the last quarter of the twentieth century makes it more difficult for the present to appreciate the porousness of Unionism and nationalism in the first half of the

---

[6] See e.g. H. J. Hanham, *Scottish nationalism* (Cambridge, MA, 1969); K. Webb, *The growth of nationalism in Scotland* (Glasgow, 1977); J. Brand, *The national movement in Scotland* (London, 1978). A splendid exception to the general trend is the pluralistic interpretation found in Mitchell, *Strategies for self-government.*

twentieth century. Moreover, the willy-nilly ascription of labels such as nationalist and unionist to figures in the past without due attention to the substance of their ideological platforms, lumps moderate nationalists with extreme nationalists, when the former might well have been more likely to associate themselves with the mainstream parties of the Union. There were, in fact, significant tensions within Scottish nationalism between fundamentalists who wanted full independence for Scotland and moderates who desired little more than a modified Union. Such tensions led to a major split in the SNP in 1942. A keen sense of wartime realities prompted John MacCormick and his moderate supporters to break away from the party when hard-liners associated with the anti-conscriptionist Douglas Young (1913–73) gained the ascendancy. In his memoir of the national movement, *The flag in the wind* (1955), MacCormick described two rather different types of Scottish nationalist. In the first place, there were the nationalists who look at Scotland 'through green spectacles' and 'despite a complete lack of historical parallel' manage to 'identify the Irish struggle with their own'. The second category was composed of those 'whose nationalism was a perfectly healthy desire for a better form of Union with England than that which had been freely negotiated in 1707'. This type of nationalist favoured Scottish equality with England within the Union. MacCormick had little affinity for the first type of Scottish nationalist, and was 'glad to say . . . that it is the latter state of mind which, in the long run, has predominated in the National Movement'.[7] MacCormick's personal recollection of nationalist opinion at the time of the merger of

---

[7] John MacCormick, *The flag in the wind* (London, 1955), p. 67.

the Scottish Party and National Party of Scotland to form the SNP was that 'while many of our countrymen were dissatisfied with the state of the Union they desired not to break it up but to reform it'.[8] Notwithstanding MacCormick's sensitivity to the unionist element in early nationalism, Scottish historians have not always gone out of their way to highlight the differences between out-and-out nationalists and those with dual loyalties to their nation and the United Kingdom, or to explore the residual sentimental attachment to the Union which existed even in nationalist circles.

Nor did nationalists in the first half of the twentieth century agree on the need for a separate nationalist party distinct from a cross-party national movement. Whereas some nationalists conceived of the need for a separate political party to advance the aims of Scottish nationalism, others preferred to use pressure groups – such as the Scottish Home Rule Association – as the vehicle for nationalist politics in tandem with support from traditional political parties, such as Labour or the Liberals. Even with the formation of the National Party of Scotland and then the Scottish National Party as party-political embodiments of the nationalist cause, some nationalists continued to regard the NPS and the SNP as pressure groups and continued to enjoy dual membership of the National Party alongside another party-political organisation. Yet both Labour and the Liberals were, in spite of their home rule commitments, ostensibly parties which endorsed the Anglo-Scottish Union. Cross-party ideals continued after the Second World War. MacCormick, the

[8] *Ibid.*, pp. 79–80.

principal begetter of Scottish Convention, an all-party nationalist organisation outside the SNP, was also Vice-Chairman of the Scottish Liberals. In the 1948 Paisley by-election MacCormick stood on a devolutionist platform as a 'National' candidate against Labour's Whitehall centralism, and found his candidacy supported not only by the Liberals but also by the Paisley Unionist Association and by prominent Conservatives such as Peter Thorneycroft and Reginald Manningham-Buller.[9] Curiously, even MacCormick's bête noire, Douglas Young, whose Scottish nationalist zeal was undimmed by the larger world crisis of 1939–45, enjoyed dual membership of the SNP and the Labour party, and left the SNP in 1948, the year the SNP banned dual membership. Nor should we forget the surprising porousness of party politics, including the interplay which existed between the nationalist parties and the Unionist Party and the shared assumptions of hibernophobia, anti-Catholicism and imperialism which, while essential components of inter-war Unionism, also proved influential in certain quarters of the early nationalist movement.

The origins of the national movement

There was no articulate or coherent 'nationalist' movement of any kind in Scotland between the demise of the Jacobite cause in the mid-eighteenth century and the formation of the short-lived National Association for the Vindication of Scottish Rights (1853–6). The NAVSR took its rise in very curious circumstances, from the campaign in 1852 of the antiquary and

[9] *Ibid.*, pp. 120–4.

historical romancer James Grant (1822–87) – supported by his brother John – protesting that England was in breach of the Articles of Union, and in particular that it had shown a cavalier disregard for the laws of heraldry in ways which clearly signalled Scotland's demotion from the status it should have enjoyed under the Treaty of Union. The Grants appealed to the Lord Lyon King of Arms, the chief heraldic officer in Scotland, to complain about irregularities in the quartering of the royal arms and other improprieties in the flying of flags and in the design of the new florin coin. However arcane these matters of heraldry and numismatics now seem, they generated publicity for the Grants' cause, which found institutional embodiment in the NAVSR. The first public meeting of the NAVSR was held in Edinburgh in November 1853 and attracted an attendance of 2,000, soon to be eclipsed the next month when a meeting of the NAVSR in Glasgow drew a crowd of 5,000. The NAVSR was a pressure group, and was beholden to no political party. Indeed, it tended to win much of its following at the extremes of Scottish political culture. Support for the organisation came from various sectors of the Scottish scene – from romantic reactionaries in the mould of the Grants and under the supposed inspiration of their late second cousin Sir Walter Scott, including the Association's President the Earl of Eglinton, who had sponsored the Ivanhoe-ish Eglinton tournament of 1839 and the poet William Edmonstone Aytoun (1813–65), author of *The lays of the Scottish cavaliers* (1848);[10] from Free Churchmen, most prominent among them the Rev.

---

[10] W. E. Aytoun, 'Scotland since the Union', *Blackwood's Magazine* 74 (Sept. 1853), 263–83.

James Begg, disillusioned with the British state's handling of the events which had led up to the Disruption of 1843; and from radical Liberals such as Duncan McLaren (1800–86) and the political theorist Patrick Dove (1815–73). This odd and unstable coalition campaigned on an equally miscellaneous range of issues. The NAVSR argued that Scotland was unduly neglected by the British state compared to the vast amount of attention devoted to Ireland and its problems; that a disproportionate amount of public money was spent in England relative to tax receipts raised in Scotland; that the number of Scottish MPs was too low; that the Scottish Secretaryship should be revived; that the United Kingdom should be known as Great Britain and not as England; and, of course, that Scottish heraldic emblems had been downgraded and ought to be restored to their former prominence.[11]

The NAVSR was typically understood as the distant forerunner of contemporary nationalism, and its somewhat eccentric and half-hearted efforts were viewed generously as a pioneering attempt to raise the issue of Scottish nationhood in a milieu of Victorian complacency, prosperity and empire-building, from which Scotland derived enormous benefit. More recently, Graeme Morton has coined the term 'unionist-nationalism' to describe the ambivalent assortment of proposals which comprised the NAVSR's platform.[12] At bottom,

---

[11] *Justice to Scotland: address to the people of Scotland and statement of grievances by the National Association for the Vindication of Scottish Rights* (Edinburgh, 1853).

[12] G. Morton, *Unionist-nationalism: governing urban Scotland 1830–1860* (East Linton, 1999). See also, G. Morton, 'Scottish rights and

indeed, the NAVSR was a unionist organisation, which stood for a strict construction of the Treaty of Union and an acknowledgement of its spirit as well as its letter. The question of Scottish nationhood only arose because of the perversion of the Union, which had relegated Scotland from a proud position as England's equal in a union of sister kingdoms to a status of mere provinciality within the United Kingdom. However, the repeal of the Union did not feature in the programme of the NAVSR. The basic issue at stake was the equality of Scotland and England within the Union of 1707. In the sphere of symbolic politics, equality meant equality of dignity, whether in armorial bearings or in the casual assumption that England had become a synonym for Britain. In the world of public policy, equality meant proportionate taxation and expenditure across the component parts of the United Kingdom. At no point did the NAVSR agitation evolve into a nationalist critique of the Union itself. Rather criticism was directed at the ways in which the Union had unfolded, in opposition to the fundamental principles of Anglo-Scottish co-partnership which underpinned the Treaty of 1707. The NAVSR expressed the irritation of some sections of Scottish society – a society which was overwhelmingly unionist – at the ways in which Scotland's contribution to the life of the United Kingdom had come to be taken for granted at the state's English core. However, there was no nationalist substance to its proposals. The NAVSR reflected the dominant and unchallenged unionism of mid-nineteenth-century Scotland.

centralisation in the mid-nineteenth century', *Nations and Nationalism* 2 (1996), 257–79.

Ironically, however, nationalism as a political ideal did flourish in mid-nineteenth-century Scotland, but not in the form of Scottish nationalism. Scots were, it transpires, enthusiastic supporters of nationalist movements abroad. Glasgow alone was home to the Glasgow Garibaldi Italian Fund, the Glasgow Polish Association, the Glasgow Polish Committee and the Glasgow Working Men's Garibaldi Committee.[13] The principle of liberal nationality found its way into the hearts – and pockets – of Scots; yet it was not accompanied by any sense that Scots themselves did not enjoy the benefits of liberal nationality. It was part of the curious amnesia which enveloped Scottish political culture in the era of banal unionism that Scots – however solicitous of the suppressed rights of the other historic nationalities of Europe – were not conscious of any shortcomings in their own political status. Contemporary political logic seems to have run as follows: that Scots enjoyed the full rights of liberal nationality as free Britons within a Union of sister kingdoms. Scots were clearly exposed to nationalism and aware of nationalist campaigns in other parts of Europe. Nevertheless, nationalist agitation was a political option mid-nineteenth-century Scots chose not to exercise, except in its most diluted and lukewarm form as a kind of strict unionism.

One of the principal legacies of the short-lived NAVSR was an ongoing concern that the term 'England' had become an all-too-familiar synonym for 'Great Britain' or the 'United

---

[13] See e.g. J. Fyfe, 'Scottish volunteers with Garibaldi', *Scottish Historical Review* 57 (1978), 168–81; J. Fyfe (ed.), *The autobiography of John McAdam* (Scottish History Society 4th ser., 1980).

Kingdom'. Leading the Scots campaign against this abuse was William Burns, a Glasgow solicitor and a leading supporter of the Scottish cause from the rise of the NAVSR in 1853. During the mid-1850s Burns got into a debate with Lord Palmerston about the misleading – and quasi-imperialist – substitution of England for Great Britain. Burns complained that 'by constantly speaking of, and representing, the United Empire, its sovereign and institutions, as English', that England's 'public men' appeared to regard Scottish people not as England's partners in the Union, but as if 'annexed as appendages to England'.[14] Burns revisited this theme in a series of speeches and pamphlets in the following decades, including *What's in a name? Being an inquiry, how far the practice of substituting the name of England for Great Britain, as that of the United Kingdom, is legitimate in itself, or injurious to Scotland*. Others echoed Burns's anxieties. In 1884 the Reverend David Macrae (1837–1907) of the Scottish National Rights Association lamented in his pamphlet *Britain not England: a word on the misuse of our national names* (1884) that even in school histories issued by Scottish publishers the Union appeared 'in the middle of the book as if it were a mere incident in the history of England'.[15] This apparent pedantry about names was indicative of a deeper political problem: that Scots were conscious that the English misunderstood the principles upon which they believed the Union to be founded and, as a result, contemporary English

---

[14] *Letter by a North Briton to Lord Palmerston, as published in the Times of 22nd October 1853* (Glasgow, n.d.), p. 6.

[15] David Macrae, *Britain not England: a word on the misuse of our national names* (1884), p. 6.

politicians and journalists had little appreciation of Scotland's proper status within a union of equals. Was Scotland treated as a sister kingdom of England, or looked down upon as a subordinate province?

Notwithstanding the emergence of this type of anti-English grievance, late nineteenth-century Scottish nationalism did not arise out of a profound sense of difference from England as an ethnic other. Ironically, indeed, some early nationalists appeared to be complaining about anglicisation as a trend which threatened to dilute the existing Englishness of the Scottish Lowland character. In an article entitled 'Scotland's version of home rule' W. Scott Dalgleish argued that

> [t]he union was not contracted between two nations of different race, but between two nations of the same race, speaking the same language, professing the same Protestant faith, and having political institutions of the same kind. The Scots who were then the dominant race in Scotland were not Celtic Scots, but were English Scots, in some respects more English than the English themselves.

Both nations had emerged from a 'common nursery', the old Anglian kingdom of Northumbria, which had stretched across much of northern England and Lowland Scotland, from the Humber to the Forth. Although the later middle ages had witnessed an 'estrangement' between the two Anglian nations of England and Scotland, Dalgleish contended that this alienation had in fact preserved the Anglian character of the Scottish Lowlands, meaning that 'the mass of the English-speaking population north of the Tweed were more purely English than their southern kindred'. Ironically, the post-1707 anglicisation of Scotland, he believed, was diluting the Anglian character of the Scottish nation. Dalgleish hoped to preserve Scottish nationality by way of some new machinery of governance, though without 'impairing or imperilling the feeling of loyalty to the imperial centre'.[16]

When a campaign for Scottish home rule first emerged during the 1880s, it arose in large measure as a response – a somewhat ambiguous response, as we shall see – to the campaign for Irish home rule and as an offshoot of concerns about the future consolidation of the British Empire. Many Scots home rulers took the view that devolving the governance of the home countries to domestic home rule parliaments would enhance the capabilities of the Westminster legislature as an effective imperial parliament. For some, indeed, Scottish home rule was part of a wider project of imperial federation. Generally, Scottish home rule was envisaged as a pillar of a revitalised British Empire. The consolidation of a far-flung Empire might entail a new distribution of domestic responsibilities within the British mother countries.

Indeed imperial issues constituted one of the central pillars of the Scottish Home Rule Association, a pressure group which was created in 1886, whose connections lay largely with advanced liberalism. The four objects of the Association were:

> To foster the national sentiment of Scotland, and to maintain her national rights and honour.

> To promote the establishment of a legislature, sitting in Scotland, with full control over all purely Scottish

[16] W. Scott Dalgleish, 'Scotland's version of home rule', *Nineteenth Century* 13 (1883), 14–26.

questions, and with an executive government responsible to it and the Crown.

To secure to the government of Scotland, in the same degree as is at present possessed by the Imperial Parliament, the control of her civil servants, judges, and other officials, with the exception of those engaged in the naval, military and diplomatic services, and in collecting the imperial revenue.

To maintain the integrity of the Empire, and secure that the voice of Scotland shall be heard in the Imperial Parliament as fully as at present when discussing Imperial affairs.[17]

The SHRA, which had links with the Federal Union League for the British Empire, stood as much for 'the integrity' of the British peoples as it did for the special status of Scotland within this ensemble. In particular, home rulers prized decentralisation as a means of preserving the unity of a growing Empire. The imperial parliament, it appeared, had become congested, and was unable to take proper account of the affairs of the four home nations in addition to the business of the Empire. William Jacks (1841–1907), a one-time Liberal MP for Leith, argued that home rule would release time and energy in the imperial parliament, which might then become the 'nucleus for a great federation of the Anglo-Saxon or British race'.[18] As John Kendle has argued, Scottish home rulers tended to

---

[17] *Scottish Home Rule Association objects* (Edinburgh, 1892?).
[18] William Jacks, *The House of Lords and federal home rule* (Glasgow, 1889), p. 18.

be 'more concerned with relieving parliamentary congestion than realizing a national dream'.[19] Sometimes, indeed, in home rule rhetoric of the 1880s and 1890s it seems as if a devolved parliament was valued less as an end in itself than as a means to preserve the cohesion of the Empire. Indeed, contemporaries argued there was a logical connection between federation of the Empire and federation of the home countries of the British Isles.

The first wave of Scottish home rulers insisted on their unionist credentials. William Mitchell, the Treasurer of the SHRA, insisted that it was 'a mistake to suppose that the Union with England was not in many ways an advantage to Scotland. All that is maintained by Scottish home rulers is that the same advantages might have been obtained without sacrificing the inestimable benefits of self-government by Scotland in its own domestic affairs.' Unlike many modern Scottish nationalists who invoke the Wars of Independence as a golden age of active Scottish nationality, Mitchell proclaimed that the 'crowning blessing of the Union was the termination of the disastrous wars which had so long desolated both kingdoms'. Nevertheless, he thought that the Union ought not to have been on incorporating lines, but ought to have preserved a legislature in Scotland responsible for domestic matters, which would work in tandem with a parliament at Westminster charged with 'common and imperial purposes'. Indeed, Mitchell envisaged home rule working in tandem with imperial federation for the greater of the whole British Empire. He denied, moreover, that

---

[19] J. Kendle, *Ireland and the federal solution: the debate over the United Kingdom, 1870–1921* (Kingston and Montreal, 1989), p. 68.

home rule was a 'centrifugal' force.[20] Similarly, Charles Waddie, the secretary of the SHRA and author of *The federation of Greater Britain* (1895), favoured 'a true British parliament' for the Empire as 'the guardian of the interests of the whole dominions of the crown'. Despite Waddie's use of the language of federation, what he envisaged was in fact a scheme of devolution across the Empire – both within the British Isles and overseas – under the ultimate sovereign authority of the British crown-in-parliament: 'The constitution of every state under the crown being statutory, parliaments are its own creation, and what it made it can unmake. If any of the colonies or home countries overstepped the delegation, they would be called to order by this supreme tribunal.'[21] Home rule was, if anything, a symptom of creative imperialism, a desire to rethink the institutions of a global empire and attendant responsibilities acquired in a fit of absentmindedness. With great plausibility, B. D. Mackenzie, a Vice-President of the SHRA, invoked Scots imperialist sentiment to deny the charge of separatism directed at home rulers, arguing that Scots had invested too much effort in 'building up' the British Empire to sacrifice any share in 'its honour and glory'.[22] Indeed, it is worth noting the activities of the SHRA were part of a wider culture of imperial reform in late nineteenth-century Scotland, which was not confined to home rulers, but rather whose agenda home rulers reflected

---

[20] William Mitchell, *Home rule for Scotland and imperial federation* (Edinburgh, 1892), pp. 18–19, 79; William Mitchell, *Seven years of home rule legislation* (Edinburgh, 1893?), p. 9.

[21] Charles Waddie, *The federation of Greater Britain* (Edinburgh, 1895), pp. 3–4.

[22] B. D. Mackenzie, *Home rule for Scotland* (Edinburgh, 1890), p. 15.

in their own campaigns. A Scot – Lord Rosebery, the future Liberal Prime Minister – was President of the Imperial Federation League, set up in 1884 to consider strengthening the bonds of the Empire by way of wide-ranging imperial reform, and Rosebery also served as President of the Edinburgh Unity of the Empire Association, which flourished during the late 1890s.[23]

It is also highly significant that much of the intellectual energy behind the case for Scottish home rule came from Scots with Australian backgrounds. Two Scots-Australians stand out for the vigour of their advocacy of the Scottish home rule cause, Thomas Drummond Wanliss, a publisher from Ballarat in Victoria, and Theodore Napier, the Treasurer of the Scottish National Association of Victoria. Wanliss, who had been born in Perth and had strong connections with Dundee and Edinburgh, was active in Australian politics not only as proprietor of the *Ballarat Star*, but also as a politician, sitting for five years as a representative on the Victoria Legislative Council. Back in Scotland Wanliss became the publisher of *The Thistle*, a nationalist journal published in Edinburgh between 1909 and 1918. Napier was born in Australia and owned land there, but had been educated in Scotland. Napier was introduced to Scottish nationalist politics by Wanliss, and their early works shared a similar imperialist outlook on the predicament of Scotland and

---

[23] See e.g. Robert Lockhart, *Closer union with the colonies* (Edinburgh, Edinburgh Unity of the Empire Association, 1898); *Edinburgh Unity of the Empire Association Report of the Executive Committee for the year ending March 1898*. Cf. D. S. Forsyth, 'Empire and union: imperial and national identity in nineteenth-century Scotland', *Scottish Geographical Magazine* 113 (1997), 6–12.

the potential for home rule. However, Napier later struck out on his own and his nationalism developed in a Jacobite direction. Eventually he became secretary of the Legitimist Jacobite League of Great Britain and Ireland and started up an eccentric Jacobite magazine, *The Fiery Cross.*

Whatever the oddities of his later Jacobitism, Napier started out as a more conventional supporter of imperial federation. Napier argued that Australia enjoyed the benefits of a form of 'local national self-government under the crown', and Scotland too should enjoy the benefits of a similar measure of local self-government. At this stage of his career Napier was no nationalist. Indeed, he presented home rulers as the true unionists; for he termed those who opposed home rule as 'pseudo-unionists'. 'In no sense', argued Napier, does home rule 'imply separation from the united body'.[24] Napier was a key organiser of the petition to the Queen launched in 1897 which called for a strict observance of Article I of the Union. The 'general and continuous use of the terms "England" and "English" in an imperial sense [was] a direct aggression on the national honour of Scotland', for such usage implied that Scotland was merely a 'province' of England. There were also imperial implications, for 'national sentiment' – whether English, Scots or Irish – was one of the principal bonds of Empire: yet 'this unjust and unconstitutional attempt to anglicise the United Kingdom, and to make England and Englishmen the sole representatives of British power and of the British name, must necessarily

---

[24] Theodore Napier, *Scotland's demand for home rule or local national self-government: an appeal to Scotsmen in Australia* (Melbourne, 1892), pp. 5, 11.

have a more injurious effect on the all-important question of unity between Britain and Further Britain, or Britain-beyond-the-seas'.[25] It mattered greatly to the Scottish diaspora that the Empire was genuinely British. Wanliss too was a convinced opponent of 'Anglo-Jingoism', the assumption that the Empire was English and that Scotland too was simply an acquisition of the English imperial crown. According to Wanliss, the modern school of English historians – Freeman, Green and Seeley – had presented the history of the Empire as part of the ongoing expansion of England's 'imperial race' since the Saxon era. Oblivious of empire as an Anglo-Scottish partnership, these historians had traced the beginnings of empire back to the English absorption of the subordinate nations of the home countries. In this light, Wanliss interpreted the 'home rule cry' not as a demand for 'the separate and individual sovereignty of Ireland, Scotland and Wales', but as a plea for 'the restraint of a usurping and unjust English sovereignty of these nationalities'. Home rule governments within the home countries would help to restore the Britishness of the Empire. Here the complaints of Wanliss – against English rather than against British imperialism – were in substance indistinguishable from those of the unionist critics of the English imperial crown discussed in chapter 3, and serve as a reminder that several core arguments featured on both sides of the supposed ideological divide between Scottish 'unionism' and 'nationalism'.[26]

[25] *The petition to Her Majesty the Queen from her Scottish subjects* (Edinburgh, 1897), p. 6.

[26] T. D. Wanliss, *The bars to British unity or a plea for national sentiment* (Edinburgh, 1885), esp. pp. 105, 118, 164–72; Wanliss, *A colonial view of home rule* (Dundee and Ballarat, 1890), p. 7.

The SHRA was also a by-product of domestic issues. In particular, Scottish home rulers resented the vast amount of attention lavished on the question of Irish home rule. Scottish home rulers rejected Gladstone's 'lop-sided'[27] approach to Irish home rule. Mitchell contended that 'Home Rule cannot be given to Ireland alone without inflicting injustice on Scotland', and even expressed some sympathy for the Unionists, because their rejection of home rule for Ireland alone was not so far out of step with the position of the SHRA.[28] The SHRA favoured home rule all round, whether through a wholesale plan of devolution or a federal reorganisation of the United Kingdom. Waddie complained that home rule for Ireland alone was not a sensible way forward for reforming the obvious defects in the machinery of British government. He denounced the selfishness of the Irish for frustrating the essential reform of home rule all round without which imperial federation was an impossibility.[29] A further factor which energised the SHRA was the cause of Scottish church disestablishment, another issue which rose to prominence in the 1880s and was, in fact, a much bigger concern to late nineteenth-century Scottish Liberals than the question of devolution for Scotland. Nevertheless, progressive Liberals in Scotland tended to favour both home rule and the disestablishment of the Church of Scotland; but the relationship between these two positions was far from straightforward. Scottish home rulers insisted

---

[27] William Mitchell, *The political situation in Scotland* (Edinburgh, 1893), p. 3.
[28] *Ibid.*, p. 7.   [29] Waddie, *Federation*, p. 2.

that the British parliament had no authority to disestablish the Scottish church, an issue which could only properly be dealt with by a devolved Scottish legislature.

In 1900 – in the wake of a general election defeat – Scottish Liberals established the Young Scots Society to inculcate in 'young men' the core principles of Liberalism.[30] The Young Scots Society was from the outset on the radical wing of Liberalism, and it was active on behalf of land reform and social issues. These were the primary concerns of the Young Scots, but Scottish home rule also came to claim their attention. However, the Young Scots disavowed any attention of undermining the Union. Rather, they asserted, their aim was to 'make the Union complete and impregnable'.

> Modern Scottish Home Rulers do not propose to repeal the Treaty of Union. They do not even propose to repeal Article III, under which the ancient sovereign parliament of Scotland came to an end. They simply propose to extend the Treaty of Union by creating subordinate national parliaments for the two contracting countries. This will make the Union more harmonious and more beneficial, by removing causes of friction, and leaving the two countries free to work out their national development under a common flag.

Indeed, the Young Scots, like the SHRA before them, viewed the question of Scottish home rule largely as a dimension of a wider vision for reform of the Empire as a whole.

---

[30] For the Young Scots Society, see R. Finlay, *A partnership for good? Scottish politics and the Union since 1880* (Edinburgh, 1997), pp. 52–61.

'Home Rule', proclaimed the Young Scots Society, 'is true imperialism.' The safeguarding of nationality within the home countries was in fact a necessary step towards a more efficient and resilient Empire. The Young Scots argued that '[I]n the interests of the four nations separately, of the United Kingdom as a whole, and of the Empire, all-round devolution is imperatively required.' Their aim was what they called a 'Home Rule Empire', to be achieved by adding 'a British Federation to the other great federations within the Empire'. After all, the Young Scots argued, Nova Scotia, which had half the population of Glasgow, already had 'full control of its own affairs under the dominion of Canada', while 'Old Scotland' itself lacked self-government.[31]

The rise of nationalist parties

During the inter-war era Scottish nationalism retained an imperialist hue. In October 1918 the Scottish Home Rule Association was re-founded by Roland Muirhead (1868–1964), a former Young Scot and now a Labour supporter. The revival of the SHRA was inspired in part by contemporary international principles of self-determination, but the organisation also bore the traditional stamp of the earlier SHRA, particularly with regard to the importance of the Empire and a wariness about outright separatism. Indeed, in 1920 the Scots National League was formed by anti-imperialists in reaction

---

[31] *Sixty points for Scottish home rule* (Young Scots Society, Glasgow, 1912), pp. 8–10, 29.

to the imperial – and unionist – character of the revived SHRA. As Richard Finlay has shown, inter-war nationalism was riven by disputes over the future of the British Empire and Scotland's place in it.[32] On one extreme stood outright anti-imperialists, but there were also many nationalists who expressed a positive vision of the Empire, but differed over the nature of Scotland's contribution to the imperial project. Would Scotland become an autonomous dominion within the Empire like Canada or Australia or would Scotland acquire a parliament for domestic affairs only, while continuing to look to Westminster in imperial and foreign policy matters? Another alternative envisaged a Scottish parliament sharing in the overall direction of the Anglo-Scottish Empire with an English parliament. Most nationalists aimed at the restoration of Scottish nationhood within the British Empire and valued the continuation of some form of connection with England. In his pamphlet *Albyn* (1927) Christopher Murray Grieve (the real name of the stridently nationalist and otherwise anglophobic poet Hugh MacDiarmid) made the case for Scottish nationalism within the framework of a 'British Association of Free Peoples'. Grieve insisted that '[t]he Scottish Home Rule demand is . . . strictly in accord with the very life-spirit of the Empire'. Adherence to a bland uniformity across the Empire was, by contrast, 'anti-Imperial'. The Empire would only flourish, Grieve argued, by way of the encouragement of a diversity-in-unity.[33]

---

[32] Finlay, 'For or against?'.
[33] C. M. Grieve, *Albyn, or Scotland and the future* (London, 1927), pp. 59–60.

In 1928 the National Party of Scotland was formed out of the coalescence of the SHRA, the Scots National League, the Scottish National Movement and the Glasgow University Scottish Nationalist Association, whose driving force was an energetic law student, John MacCormick.[34] The establishment of a separate party to advance the cause of Scottish nationalism was not a sign of the rising expectations of the Scottish nationalist movement. Rather it was a sign of failure. Neither the Liberals nor Labour had been sufficiently committed to the home rule cause, and a number of Scottish home rule bills had flopped. Thus a number of Scottish home rulers had come to the conclusion that a separate nationalist party needed to be formed. Pressure groups were not enough in themselves to see the job done. The NPS advocated 'independent national status within the British group of nations', promoting the ideal of '[s]elf-government for Scotland on a basis which will enable Scotland as a partner in the British Empire with the same status as England to develop its national life to the fullest advantage'. In practice, what the NPS aimed at was dominion status for Scotland, similar to that accorded Canada or Australia. The NPS immediately adopted a vigorous imperial policy, under the influence of Tom Gibson. Although a convinced nationalist who rejected home rule as an unacceptable half-way house, Gibson nonetheless wanted to assert the rights of an independent Scottish nation to a role in the governance of the Anglo-Scottish Empire that it had helped to create.

[34] R. Finlay, *Independent and free: Scottish politics and the origins of the Scottish National Party 1918–1945* (Edinburgh, 1994), pp. 76–7.

On 17 November 1928 the NPS policy committee adopted a resolution that

> The party, having regard to the large contribution made by Scotland in building up the British Empire, is desirous of increasing the interest of the Scottish nation in the affairs of the Empire to the extent her contribution warrants and, as a Mother Nation, thereby demands complete recognition of her rights as such in that Empire... The Party cannot, in these circumstances agree to acquiesce in any situation that does not permit of a Mother Nation exercising her right to independent status and her right to partnership in that Empire on terms equal to that enjoyed by England.[35]

The idea that Scotland was a mother nation of the Empire enjoyed considerable currency in nationalist circles, not only within the ranks of the NPS; nor did it consistently lead to demands for dominion status for Scotland.

Such ideas held a certain attraction for Lord Beaverbrook (1879–1964), the Scots Canadian press magnate. Born a son of the presbyterian manse in New Brunswick, Beaverbrook had a keen sense of his Scottish heritage and of belonging to the wider Empire, manifested in his sponsorship of Empire Free Trade. In 1932 Beaverbrook also took up the cause of Scottish nationalism, using the Scottish *Daily Express* as a vehicle for a blend of populist imperialism and Scots home rule and forging close and enduring links with MacCormick.

---

[35] Quoted in Brand, *National movement in Scotland*, p. 201.

Beaverbrook's secretary, personal adviser and occasional ghost-writer, George Malcolm Thomson (1899–1996), was himself an influential proponent of Scottish nationalism.[36] In *The kingdom of Scotland restored* Thomson made the case for a return to a renegotiated treaty of Union which would be centred almost exclusively on the monarchy, as in the Union of the Crowns. The contemporary nationalist call for dominion status was an insult as far as Thomson was concerned: 'A dominion is a promoted colony; Scotland is a historic kingdom.' His aim was instead to restore Scotland to its rightful status as one of the historic kingdoms of Europe. Of course, due recognition should be paid, Thomson believed, to Scotland's imperial role – but the conferment of dominion status would serve only to obscure Scotland's role as a mother nation of the British Empire. What was needed was a declaration of Scottish national sovereignty to be followed immediately by a new Treaty with England defining the future scope of Anglo-Scottish relations. Thomson envisaged 'a union of two equal partners, two kingdoms united in a dual monarchy'. Scotland would benefit from having a viceroy – if possible drawn from the royal house – who would serve as the representative of the 'common sovereign'. While Scotland would run its own domestic affairs, matters of defence, foreign policy and, most importantly, crown colonies and dependencies, would be the joint responsibility of the Anglo-Scottish dual monarchy. Given the scale of the Scottish populations in Canada, Australia, New Zealand and South Africa, Thomson believed, 'Anglo-Scottish

[36] A. J. P. Taylor, *Beaverbrook* (London, 1972), p. 340; Brand, *National movement*, p. 217.

dual control' of the Empire would enhance the functioning of an increasingly federalised empire.[37]

In a similar vein Andrew Dewar Gibb – a close ally of Thomson's – would argue in *Scottish Empire* (1937) that Britain had been little more than England's 'alias' when it came to the direction of the Empire. Nonetheless, this was an empire which Scotsmen as individuals had helped to build, even if the post-1707 'province' of Scotland had been excluded from its proper role in the making of imperial policy. This was a pity. Notwithstanding the fact that Scotland 'was giving lavishly in men and money' to the imperial project,

> she was permitted to give nothing of her institutions, her law, or her administrative system, and in many cases even her church was but grudgingly admitted on a footing little higher than that of a dissenting conventicle. In some colonies the law of Scotland might have found ready acceptance, being simple and more nearly related to widely accepted principles than the law of England. It has been received nowhere in the Empire.

Gibb lamented the absence of any 'real dualism' within the Union of 1707. Gibb, like Thomson, favoured a 'real union' or personal union between Scotland and England, on the model of the dual monarchies found in the Swedo-Norwegian state before 1905 and in Austria-Hungary after 1867. However, that had not been the basis of the Anglo-Scottish Union. Thus the Scots were only able to participate within an essentially English

[37] G. M. Thomson, *The kingdom of Scotland restored* (London, n.d. [1930/1]), pp. 13–16.

empire in a 'subordinate' role. Yet Gibb was at pains to refute any suggestion that the Scots were unfit to rule the Empire, for the empire-building Scots had shown themselves 'no less fit to rule than any of the imperial peoples since time began'. The nationalism of the 1930s was to a large extent the nationalism of an imperial nation manqué.[38]

Although Thomson remained aloof from partisan involvement, he encouraged Gibb's involvement with a right-wing nationalist offshoot from Scottish Unionism, the Scottish Self-Government Party, better known as the Scottish Party. One of the two constituent elements of the SNP, along with the NPS, the Scottish Party was at bottom an imperial reform party, interested for example in Beaverbrook's project for Empire Free Trade. It saw the Scottish Question largely as a means towards the further reordering of the British Empire. The Scottish Party originated out of a split in the Cathcart Unionist Association on the south side of Glasgow. Under the leadership of Kevin MacDowall, a Glasgow solicitor and chairman of the Imperial Committee of the Cathcart Unionists, these dissident Unionists broke away from their party over the twin issues of Empire and Scottish home rule. They were able to gather various Scottish notables to their standard, including Gibb, the Duke of Montrose and Sir Alexander MacEwan, whose *The thistle and the rose* was published in 1932.[39] The new party had a certain populist appeal, and England was not the main target of right-wing nationalist abuse. Gibb's *Scotland in eclipse*, published in 1932, had blamed the Union for Scotland's Irish problem,

---

[38] Andrew Dewar Gibb, *Scottish Empire* (London, 1937), pp. 5, 311–12, 315.
[39] Finlay, *Independent and free*, ch. 3.

arguing that the Union had deprived Scotland of the capacity to control immigration. Moreover, MacDowall was obsessed with imperial issues, and primarily saw Scottish home rule as a stage in the much-needed reform of the Empire and its institutions. However, the Scottish Party stopped short of promoting dominion status, and instead favoured only legislative home rule in domestic matters alongside a continuing Union, with the British parliament responsible for defence, overseas and imperial affairs.

Thus by 1932 there were two Scottish nationalist parties, the NPS on the left and the Scottish Party on the right. Electoral mathematics dictated co-operation, at the very least, for the story of the NPS had been a saga of lost deposits and there was scarcely room for one nationalist party in Scottish politics. The Kilmarnock by-election of 1933 held out an opportunity for the two nationalist parties to work together for their common interests. In the autumn of 1933 the NPS and the Scottish Party issued a joint statement of principles which underpinned their immediate collaboration in the by-election, and also presaged their eventual merger as a single party, the Scottish National Party, the following year. This joint statement called for a Scottish parliament for Scottish affairs, argued against the introduction of any tariffs between Scotland and England, conceded that imperial, defence and foreign affairs would be matters of joint concern for Scotland and England, and insisted that there should 'only be such future modification or revision of the Act of Union as is necessary to achieve these foregoing objects'.[40] At the founding of the

---

[40] Quoted in MacCormick, *Flag in the wind*, p. 85.

SNP imperial issues loomed as large as national concerns. Sir Alexander MacEwan's election address in the Kilmarnock by-election noted that 'Scotland has responsibilities towards the Empire which with England she helped to create.'[41]

Agreement on a merger was reached in January 1934, and approved by the NPS in February and the Scottish Party in March. The agreed principles on which the merger took place enshrined the values of nationalism, unionism and imperialism:

> (1) The establishment of a Parliament in Scotland which shall be the final authority on all Scottish affairs, including taxation and finance;
>
> (2) Scotland shall share with England the rights and responsibilities they, as mother nations, have jointly created and incurred within the British Empire;
>
> (3) Scotland and England shall set up machinery to deal jointly with these responsibilities, and in particular to deal with such matters as defence, foreign policy, and customs;
>
> (4) It is believed that these principles can be realised only by a Scottish National Party independent of all other political parties.[42]

The Scottish National Party came into being in April 1934 as a vehicle not only for national aspirations, but also with the avowed intent of establishing Scotland as an acknowledged

---

[41] Finlay, 'For or against?', 199.
[42] Mitchell, *Strategies for self-government*, pp. 182–3. See also Finlay, *Independent and free*, p. 153.

'mother nation' of the Empire alongside England. Unsurprisingly, the terms of merger alienated some of the more extreme nationalists in the NPS and provoked departures from the party. However, in the short run the loss of these hardliners helped to ease the amalgamation of the conservative Scottish Party imperialists with the moderate core of the NPS.

Nevertheless, MacDowall left the SNP in 1935, disillusioned by the lack of support for his imperial vision, which was his primary motivation in politics.[43] The withdrawal of MacDowall and his supporters saw the SNP lurch away from imperialism towards pacifism and neutrality, a position which led to a further secession of moderates from the party in 1942 when the party elected as its leader Douglas Young, a noted conscientious objector. Yet still the siren song of the Treaty of Union – or at least the possibilities it afforded of impossibly strict construction or decidedly mischievous misinterpretation – seduced even the most anglophobic of Scottish nationalists.

Young was a charismatic figure, six feet five inches tall and bearded. A classicist, he lectured at Aberdeen from 1938 to 1941, and later at Dundee (1947–53) and St Andrews (1953–68), before becoming a Professor at McMaster University in Ontario, and then at the University of North Carolina. Young would achieve a measure of literary renown for his translations of some of the comedies of Aristophanes into broad Scots, or Lallans, notably with *The Puddocks* and *The Burdies*. Young's refusal to perform military service led to his conviction on 23 April 1942 for contravention of the National Service Act of

---

[43] Finlay, *Independent and free*, pp. 175–7.

1941. He appealed to the High Court of Justiciary on 9 July 1942, on the grounds that the National Service Act was contrary to the Treaty of Union. After serving a period of imprisonment, Young was released in 1943 and later called up for industrial conscription under the Defence (General) Regulations of 1939. Again, he declined to serve and was tried at Paisley Sheriff Court on 12 June 1944. His appeal on 6 October 1944 to the Justiciary Appeal Court contended – unsuccessfully – that the Defence Regulations set out under the auspices of the Emergency Powers (Defence) Act (1939) were inconsistent with Article XVIII of the Treaty of Union. This Article prohibited any 'alteration' in 'laws which concern private right' in Scotland, 'except for evident utility of the subjects within Scotland'. Young therefore insisted that the onus was on his prosecutors to prove 'that this invasion of my liberty was for the evident utility of the subjects within Scotland'. Young's argument was to all intents and purposes a unionist argument. He argued that the Treaty of Union was the 'governing constitution' of the United Kingdom, that all Acts contrary to the terms of the Treaty were *ultra vires* and that the Treaty had not bestowed 'omnipotence' on the Westminster parliament. Young's nationalism took the form of a strict construction of the Treaty of Union. The Union of 1707 was the 'constituent law' of the United Kingdom, and 'no provision was made for amending the Articles of Union, precisely because they were intended to be valid in all time coming', regardless of the somewhat pressing circumstances of the Second World War.[44] There

---

[44] Douglas Young, *An appeal to Scots honour: a vindication of the right of the Scottish people to freedom from industrial conscription and bureaucratic*

is also a further irony to consider here, for it was Lord Cooper, whose *obiter dicta* in *MacCormick* v. *Lord Advocate* (1953) would later open up the constitutional status of the Treaty of Union, who in 1944 found Young's arguments to be groundless. Ironically, Cooper's reasoning in 1953 bears more than a superficial resemblance to the arguments of Young which he rejected out of hand in 1944, albeit in vastly different circumstances.

The rise of pacifism within the SNP led to the withdrawal of moderates led by John MacCormick who found the position of Young and his supporters misguided and unrealistic. MacCormick and his allies founded a new nationalist organisation – Scottish Convention – as a campaigning vehicle for a Scottish parliament within the framework of the United Kingdom. Scottish Convention favoured the establishment of a domestic Scottish legislature to tackle Scotland's social and economic problems. On the other hand, it was resolutely opposed to separatism or the idea of a Scottish republic. Scottish Convention's ultimate goal, according to MacCormick, was a 'free Scotland in a federal United Kingdom'. In 1949 Scottish Convention launched a massive petition, the Scottish Covenant, which gained around two million signatures. Its signatories pledged themselves 'in all loyalty to the Crown, and within the framework of the United Kingdom, to do everything in our power to secure for Scotland a Parliament with adequate legislative authority in Scottish affairs'.[45] Yet, although as a moderate nationalist MacCormick acknowledged the Treaty

despotism under the Treaty of Union with England (n.p., 1944/5), pp. 1–5, 9, 18–21, 28, 30.

[45] Quoted in Webb, *Growth of nationalism*, p. 65.

of Union as 'the foundation stone of the British Constitution', he found the document 'lacking in self-consistency'.[46]

Indeed, MacCormick developed his own distinctive interpretation of the Union and the place of the British parliament within it. He contended that the constitutional traditions of Scotland and England differed radically. Whereas the Norman Conquest of England had placed the kings of England above the law, Scotland had never been conquered and, as a result, sovereignty had been retained by the wider community of the realm. Indeed, the existence in the independent Scottish kingdom of the custom of desuetude, whereby unpopular statutes lapsed if the people as a whole declined to adhere to them, seemed compelling evidence for popular invalidation of the will of the Scots parliament. Sovereignty in Scotland, MacCormick contended, resided with the people. If the parliament of Scotland 'had always been subject to the ultimate sanction of community assent', and had held 'no sovereign powers itself', then, he argued, it had not possessed the authority to 'convey', by way of the Union 'sovereign powers to its successor the Parliament of the United Kingdom'. MacCormick was unable to see how the Scots parliament could 'by any conceivable rule of law create a new institution with powers wider than its own'. Nor, as Scottish constitutional history differed significantly from English constitutional history, was there any reason to assume that British constitutional law was a simple matter of assuming the continuity of pre-1707 English practice. Furthermore, MacCormick insisted that the framers of the Treaty had

---

[46] John MacCormick, *Scottish Convention: an experiment in Scottish democracy* (Glasgow, 1943), p. 11.

made a clear distinction 'between the things that were to endure in all time as utterly binding and the more temporal provisions which circumstance might later alter'. The Union did indeed constitute a fundamental law of the British state. MacCormick concluded that the British parliament was limited in its authority in two ways, for it 'could not enjoy any greater powers than the parliament of Scotland' and it was also 'limited by the entrenched clauses in the Treaty which had created it'.[47] Similarly, it was this belief in the true principles of Union and his keen sensitivity to the constitutional anomalies ignored by the Diceyans which inspired MacCormick's intervention in the royal numerals case. The new royal style of Queen Elizabeth II was a manifest absurdity, given that the only previous Queen Elizabeth in either England or Scotland had preceded the Union of the Crowns, never mind the Union of 1707. Post-Union Britain, MacCormick wished to remind Britons, was not a simple continuation of the pre-Union English state.

The Union and the modern SNP

MacCormick stood at the limits of an older tradition of nationalism whose primary aim was not to do away with the Union, but to achieve a better – because less restrictive – Union, including a wider overhaul of the British Empire. The post-1942 SNP distanced itself from its imperialist and quasi-unionist provenance in the inter-war era. Nationalist ideology was no longer a special kind of reformist unionism. Independence supplanted domestic home rule as the dominant characteristic

---

[47] MacCormick, *Flag in the wind*, pp. 188–90.

of Scottish nationalism, while the aim of negotiating a looser association with England metamorphosed into the goal of ending the English connection altogether. Nevertheless, nationalists continued to obsess over a strict construction of the Union of 1707, whose legitimacy they otherwise rejected. Nationalists, notwithstanding their conversion to separatist policies, continued to take the Union more seriously than unionists, at least until the emergence of a more strident unionism in the late 1980s.

A pedantic constitutionalism continued to be a noted feature of nationalist campaigning, most famously the claim that the Scottish parliament had only been adjourned – not dissolved – in 1707, and might therefore be recalled, an argument reiterated by Winnie Ewing MSP at the opening of the new Scottish parliament in 1999.[48] However, there was also considerable substance to nationalist engagement with the Union and the British constitution. The central exponent of the nationalist interpretation of the Union state has been Sir Neil Mac-Cormick, the son of John MacCormick, who has some claim to being the most sophisticated and incisive of late twentieth-century Scotland's cadre of pioneering analytic unionists. Neil MacCormick was appointed Regius Professor of Public Law at Edinburgh in 1972, and has subsequently contested various seats on behalf of the SNP – Edinburgh North in 1979, Edinburgh Pentlands in 1983 and 1987, and Argyll and Bute in 1992 and 1997 – and served as an MEP between 1999 and 2004. In a series of incisive books and articles, MacCormick has interrogated traditional understandings of parliamentary

---

[48] Ewing, *Stop the world*, p. 291.

sovereignty and has also explored the anomalous features of the British constitution. He argues that the British constitution is to be found – albeit in rudimentary and highly minimalist form – in the Union of 1707. MacCormick's restatement of parliamentary sovereignty in the light that the Union state actually possesses a written constitution is that 'Whatever the Queen in Parliament enacts, unless in derogation from the justiciable limits set by the Articles of Union, is law.'[49]

Nevertheless, the conversion of the SNP in 1988 from a position of outright independence to a revised aim of 'Independence in Europe'[50] serves as a reminder that since its emergence in the second half of the nineteenth century the Scottish nationalist tradition has less frequently stood for separation and total independence than some form of supra-national association whether with England, the British Empire or the European Union.[51]

---

[49] MacCormick, 'Does the United Kingdom have a constitution?', 11.

[50] See Jim Sillars, 'Independence in Europe' (1989), in L. Paterson (ed.), *A diverse assembly: the debate on a Scottish parliament* (Edinburgh, 1998), pp. 196–204.

[51] A vein of unionism – indebted not to the 1707 Union but to the earlier Union of the Crowns of 1603 – seems to persist in the SNP. See the 'national conversation' initiated by the minority SNP Executive in Scotland after the election of 2007, *Choosing Scotland's future: a national conversation* (Scottish Executive, August 2007), esp. 3.4 (p. 19), 3.15 (p. 22) and – most explicitly – at 3.25 (p. 24): 'On independence Her Majesty the Queen would remain the Head of State in Scotland. The current parliamentary and political Union of Great Britain and Northern Ireland would become a monarchical and social Union – United Kingdoms rather than a United Kingdom – maintaining a relationship first forged in 1603 by the Union of the Crowns.'

8

Conclusion

Several important – and surprising – conclusions emerge from this study of the Scottish unionist tradition. In the first place, it should be clear that the subject under investigation is not the singular phenomenon of unionism, but the various unionisms in which Scots have historically articulated their wish for some form of association with England. Scottish unionist political thought is not reducible to an unambiguous ideological position shared by all unionists. Nor, for that matter, is Scottish nationalism easily reduced to a basic core doctrine of national independence. Indeed, one of the most curious findings of this study is that, for the most part, Scottish political argument has long been conducted in the vast yet variegated terrain which constitutes the middle ground between the extremes of anglicising unionism and anglophobic nationalism. While there is a huge gulf between the most extreme forms of unionism and nationalism, the most influential forms of unionism have been tinged with nationalist considerations, while the mainstream of nationalism has tended to favour some form of wider association with England, whether in a looser union, a federated empire or as a partner within the European Union. At the heart of this study is an awareness of the ways in which political unionism co-existed in Scotland with certain forms of Scottish national consciousness, most particularly a decidedly non-Anglican, sometimes defiantly anti-Anglican, Scots presbyterian churchmanship. Nor should we forget the emergence of Scots legal nationalism in the second half of the twentieth century, which not only flourished in conjunction with political unionism but was inspired by jurists with connections to the Unionist Party.

The provenance of Scottish unionism provides another surprising feature of this study. Unionism did not originate in response to the Union; nor, indeed, did it emerge in the aftermath of the earlier Union of the Crowns in 1603, or even as the by-product of an English determination to unite Britain. Far from being an offshoot of an English stem, unionism was an indigenous growth, whose flowering can be traced back to the early sixteenth century, eighty years before the Union of the Crowns. Unionist ideology emerged in conscious reaction to the vision of Britain as an English empire which the English political nation inherited from the writings of Geoffrey of Monmouth and the deeds of Edward I. Much of the history of unionist political thought depends, it transpires, on the Scots awareness that union was not the same thing as absorption, and that unionism was at bottom a type of anti-imperialism. However, unlike Scottish patriots of a more traditional stamp who favoured a direct defence of Scotland's independent nationhood, unionists took the view that the best long-term defence of Scottish nationhood from the pretensions of English imperialism lay in some form of equal partnership with Scotland's southern rival. In other words, unionism was inspired by Scottish – not English – concerns and took its rise in opposition to English desires to rule Britain as an empire. After 1707, of course, Scottish unionists became enthusiastic proponents of a transatlantic, and then of a global, British Empire; but they nevertheless retained a measure of suspicion about

English imperialism over the home countries. The Union of 1707 was both a grand opening to overseas empire and a constitutional prohibition on English imperial overreach within the domestic political sphere. While unionists differed over issues of assimilation within the post-1707 British state, particularly when it seemed that the extension of certain English rights to Scotland might benefit the Scottish people, the Union was generally prized as a settlement which had come to the rescue of Scottish nationhood, and which preserved some of its central institutions, the Kirk not least, within a more viable, stable and enduring union state.

While the unionism of popular stereotype appears to be a rather passive ideology, the unionisms which come into focus in this study reveal the enormous creativity, ingenuity and conceptual richness which have underpinned the Scottish unionist tradition in its various manifestations. The very mysteriousness of the Union of 1707 – a treaty which expired with its parties at the very moment when it came into effect, a foundational document whose constitutional relationship with the parliament which it created has never been clearly defined – helps to explain the fertility of unionist political thought at those points where the Union called out for interpretation. On the other hand, the quiet acceptance of the Union by most Scots for most of its history produced the 'banal unionism' described in chapter 1. In turn, the absence of consistent pressure on the Union or its interpretation kept the mysteries of the Union and the unresolved paradoxes of the British constitution out of the public gaze or the scrutiny of Scottish constitutional experts. Here is the unexpected and indirect connection between the two puzzling faces of Scottish unionism: the inarticulacy of banal unionism and the sophistication of the Union's more articulate interpreters. The superficial irreconcilability of these two broad types of unionism has been the most difficult part of this topic for the historian to resolve. Indeed, it might well seem unpersuasive to the reader that this account of Scottish unionism insists both that the primary legacy of Union was over the long term an imperceptible background radiation – in the form of a casual and unquestioning silence on the topic – and that this inarticulate loyalism was punctuated by moments of intense creativity. Eventually, in the second half of the twentieth century, there was another ironic conjuncture. The ambiguities within the Union became more apparent to constitutional commentators, and were incorporated within the canon of Scots jurisprudence and political theory. The interpretation of Union was now a topic of immense richness and subtlety; however, unionism itself as an ideology – at least as expressed by its overt champions within the ranks of Scottish Conservatism – became more overt, yet also shriller and less tolerant of ambiguity and complexity.

Of course, some of the puzzlement associated with unionism evaporates when one realises that most of the political and constitutional debate about the Union until around 1930 centred not on the political relationship between Scotland and England, but upon matters of ecclesiastical polity. To what extent did the Union create a measure of space for the free exercise of Scots presbyterian churchmanship beyond the authority of a sovereign – and otherwise Erastian – British parliament? The central moments in the unfolding constitutional interpretation of the Union were the Disruption of 1843 and the concordat between the British state and the Kirk enshrined in the Church of Scotland Act of 1921. Much of the richness of Scottish unionist argument, therefore, takes the form of ecclesiology. Banal unionism in the political sphere is not matched by a similar silence on the relations between the temporal and spiritual realms and the privileges supposedly guaranteed to the Kirk within the Union. Unless Scottish historians pay due attention to the salience – sometimes the primacy indeed – of ecclesiastical issues in the relatively recent past, they will fail to make proper sense of the place occupied by the Union in the history of modern Scottish political thought.

The history of political thought is, in fact, one of the most underdeveloped areas of modern Scottish historiography. It is one of the larger claims of this study that the history of political thought has the potential to reshape some of the recognised contours of Scottish historical interpretation. When one leaves behind the history of political partisanship to examine the ideas and arguments which provided the stuff of political debate and disputation, the proclaimed differences between political parties, and between nationalists and unionists, begin to blur. If Scottish historians finish this book feeling unsettled about their basic categories of political analysis, this study will have served its purpose.

INDEX